MY SHRINKING BRAIN:

DANCING AS FAST AS I CAN

...A Book About Alzheimer's Disease

ALSO BY BARBARA SHARIK

THE BOOCAT SERIES
Visit www.bbooctunleashed.com
LIKE BooCat Unleashed on FACEBOOK

BooCat Unleashed
(Camp Pope Publishing, Iowa City, Iowa) 2010

BooCat: Dancing Naked in the Rain
Co-author: BooCat
(It's Barbara's Business! Jones, La.)
Printed by CreateSpace, USA 2011

BooCat: Living in My Lap
Co-author: BooCat
(It's Barbara's Business! Jones, La.)
Printed by CreateSpace, USA 2012

BooCat Throws a Frisbee
(The BooCat Chronicles: A Fictional Flight into Feline Fantasy)
Co-author: BooCat
(It's Barbara's Business! Jones, La.)
Printed by CreateSpace, USA 2012

EROTICA ROMANCE

Unquenched Thirst: The Crush that Lasted Fifty Years
Co-author: Dennis Claiborne (11/03/44-01/20/13)
(It's Barbara's Business! Jones, La.)
Printed by CreateSpace, USA 2010

PSYCHOLOGICAL THRILLER

NORMAL
...A Novel
(It's Barbara's Business! Jones, La.)
Printed by CreateSpace, USA 2013

MY SHRINKING BRAIN:

DANCING AS FAST AS I CAN

...A Book About Alzheimer's Disease

BARBARA SHARIK

It's Barbara's Business!
Jones, Louisiana

MY SHRINKING BRAIN: DANCING AS FAST AS I CAN
...A Book About Alzheimer's Disease
Copyright © 2013 by Barbara Sharik

This book is a work of emotions. The characters, incidents, and dialogue are not drawn from the author's imagination but instead are presented as best the author recalls through the membranes of her shrinking brain.

Cover Design by CreateSpace

Front Cover Photograph by Robert Arrington
Interior Photographs by Ann Hamilton
Author Photograph by Mona L Hayden

ISBN-13: 9781491047828
ISBN-10: 1491047828

Published by: It's Barbara's Business!
Jones, Louisiana

Printed in the United States of America
By CreateSpace

Dedication

To Theresa
&
In Memory of Tony

In Gratitude

To Chuck
… for building my marble fence
And keeping the pickets in my life-fence whitewashed & semi-upright

Remembering

Jon H McNeil and Dennis W Claiborne

You cannot truly open your heart
without first opening your mind.

-Barbara Sharik 07/01/13

Somebody should tell us, right at the start of our lives, that we are dying.
Then we might live life to the limit, every minute of every day. Do it! I say.
Whatever you want to do, do it now! There are only so many tomorrows.

-POPE PAUL VI

Death is not the greatest loss in life.
The greatest loss is what dies inside us while we live.

-NORMAN COUSINS

THE COVER

"STRONGHOLD"

South central Alaska's Knik Glacier is a 25-mile towering fortress of ice whose impenetrable kingdom tears across the landscape, flooding valleys and crushing mountains into powdery ash.

In the summer the melting heat of the sun transforms the ice into spectacular sculptures as hanging icebergs succumb to gravity and plummet into the mouth of the lakes below.

"Stronghold" was taken during the summer of 2013 on a spectacular helicopter flight across the sprawling glacial ice field.

For a brief moment the helicopter settled atop the icy towers and we stood temporarily suspended by its blue brilliance as 1200-foot crevasses plummeted below our feet.

Facing the enormity of the surrounding ice field, I reflected on the reality that without our miraculous airship, escape from this stronghold would be futile.

The slowly eroding glacier that succumbs to earth's changing environment is not unlike what one must feel as they stand alone facing the realities of a rapidly shifting, slowly melting mind, where uncertainty and strange other-worldly realities begin to emerge.

Where are the tools to navigate this ever-changing paradigm?

Those who love the one afflicted stand alongside her in the perilous wilderness. Together they seek a means of escape and the tools to navigate this difficult terrain.

Fortunately Barbara Sharik has lovingly written this incredible book which, in effect, gives wings to those who are lost and helps them to navigate their way back home.

-ROBERT ARRINGTON
Fine Art Photography • Digital Imaging • Web Development
www.robertarrington.com, robert@robertarrington.com

"Glaciers are delicate and individual things, like humans.
Instability is built into them."
-WILL HARRISON

AUTHOR'S NOTE

I joke, but Alzheimer's disease is a serious thing.
Forgive me my humor. Humor is my way of coping.
Anything cried can be smiled.
Alzheimer's will eventually make me cry,
but for now, while I still can,
I am smiling…
even as I am dancing as fast as I can.

Painfully shy as a child, as I grew into adulthood, I knew no one could put away childish things, such as shyness, except me.

Funny retorts often popped into my head but too self-conscience, I kept silent. Then when I heard a radio advertisement for the Jay Leno Comedy Challenge, I resolved it was time to open up wide and let the humor out.

I entered, performing in front of a live audience. One of eight semi-finalists, I didn't place first, but I had met the challenge, and deep inside I was a winner.

Two elderly women, Ann and Rose, are out driving their big old Lincoln, barely able to see over the dashboard.

As they're driving along, headed to Walmart, they approach an intersection. The light is red, but Ann drives right on through, not hesitating for a second.

Bewildered, Rose thinks to herself "What the heck? I could've sworn we just ran a red light."

A few minutes later, they come to another red light. Again, Ann drives right on through.

Rose is alarmed, but still, she is not sure if she's imagining things. She reasons, it happened so fast…

However, at the next intersection, Ann drives through another red light and Rose can stand it no longer. She turns to her friend and asks, "Ann, did you know that we just ran through three red lights in a row?"

Ann replies, "You know, I noticed that too!"

Rose, flabbergasted, says, "Good golly, you could have gotten us both killed!"

Ann turns to Rose and says, "Me? I thought you were driving!"

IN APPRECIATION

Dr. Vipul Shelat

Death is inevitable and coherency is not guaranteed. I passed the sign for *Easy Street* a long time ago, now I am working my way through the *Detour*.

I look at the man who handed me the fearful death sentence, but who also handed me the prescription for life. This man diagnosed my *road closure*, but he also rerouted me safely back home with lucidity. Through his caring knowledge and dedication, he is giving me a second chance, granting me a little more time.

So often, when someone asks how I am doing I jokingly respond, *"I was doing alright, but I got over it."*

Although meant as a joke, I really *was* doing alright and then I *did* get over it. My brain began shrinking. However, now, I am in the process of getting over the *"getting over it."*

I am in the midst of living and celebrating a cognitive life before death.

I will die. Everybody dies. But, dignity is mine for a while. Dignity and grace.

So, let the music begin. Let the music continue. And, because time is of the essence and I know this is my last dance, I am dancing as fast as I can.

Thanks, Doc.

PREFACE

Until the moment he died, I believed my dad was the smartest man I ever knew. He was my go-to person, my Google in life before Google, the answer to my daily questions. Although he wasn't educated, he was brilliant – a self-made man who supported a wife and five children as a builder. The day we buried him, a desperate panic set in when I thought all that knowledge and experience, that wealth of information and common sense, would go with him. I was 25 and he was just 61, not enough days shared between us.

As the years passed, I realized that I could indeed maneuver my way through life because of his words and ways. His independence and fearlessness were passed to me through his immense presence, and hopefully will live forever through those I may have influenced along the way.

As I read this brave and insightful account of Barbara's shrinking brain, I couldn't help but believe that even though our bodies weren't designed to live forever, her imprint most certainly will. Barbara is one of those people like my dad, that you feel privileged to have crossed paths with. The eternal optimist, she has survived much and lived life as we all should – authentically and with eyes wide open.

Barbara always brings a smile and laughter, never one for showing up empty-handed. Also not known for dipping words in chocolate before serving, she's quick to challenge a thought, a belief, or a theory such as 'everything happens for a reason vs. luck and chance'. We've gotten a lot of mileage out of that one. Now we simply agree to disagree and wouldn't have it any other way.

She's the voice of reason and logic, intelligent and well-read. She's that glimmer of hope, knowing the exact words of comfort and healing. And for this alone, her indelible imprint will remain forever cemented in my heart.

My prayer is that when the end inevitably comes, as it will for us all, this courageous and beautiful woman will have left no words on the table, instead choosing to gift us by strategically placing them where they best fit.

-MONA L HAYDEN
Publisher of LOUISIANA ROAD TRIPS Magazine
Independent Writer, publicist
www.laroadtrips.com

Pushing up Daisies

Photo by: Ann Hamilton,
Anchorage, Alaska

There will be time enough for pushing up daisies, the expression referring to dying and being buried... Instead, take time to smell the flowers with every breath every day. Tomorrow is not promised, but, we have today; live it with optimism.

PROLOG: UNCHAINED MELODY

There is a sign in the distance. As I get closer, I read: *Warning. Roadblock ahead.* How annoying. I have no time for roadblocks; I have a life to live.

Shrugging my shoulders, much as *Atlas Shrugged*, I determine when I get to the roadblock I will handle it. I have spent all my life handling things. This should be no different.

I keep on keeping on.

I sing in the sunshine and I dance in the rain. I count the stars above and find four-leaf clovers below. I skim across the water like a flat stone and sail over the waves like a tall ship. Somebody carved my name within a heart on a big tree beneath a bigger sky. The world is mine. I may be insignificant in the overall scheme of things, but still, I have a purpose. Everyone has a purpose; they must only discover what it is.

Suddenly, I am stopped in my tracks. Another sign looms: *Detour*.

Well, that makes sense. If there is a roadblock, of course it means I have to detour, find another way to get where I am going.

No problem.

Life is full of detours.

Taking the detour, I am routed way out of my way, but not so far I cannot find my way back home. I follow the moon. I know it will guide me home. See the stars? Navigation tools used for centuries.

Besides, my new little car has a GPS plugged in and I have only to program where I am going and the disembodied voice will advice, *turn left, turn right, three steps forward, one step back.*

Besides, what is a little roadwork along the road of life? All through life, I have encountered roadwork. Life is a work in progress.

Thus, I follow the signs, continuing until I eventually reach my road home.

But, wait. What is this? Another sign: *Road Closed.*

When did they close my road? How am I supposed to get home now?

I have been making this trip for so many years I should be able to travel it with my eyes closed, but now, now, everything is fuzzy.

Still, I figure if I can maneuver my way up the driveway, pull beneath the carport, I will be just fine.

Carefully, ever so carefully, this is what I do. Then I park, open the car door, get out and head toward my front door.

But wait! When I attempt to unlock my door, I am stymied. My door key doesn't fit.

Who changed the lock?

I look around in confusion.

I finally make my way home, traversing roadwork and detours, only to find the front door locked and my house key useless.

This is my house, is it not?

Why does the key no longer fit? Why can't I get into my house, my sanctuary?

I look around, feeling confused. I am standing in front of my house, but I am lost. How can I be lost, standing in front of my house?

I want to cry, but tears will not come. I gave up crying years ago.

Casting my eyes skyward, I say, *Please, I just want to go home. Somebody, please help me find my way back home. Please, take me home. I am lost.*

I listen.

The sound of silence fills my confounded head.

Please.

The Old Man

Photo by: Ann Hamilton,
Arches, Utah, May 2013

There is an old man with gnarled fingers, swollen joints, a nose that drips, eyes that water... teeth that clack when he talks. He shuffles when he walks, his shoulders humped. He wasn't always this way. Once, he was strong as a young pine sapling. He grew tall and reached as high as the sky.

The sun beamed down, warming the earth. Then, day turned into night. Silent moonlight glowed. Stars flickered. Some shot across the sky. Others fell. The old man wished upon the stars in the sky.

Days turned into months, months into years. With the passing years, the young sapling becomes a twisted old tree, bent, drying out and drying up. Terra Firma becomes less firm and a gusty wind will come one day and he will topple... Everything and everyone topples with time.

OUTLIVING MY OWN MEMORY

Initials abound. However, I am not OCD. On the other hand, if I were, alphabetically, it should be CDO. People suffering with OCD probably would insist the initials be arranged alphabetically. They also make lists, and admittedly, I have always made lists, especially what I call my To-Do list. I make it and then cross things off as each task is completed.

The difference between individuals suffering from OCD and me when it comes to list making is that sufferers of OCD would be compelled not only to complete and cross off each task, but if they did something not on the list, the task would first have to be added—and then—duly crossed off.

Do it.

Write it down.

Cross it off.

Who will ever know whether or not that particular task was on the list in the first place? Just you. The having to write-it-down, then cross-it-off, even though it is already done, that is an obsession. You see, OCD stands for Obsessive-compulsive disorder.

Certainly, OCD is nothing to make fun of, and I am not. Yet, if I did not know better, I might suspect I am developing it. Not just the list making, but also the double-checking. If it is not OCD, does it verge on it?

When is it just being cautious rather than a compulsion?

Let me explain. For example, sometimes I am compelled to double check, making certain I locked the door, or perhaps, that I emailed my weekly humor newspaper column to the editor.

5

Simple routine things, done unconsciously so to speak, without a second thought. Someone suffering from OCD would have to check repeatedly to verify that the door is locked and that the column has been sent. *Repeatedly* is the definitive word.

One double-check is enough for me.

So far.

I do the deed then because sometimes I cannot recall if I did it or not, I double check. Why this is not OCD is because it is not a compulsion driving me to double check. No. My disorder has to do with memory loss.

Memory Loss.

I cannot remember whether or not I locked the door. I cannot remember whether or not I mailed my newspaper column.

Well, it turns out that the reason I cannot remember is because my brain is shrinking. I call my disorder ISB… Incredible Shrinking Brain.

ISB sounds better than OCD. However, OCD does not kill you. ISB does.

Brains really are incredible. Nonetheless, all brains shrink with age. Some, more than others. What portion of the brain shrinks has a bearing. In other words, not all brains are the same and likewise, not all brains shrink in the same way.

What does it mean… this shrinking brain thing? How are we affected? What can be done to halt or slow the process? Perfectly logical questions, especially when you learn your very own brilliant brain is beginning to grow smaller through shrinkage. Until faced with this reality, likely you never gave the size of your brain a second thought.

I know I never did. Malfunction-junction stops the train. But, so long as it is functioning, as with every other part of my body, it is taken for granted.

Who notices their little finger until it gets bent backwards with a bad basketball catch? Who notices their skin until it is sunburned? Who notices their belly button unless they are into contemplation of such objects?

Sorry, I jest.

What I am saying is that we take our body parts as a matter of fact. So, suddenly, I learn something extraordinary about my brain. In fact, about everybody's brains.

As we age, like death and taxes, the inevitability also encompasses brain shrinkage. Simply put, it is unavoidable. The scary part is that memory loss and mental confusion, which comes because of brain shrinkage, are the first overt signs of Alzheimer's disease.

There, I said it. Alzheimer's Disease.

Shrinking Brain.

SAY AGAIN?

Three sisters, all hard of hearing, were playing badminton one sunny spring morning.

One says to another, "Windy, isn't it?" "No," the second sister answers, "it's Thursday." The third sister, listening in, pipes up, "So am I. Let's go get a root beer float."

SILLY PUTTY

Alzheimer's disease is practically a household word, in that we keep hearing more and more about it. But, what is it? What is Alzheimer's disease?

In a nutshell, it is an incurable and fatal brain ailment. No beating around the proverbial bush. Cut and dried.

Brain ailment.

Incurable.

Fatal.

The term gives me pause because I now know that this diagnosis is an inevitable death sentence.

Here's your card.

Whoa!

Fatal brain ailment?

Inevitable death sentence?

Drop an ice cube into a cup of hot coffee, it will inevitably melt. We are each, using an axiom, nothing more than an ice cube, starting solid but along the way, we begin to melt. Likewise, the heat of life begins the melting process long before the final plunge into the unavoidable cup of hot coffee or glass of tea waiting to be iced.

How much simpler life was before I gave Alzheimer's a second thought. Now, I am giving it a third and fourth thought.

Actually, you think about it, being born always leads to an inevitable death sentence. We are not born into adulthood, moving backwards through the years. No. We are born as innocent babes, spend the first half of our lives maturing, growing up.

Then, we spend the next half reversing the process in a manner of speaking. We grow up and out, and then we shrink up and inward.

Grow up, as in maturing and becoming an adult… and out, budding, blossoming, expanding.

Then, with time, we begin to shrink up, as in shriveling, actually losing inches in height… and inward, our abilities diminish, decrease, lessen.

I used to be able to pick up a fifty-pound bag of dog food. Now, I strain with a twenty-five pound sack. In fact, I tried so hard to put a forty-pound bag of wild birdseed into my shopping cart just yesterday, and could not lift it high enough to get it over the sides. For one fleeting split second I wanted to cry.

It slipped to the floor.

I regrouped and made a second attempt. Naturally, it was useless. If I was unable to move it from the shelf, there was no way I could lift the bag from the floor where it now sat.

I looked around. A man turned the corner, headed down the aisle in my direction. I opened my mouth to ask for his help when I noted his arm was in a sling. He never looked in my direction.

Ah well, put another brick in the wall.

How tall will the wall rise before I can no longer peer over the top?

I used to read three-four books a week. Now I read myself to sleep and wake in the morning with more chapters left unread than read.

These are the changes. They are not exactly subtle. They seem to be very sudden. They seem to be coming in a deluge. Bowing me over and blowing me over.

Wipe out!

Still, on a positive note, even as this inevitable brain shrinkage is happening, I am fortunate to be living in an age when science is making it possible to find evidence of Alzheimer's disease long before symptoms actually appear.

Think about this. Discovering a disease that, even though developing within one's body, has not yet taken its toll, gives the effected individual a fighting chance to take positive steps—no matter how limited, steps nonetheless. This is such a plus. A light at the end of a former forever-dark tunnel.

In addition to being made aware of this malady in advance, before complete damage is done, I am most fortunate to have been referred to a neurologist who knows this.

What this means is that he knew what to look for, found it, and is treating it.

With the recent advent of longitudinal MRI (magnetic resonance imaging,) results now can reveal telltale signs in brains a decade before memory and thinking are actually affected.

I thank my lucky stars and my brilliant and most caring physician, coupled with his astuteness, that I have been diagnosed early and have begun such treatment as is available.

What does this mean?

Will I live forever? Has the secret of longevity been discovered? No. I will still die. My brain will continue to shrink. The aging process cannot be reversed. However, perhaps I shall be able to die of something other than Alzheimer's. Nobody wants to die of Alzheimer's. It is a dreadful way to end ones life.

Quite frankly, it is better to go out with a bang, than to melt away into a glob of silly putty.

PERPLEXED

A sweet little old lady calls 911 on her cell phone to report that her car has been broken into. On the verge of hysteria, she explains her situation to the dispatcher. "They've stolen the stereo, the steering wheel, the brake pedal and the accelerator," she cries.

She pauses, gulping a fresh breath of air she cries, "Oh my goodness. Even my fuzzy dice are missing!" The dispatcher replies reassuringly, "Don't worry, ma'am. An officer is on the way." A few minutes later, the police officer calls in. "Disregard," he says. "She got into the back seat by mistake."

Entering the Unknown

Photo by: Ann Hamilton,

Monument Valley, Utah, May 2013

Traveling this straight road, entering Monument Valley, Utah, was our first glimpse of this magnificent place. Upon seeing this for the first time, Goosebumps covered my body and tears started to flow. Bobby said he was the same way. Something about this place gripped my soul. -Ann Hamilton

And so it is, in life, we cross the border, we enter the unknown, every day of our lives. We may think we know, but we do not. We grow accustomed, acclimated even, but, like a bolt of lightning from the sky, we never know what the very next second will bring. We go to sleep each night hearing someone singing, *Will you still love me tomorrow...* intending to awaken in the morning, but for some, morning never comes. The love song ends.

GRAY MATTER, WHITE MATTER, WHAT'S THE MATTER?

Human brains are big and powerful. They have come up with cures, causes and complexities beyond belief. Yet, the thought of slowly losing my mind is one-half of my two greatest fears.

Anyone who knows me knows I have said many times over the years only two things scare me: Tornadoes and losing my mind.

I have suffered several tornadoes resulting in various degrees of damage but never complete destruction. I never hollered, *Wipe out!* The waves were big, white cappers beating relentlessly against the shore, but the shore remained.

Everything damaged was eventually repaired or replaced. That is a good thing. My motto has always been to face things with a modicum of acceptance at the very least. Not to do so, the weight of every disaster would bury each of us alive. We would never get out of bed in the morning. I know I cannot live my life in bed. Even with the shades drawn, the sun will shine. Dust motes will dance, and shadows will fall. You cannot have shadows without sunshine.

No, I have learned to accept and if not accept, then to adjust.

The house was reroofed, new trees planted, windows replaced. The wind slowed, the rain and hail ceased. Every day is a new dawning. The sun shined again.

"Sunshine on my shoulder makes me happy..." (*Bob Denver)

Now, I turn to the second fear: Losing my mind.

Losing. My. Mind.

There is no *Lost and Found* department where I can go, give a description, offer a reward, and expect it to be returned. Once lost, it is going, going, gone. Forever. And ever. Amen.

Excuse me, ma'am. Is this yours? I found it freefalling down the mountain-side. It was the screaming that alerted me.

What was that old commercial about drug abuse? *A mind is a terrible thing to waste.* Likewise, it is a terrible thing to lose. What, other than death itself, could be worse than becoming a turnip?

No. No. I am not being flip. I am telling it like it is. In layman's terms. The expression *turnip* is synonymous with vegetable. The shrinking brain vegetates. A person with a brain that slips into oblivion is referred crudely to having become a vegetable. It is crass, but it is understood by one and all. We get the picture.

Write that down for me, Daddy.

Once the first wave of fear that accompanies realization diffuses and the wave washes back into the ocean, kept under control with the phases of the moon, I catch my breath and face facts.

Losing our minds, as it were, some say is the price we pay for living longer. However, not everybody suffers equally. Just like catching any dread disease, not everyone is vulnerable to this malady, or if so, not always to the same degree.

Some children in my childhood days, when chickenpox was considered a disease every child would suffer, were left scarred while some escaped unscathed. It was said that the first child in a family who contracted chickenpox would likely have a light case, while each subsequent child would suffer more profusely.

We were the chickenpox kids. We were the kids who received the first polio vaccine… and grateful for its discovery because many of our classmates were stricken prior to its discovery and were left crippled. Indeed, there were many crippled children before Jonah Salk found the cure for polio.

So far, there is no vaccine to halt or prevent Alzheimer's disease.

I recall reading about a study using MRI scanners to measure the sizes of different brain regions in both humans and chimpanzees, and finding that chimps showed no significant age effects while *all* human brains showed dramatic age-related effects.

Even if I was a believer in evolution there is too much about that scientific proposal that causes me to ask too many questions, so I cannot accept blindly. First, I would be asking how come the brains of chimps do not shrink if we are supposed to be evolved from chimps and apes.

Next, I would ask if we evolved, why are there still apes? Are they just slow learners? Sorry. Remember, I write humor columns.

In any case, at this point in time, I do not believe a Supreme Being created mankind either. I write off a supreme being and I write off evolution as simply as I write off everything happening for a reason. I cannot answer any of life's questions in any single way. I am left with a lot of eraser litter on my thesis as I attempt to figure out how humanity came to be.

In other words, I have no idea. I am too logical to believe either the Supreme Being theory or the evolutionary theory. Now, on the other hand, and my other hand is dripping with ideas, thoughts and beliefs, I am just a drop in the millennium bucket. Therefore, what I believe or do not believe matters not.

One ant among many in the anthill.

What is it they say? Everybody's got an opinion, but that does not mean a thing in the grand scheme of things.

So, where does that leave me? Confused, bemused and human. A human with a quest to know, but unable to believe in anything blindly. I want black. I want white. None of that gray in between.

Hmmm. Gray in between. *Gray matter?*

It boggles the already addled brain; however the MRI brain scan gives me black and white. Also, it appears that the older humans live, the more shrinkage occurs.

Think about it. That makes sense. The more you sharpen a pencil, the more it shrinks. Eventually, your No. 2 pencil is nothing but a nub, the eraser long gone.

Not being qualified in fine points (no pun intended), I can only report that I have read that some regions of the human brain shrink more than others. In other words, not all shrinkage is equal. Gray matter and white matter differ. I cannot quote where I read that. I read so much, so continuously.

Nonetheless, we have all heard the term *gray matter.* The gray matter contains the nerve cell bodies and their nuclei, along with auxiliary cells such as microglia.

White matter, consisting of the long neural axons, makes the connections between the different brain regions.

The gray matter is the meat and the white matter, the mayo.

One BLT to go, please.

RECOLLECTING

I said to my doctor, "Doctor, I lost my memory." He asked, "When did this start?" I said, "When did what start?"

"DON'T ROCK THE JUKEBOX"*
(*Alan Jackson)

Do not stop reading. I promise I will not get technical. I will only brush gently like dusting powder on a freshly showered body… just a light sprinkle, a slight scent, a little puffy cloud quickly dispersed. Besides, my shrinking brain does not allow too much technicality, nor do I have the patience to delve so deeply.

Not yet, in any case. Not yet.

Although, I have a penchant to learn, like the books I read, I gobble them up veraciously but often do not remember more than the gist. I am entertained at the time of the reading but I do not want to overfill my head. I drink, am refreshed, and that is sufficient.

A good book is like a tall, cool, drink of water. It saturates my gray matter. This was the extent of my knowledge about gray matter until learning about *my* shrinking gray matter. Confronted with this fact, everything started changing.

It is like what? Everything? Nothing? Awareness is like unlocking a door, even as the tumblers in the lock fall back into place; relocking. You stick your foot into the door, hoping to hold it open long enough to gain what you know will soon be lost.

Convoluted? Complex? Multifaceted?

Yes, to all of the above.

Once I was five-foot-seven and a half inches tall. Now, I am five-foot-six. Or, should that be five-feet-six? Apparently, more than my brain is shrinking.

In some tests taken and results reported scientifically, white matter shrank more dramatically than grey matter. White matter, grey matter, all technical gobbledygook to most of us. Whether the gray shrinks more slowly and the white more drastically, the bottom line is that our brains shrink as we age.

As do our bodies.

Period.

Did you ever make an apple-head doll when you were a kid? I did, but the fine points of how the apple was allowed to shrink up until it resembled the face of a really old person without spoiling, eludes me. Of course, with the ease of Googling something, I could do a search: *apple-head doll* and most assuredly the instructions would be available. *I have never searched for anything that I did not find.*

Forgive me. I am forever using double negatives. This has nothing to do with my shrinking brain. It is a longtime speech pattern. What I should have said is that I have found information to some degree or another for everything I have searched online.

I marvel over and over, even as I glory, how fortunate I am to live in the age of computers and the Internet. My thirst is quenched.

The Internet is indeed a tall drink of water, quenching my thirst for knowledge. Literally, rather than figuratively speaking.

By the way, a few paragraphs previously, I claimed a good book is like a tall, cool, drink of water. It stops me in my tracks to realize I am repeating myself. Either I lack examples other than glasses of water, or my memory failed and I forgot what I wrote a couple paragraphs ago.

Which is it? Repeating my examples in particular or repeating myself in general? You might become impatient with me and ask, *What difference does it make?* When you become my age, you will know what difference it makes.

Anyway, Google that. *Tall drink of water.* You will find figuratively speaking, *similar to 'tall, dark, and handsome.'* If you are a tall drink of water, you are a good catch.

I am sticking with the quenching of my thirst. I am referring to that glass of water literally instead of figuratively. It overflows like water pouring down a mountain side, with knowledge. Some stuff is subject to a double-check, but for the most part, it is accurate.

Again, a little of this and a little of that, was the sum total of what I knew in the beginning about Alzheimer's disease. Unless someone has a vested interest, likely most folks are like me.

There is the saying; *A little knowledge is a dangerous thing.*

In my opinion, no knowledge is dangerous. In learning, in this case, there is no danger. Knowing anything at all is a plus. The more we learn, the more enlightened we become about a disease that has been shrouded in mystery for decades. Mystery, fear, wild conjectures and always with a bad ending.

Learning will not change the inevitable ending but it will allow for a safer journey en route. Like crossing a creek bed, stepping from one stone to the next. Beware the moss-covered rocks. Watch out for the loose pebbles. While, the map is not yet complete, it does offer guidance. It points out detour signs… *Turn around, don't drown.*

Simply using my common sense I consider, gravity might account for the body shrinking. Pounding the pavement for so many years. Wearing down. But, the brain? Is the connection merely the aging factor at work? Have I overused it? Surely not. In most cases, if something is unused it shrinks more quickly. Is this how the shrinking brain works?

Thus, my quest to know more begins with another thought, because I am always thinking. If longevity has a bearing on shrinkage I cannot help but wonder about the little Musk turtle I rescued recently. He will undoubtedly outlive me considering the fantastic aquatic terrarium habitat I set up for him (not to mention a turtle's natural known longevity); but whether or not his brain shrinks over the years would have meant zilch to me six months ago. Just another statistic. I appreciate statistics but I have learned they can be subjective. Seriously. Read a finding, then learn it was obtained by testing six little turtles for six days out of six months during a six year period. The monetary grant for this study likely amounted to more than I will earn in a lifetime.

In other words, I take statistics with the proverbial grain of salt. I grew up believing two plus two makes four. Then, upon adulthood, I learned with enough factors, it is not always the case.

Truth be told, it did not interest me whether or not any other species with extreme longevity suffered from brain shrinkage either. Now, I am interested. I want to know everything there is to know. It is like lightning striking. Suddenly, out of the blue it matters, and what matters most is that this brain shrinkage is happening to me, right now.

My brain is shrinking.

Isn't that the way it often is? Unless you are directly involved, unless it is happening to you personally, it is just background noise. Static on a radio station.

Bzzzzzzzzzzzzzzzz

Now, I am dancing as fast as I can.

⌁

FOUR-STAR RESTAURANT

Two senior couples are walking along, wives in front, husbands in back. Larry says to Chuck," Gee, we went to a new restaurant last night and had the best meal ever. Good prices too." Chuck says, "Well, we like to eat out too. What was the name of the restaurant?" Larry says: "Wait a minute… let me think. Help me out here. What's the name of that pretty flower, smells sweet, grows on a thorny bush?" Chuck says, "You mean a rose?" "Yes, yes, that's it!" cries Larry happily. Then he calls ahead to his wife, "Rose. Hey, Rose. What was the name of that restaurant we ate at last night?"

⌁

Life's Highway
Photo by: Ann Hamilton,
Monument Valley, Utah., May 2013

As innocent babes we are carried, then we crawl and eventually we dare to stand. Still holding on we take a step. Then another. Finally, we let go and walk forward. One footstep at a time. Soon we learn to run, skip and jump. We leap so high, sing at the top of our lungs, live with joy as we begin our journey, traveling life's highway... from beginning to end.

What lies over the horizon? We will not know until we get there. And so, we go until we can go no more. One stride at a time.

SUBJECT: WHEW!

Email
From: Dennis Claiborne
Date: Thursday, December 23, 2010 6:49 PM
To: Barbara Sharik
Subject: Whew!

Had a moral victory today; I made a bit of money, but I did not quit trying. The thought and title of your column, if you haven't already got one, DON'T STOP. If you do you start dying, and prematurely. I won't allow myself a recliner. Too snug and comfy. I intend to work until I die one day, take 15 minutes off for the funeral, and then get back to work.

⌒

Email
From: Dennis Claiborne
Date: December 23, 2010 7:06 PM
To: Barbara Sharik
Subject: Re: Whew!
The day was not good, only mediocre but the point is, I DID NOT STOP. It does not make me a hero, but only a person who has not given up.

⌒

THE "DON'T STOP" COLUMN...
YOU'RE ONLY AS OLD AS YOU THINK YOU ARE

The many columns I have written about being old, aging, traveling in the last lane, would fill a dozen books themselves. However, this is the column I wrote in response to this particular conversation and email exchange with Dennis.

How old do you want to be?

I've been calling this column 'Life in the Last Lane' for a number of years. Because I felt myself traipsing along that lane and because aging is inevitable, I chose to pen a column poking fun at the process. Although I must go where life inevitably takes me, I'm determined not to go lightly in the night. Instead, I'll go kicking and screaming, with tongue in cheek, traveling with a large smile on my face every step of the way.

Recently I discussed aging with a former school mate, Dennis, whose friendship was recently renewed after a 50 year absence as we each navigated roads in significantly different directions. He asked me, because we've found a joint penchant for engaging in deep philosophical discussions, "How old do you want to be?"

Do I have a choice? I asked. He summed his answer by saying too often we decide to get old and we get old. That simple. Does age creep up on us? Do we wake up one day and decide we are 66 years old, so we are old? And does that mean we have to behave like old people?

Dennis holds that over the years he's watched too many people get old who didn't have to. He's a proponent of the think young and you'll feel young; think old and even your physical disposition will become elderly.

He considered maybe our generation believes we must follow in our parent's footsteps. They became old at a certain age, and perchance it's expected. But it's a lot more fun to do the unexpected and to think and act however young you want to be. There's no written rule that you have to become old at a certain point in your life.

Totally against the popular chair commonly known as a recliner, Dennis said he wouldn't have one in his house. You sit down in a recliner, kick back, turn on television to some mindless show and it's all over except the funeral. He also doesn't believe in scooters unless a person is literally unable to walk any longer, insisting scooters eliminate the natural ability to maneuver upright, getting much needed exercise and staying mobile. They first become a crutch, then a way of life. Instead of self-sufficiency, they create dependence.

Moving about improves the blood pressure and creaky muscles. Besides the physical effort involved in his profession, because he's single, he said doing his "wifely chores" as he jokingly refers to necessary household tasks, helps keep him vigorously active.

In the 1800's, people rarely lived past age 30. This isn't what we're doing any more. Hence, he's adamant we eliminate the term "geezer" from our vocabulary and think positive. Dennis is quick to say he isn't advocating anyone act like a teenager; just that there's no written rule that upon reaching a certain biological age we must be considered "Senior Citizens" (a term I dislike).

Go ahead and collect the discount at lunch time, but stay sprightly while doing so. Keep your mind young. Read. Do crossword puzzles. Play Chess. Pore over the daily newspaper and watch the news. Think. Have conversations beyond Corns, Calluses and Cataracts.

Friend Dennis firmly believes when you think you've tried your very hardest, push harder. Final advice for this year's New Years resolution, he adds, "If you look around and everybody's acting like old geezers, resolve to find some new friends."

Bastrop Daily Enterprise, December 21, 2010

SUBJECT: RE: 12-21.COLUMN.BARBARA.OLDAGE

Email
From: Rosemary Ross
Date: December 24, 2010 11:26 AM
To: Barb Sharik
Subject: Re: 12-21.column.barbara.oldage
Uh oh, I act pretty old a lot, are you going to find new friends that are not me?? I like my Mom's view on aging, she is 91, she says, "I wish I felt the way I did when I was 75!"

I tell her, I wish I felt the way you did when you were 75! She was totally young then, used to out walk me. Only got less active when my dad got bedridden and she had to take care of him, and became housebound…

I agree totally you are only as old as you think you are, and let me tell you, if you think you are old you will be so! One thing I read once and believe is when we think more about what we DO want than what we don't want all our dreams will come true. The majority of people spend ten times more thinking of what they don't want; I am working on it… Have a great weekend!

$\smile$

ALL THINGS CONSIDERED

A group of senior citizens were exchanging complaints about their ailments: Jan: "My arm is so weak that I can hardly hold this coffee cup." Linda: "Yes, I know. My cataracts are so bad I can't see to pour my coffee." Bob: "I can't turn my head because of the arthritis in my neck." Pat: "My blood pressure pills make me dizzy." Carolyn: "I guess that's the price we pay for getting old." Mona: "Well, it's not all bad. We should be thankful that we can all still drive."

$\smile$

"GET OUT IN THE KITCHEN AND RATTLE THOSE POTS AND PANS"*
(*Bill Haley & the Comets)

There have been articles written and suppositions put forth about the causes of Alzheimer's disease. I recall many years ago reading something about cooking with aluminum pots and pans possibly being responsible for strange white spots found in brains after the death of some elderly. So much was unknown just a relatively short time ago. No matter how much we now know there is still so much yet unknown.

Like the song *"Tell me why... why do fools fall in love..."** (*Frankie Lymon), I am asking why. Tell me why.

And, while I am asking why-oh-why, at this point, what I am interested in is not necessarily the cause—not personally, not now, it is too late for me to consider the cause, or even the prevention. No, instead, I am more interested in the cure. If not the cure than at least the curtailment.

If the progression cannot be stopped, at least, install a guard rail. Close the gate. Seal the windows. Slow it down. Give me quality.

Remember double knit? A great innovation in the clothing world. Wash and wear. I retired both my iron and ironing board with glee. Pantsuits for women became standard fare for everyday, for church, even formal wear. The whole fashion world changed.

However, with time other lighter variations of material materialized with equal popularity... eventually overriding the heavy double knit everybody went wild over.

Even the nicest pantsuit becomes worn with wear.

Like the musty pantsuit still hanging in the back of my closet, likely rotting with time, I ask if the progression cannot be stopped, at least sew on that missing button. Install a guard rail. Close the gate. Seal the windows. Slow it down. Give me quality but do not leave me smelling like mothballs.

Do not let me become an old woman with drool running down my chin even as I put the ice cream in the microwave and call my child by another name because I do not recognize her beautiful face.

I remember reading, because I am always reading, that healthy diets high in omega-3 fatty acids and rich in vitamins found in vegetable and fruits... all good for our overall health... are considered beneficial not just for normal longevity, but in possibly contributing to keeping Alzheimer's at bay.

Truthfully, I have not been particularly interested in Alzheimer's, only in passing. I read bits and pieces. Perhaps that is all that was available over these past ten years. Bits and pieces; nothing specific. Perhaps that is because for a very long time there has been nothing specific known. A disease shrouded in mystery and conjecture for the most part.

Not until now. Now it is personal. Is that selfish? Perhaps. I mean, no one can take on every needy cause under the sun. We must pick and chose the things that concern or move us most.

You have a child who wants to join Girl Scouts and there is no local troop, so you start one, become the leader.

Your mother is diagnosed with breast cancer, has a mastectomy, you campaign to stamp out this terrible disease. You accept challenges. Act accordingly.

You find out your brain is shrinking, you want to do something, to be involved on some level to help others, even as you hope to be helping yourself or a loved one.

My late best friend, Dennis Claiborne, used to tell me he read that Einstein never memorized anything he did not have to; it only used up valuable brain space.

He told me this when I began complaining of occasionally forgetting something that I should easily recall. He tried to assure me (reassure me?) if I forgot something, it is of no great consequence. He said it did not mean I was on the verge of senility.

So, you see, upon reflection, I was already beginning to worry. Mostly it was because I misplaced my keys a time or two, and sometimes could not bring to mind the right word… Simple things that he insisted meant nothing more than a full brain, too many different things on my mind. In my head.

On the other hand, when we talked, and we talked every day, he would occasionally have trouble finding a word, begin getting impatient with his

own self, and somehow, some way, I always manag[ ]
word. It just seems that now, *my* words are becom[ ]
ficult to lasso and rein in.

When we talked about this, before his unt[ ]
2013, I did not yet know that my neurologist wa[ ]
He advised me of the shrinkage of course, but at that point, he had not used the "A" word. Therefore, I never suspected. I never even considered it. Senility, a word I was more familiar with, blurred the edges but not Alzheimer's disease. I never considered Alzheimer's. We never wrapped our elderly minds around this particular thing ever happening to either of us. We were too smart. We were constantly reading and learning, a thirsting knowledge and we constantly kept the water flowing.

In a nutshell, Dennis and I were both intelligent enough to know the current output about all brains shrinking to some degree but we did not apply it to anything more than a standard part of aging.

He tried to reassure me and I tried to accept his reassurance. I have not had a shoulder to lean on for many years. One shoulder angled off leaving me on a slippery slope. Others disappeared altogether.

His shoulders, connected to his magnificent brain, were broad and enlightening. They were made of sturdy stuff. He fed my brain. I fed his. We maintained a degree of constant intellectual discourse. I thrived mentally. He did also.

You see, I have a habit of floating through life with eyes wide open but seeing only the good. I see only the good as a defense mechanism. I have never suffered from depression. I have never had the urge to pull the covers over my head and burrow deeply into the bed. No. I jump up cheerfully every single morning.

When bad things happen, and they have, I find staying busy, keeping my mind sidetracked, keeps it from becoming log jammed and drowned in misery.

optimistic. My glass if always three-quarters full. Life gives me
ns, I make lemon meringue pie. It has been my coping mechanism as
r back as I can recall. A frown is simply a smile turned upside-down. This
does not make me special in any way and although it sounds fortunate, the
fact is, I do not suffer depression because in many instances I block. I do
not wallow; I departmentalize and hide away the sadness.

It is still there. It is always there. I can draw it to memory if I need to.
But, I do not dwell. I simply could not survive if I did. My shoulders are
not so strong they could tote the weight. I just take one day at a time, write
stuff down so it does not overload my circuitry, and do it as I get to it.

You know, I liked Dennis' diagnosis. I had filled my brain so full—
because we both were voracious readers and seekers of knowledge—he
insisted there was bound to be an overflow on occasion. We had many
deep, philosophical discussions and he provided me with much column
fodder.

Dear Dennis.

We were in high school together. I had a crush on him at one time, and
was good friends with his sister, Pat. Pat and I stayed in touch for all these
years, but it was only about three years before Dennis died that he and I
became reacquainted and recharged our friendship.

We had so much in common, felt so comfortable together and in conversation, we naturally came to consider ourselves best friends. The term
soul-mate comes to mind, because we were so in tune we automatically
knew what was on one another's minds without a word, even over the
miles, on the telephone. It was uncanny.

I would start a sentence. He would finish it. He had a thought. I
revealed it before he spoke a word.

We never missed talking each day. Sometimes three or four times a day.
Often for several hours at a time. I remember the many times when he got
in from work and would call and say, *Lucy, I'm home.*

It was corny but it made me laugh every time. He had such a good sense of humor. I loved his sense of humor. He made me smile so much during those three years.

He also broke my heart. He was an alcoholic and he fought this disease daily. Some days he won. Other days, he lost. In the end, selfishly, I lost. I miss him very much.

BEHIND THE WHEEL

Mike was driving down the freeway when his cell phone rings. Picking up, he hears his wife, her voice high with anxiety as she warns him, "Mike, I just saw on the news that there's a car driving the wrong way on Highway 165. Please be careful!" "One?" replies Mike, "You've gotta be kidding. I see at least a hundred!"

DENNIS: SOMETIMES HE PUSHED TO THE LIMITS
EMAIL: POETIC INJUSTICE

Email
From: Barbara Sharik
Date: September 1, 2011
To: Dennis Claiborne
Subject: Poetic Injustice
Dennis,
When I'm out beneath the soothing shade with the live oaks over my head and shoulders, the dogs at my feet, I ask myself what I should do.

I look around and the countryside seems asleep in the sun. Even the breeze has abandoned this place where the dogs and I seek some semblance of coolness.

Like lace, the sun flitters through the tiny live oak leaves and settles on my arms, the backs of the dogs, the dusty ground. This is the only cool place in the whole world. And it is dry. So very dry. The grass crackles beneath our feet. How many days did you say it has been since Texas got any rain? Louisiana is not far behind this year.

What am I doing out here in this sadly beautiful place? Of course, I am communing with nature and spending prime time with my furbies. But, my mind is in constant motion even if all else is still.

Dennis, you are the lover who made me adore your body and accept my own without inhibition after my years of relative solitude, the person for whom I gave up my old self.

But, there is so much more. You know that. You know everything. You even know how you are breaking my heart. And, it isn't even that you want to, it is just that you must. Because you are so sad and I can do nothing to help you. I cannot make the sadness go away. It has been there so long it is a part of you as sure as the sun sets with fire filling the sky every single evening. The sun will set, and you will have an emptiness that cannot be filled.

I know all this, Dennis.

I do.

And as best I can, I accept that one day you will leave and I will be powerless to stop you. By choice, by divine power, by evaporation... you will leave... you will cease to exist.

And Dennis, I will cry beneath my live oak trees with the dogs at my feet, the sun filtering between the tiny green leaves laying lace upon my face mixed with the tears.

Please don't go.

EMAIL: A QUESTION

Email

From: Barbara Sharik

Date: September 1, 2011

To: Dennis Claiborne

Subject: A Question

A question… so many questions. I consider myself a writer & artist & fortunately have some brains & unfortunately a bleeding heart.

And you, Dennis, you are filled w/brilliant brainpower and compassion but also confusion. A lonely boy.

But, you have more talent in your little finger than most people, including their father, grandfather, great grandfather and great-great all rolled into one… But you turn your back and wash it all away with useless drink. Why?

For a little while you wrote. And wrote well & had fun. You started *Behind the Wire* & you were doing wonderfully well and then you turned your back and washed it all away with poisonous drink.

Again, why?

Why do you let drinking win? Don't wear the title *Alcoholic* like it's a badge of honor. It isn't. Take charge. That's all you have to do: take charge. Don't wash your life away.

You would not be so tired if you lay the enemy down and get on with your life without it. You can do that Dennis. You don't have to be a lonely boy with the bottle your only companion. Be strong.

EMAIL: QUERY... IRRESPONSIBILITY?

Email

From: Barbara Sharik

Date: September 16, 2011

To: Dennis Claiborne

Subject: Query... Irresponsibility?

I have always set relatively high standards of personal achievement for myself & if I don't accomplish what I believe I should, then yes I feel I have failed myself & feel irresponsible... No one else is even aware, but I am. It's a matter of my own self-esteem and what? Personal pride. I suppose.

For example, I don't have to write columns for the La Rd Trips. I don't get paid – except for personal satisfaction. The wkly newspaper? For a time, $10 a column. Then the newspaper print business went to hell and I don't even bother to submit an invoice. So I'm not getting rich. But, I set my goal & I meet it. It's my own goal.

And, people like what I write. Personal pride and satisfaction.

And now, having an upcoming magazine column in La Rural Water Assn magazine... That was me on the recommendation of someone who works with LRWA. No pay. Just personal satisfaction.

And my books. If I weren't dedicated to my own projects I would be disappointed in my own self. What is there in life if not to do the best you can for your own self. Doing it for other people is often disappointing because you are just another person in their pile of people – if they decide they don't need you it doesn't matter how responsible you've been – you're out of there.

Even though much is within our own selves, if we don't try to meet the goals we set, we are being irresponsible even if no one knows it except ourselves.

I'm never going to be rich or famous but if I can do the best I can then there is personal satisfaction... And that's better than nothing... because when I stop & look at my life, it is nothing & it matters to no one but my pets. If I dropped off the face of the earth – 2 or 3 would mourn but they'd soon forget I ever existed. Therefore, it is, in the end between me and me. Period.

A SMILE IS MORE THAN JUST A SMILE

"Suddenly it seemed to me that I looked back from a great distance on that smile and saw it all again - the smile and the day, the whole sunny, sad, funny, wonderful day and all the days that we had spent here together. What was I going to do when such days came no more? There could not be many; for we were a family growing old. And how would I learn to live without these people? I who needed them so little that I could stay away all year - what should I do without them?"

(Jetta Carleton, The Moonflower Vine)

A Far and Distant Shore

Photo by: Ann Hamilton,

Sunset in Maui, Hawaii, December 2011

We build sandcastles. We build our castles high. Then the erosion begins. Even as the waves lap the shore, wearing it away with every swell, the tide of time surges and like grains of sand, our lives also erode.

From sea to shining sea, man is born, man dies. Still, the tide comes in and the tide goes out, for many millenniums before and for many millenniums yet to come.

INSANITY BEGETS INSANITY. SO DOES LOVE

Dennis and I continued our daily phone calls, our emails, and constant communication. We were addicted to each other. Was it the conversation we each lacked otherwise, and found so refreshing between each other? I do not know. I simply know there was something that drew us to each other, like lifelines in the middle of the ocean.

The last time he visited over the Memorial Day weekend of 2011, I wound up in the hospital again, but this time it was not related to my shrinking brain. The E.R. doctors threw the term *Diverticular Bleed* around (I had suffered bouts of diverticulitis/diverticulosis so it made sense to me), but my gastroenterologist diagnosed it as *Ischemic Colitis*. He did my endoscope—about seventeen-years later than recommended—so I supposed he knows my innards better than I do.

He also did the upper gastro-intestinal endoscope exam, and had to stretch my throat three times in two years. I believe it is properly termed having my throat dilated. When I can no longer swallow my vitamin pills, it is time to be dilated again.

Why does my throat close up, draw up? My neck is not particularly large nor is it particularly fat or muscled. It is definitely not muscled like a football player or wrestler. It is just a neck that requires a neck pillow due to the compacting, degenerating discs and accompanying growth of spurs. Likely there is a reason but I have not deemed it significant enough to research. He puts me under and does what he does. Except now I am questioning the consequences and results. I wonder about once again and again and again being put under anesthetics. Does this practice distress the brain and its cells? Does it impact the brain cells negatively? Does it contribute to the shrinking process? Or like a lizards tail and some virgins, does it regenerate itself without any adverse reactions. (Excuse the virgin humor. An old joke popped into my shrinking brain from the days of yore; back when naughty jokes were just naughty enough they did not gross you out but instead left you chuckling. The rejuvenating virgin joke is one, although the joke itself is long forgotten, I know it was funny at the time. All that remains is the phrase: *rejuvenating virgin*).

I was hospitalized for five days and Dennis stayed by my side each day. He spent the night at my house, sleeping with Rosie, TacoBelle and BooCat. Rosie loved Dennis. Who else would sleep with my furbies? That made him even more special in my eyes. He was owned by cats all his life, which also ranked him high in my eyes right from the git-go. A man who loves cats has got to be a good man.

Dennis was so tenderhearted. I admired his brain and I loved his heart.

He also bought a copy of my first book, *BooCat Unleashed* but ended up telling me it had too much stuff in it. I explained that I thought it was going to be my only book so I had to cover everything.

However, it was not my last book. Immediately afterward, I wrote *BooCat: Dancing Naked in the Rain*. The next book, *BooCat: Living in My Lap* was so titled because Dennis was always saying his Alpha Cat was living in his lap. I asked if I could use his phrase for the title, and of course he was flattered and agreed. It was perfect because, BooCat was also a lap-living cat for the most part. A cat person understands that qualification: *for the most part.* Cats are wonderful companions but are independent creatures. They will let you follow them out to the food bowl. BooCat does that every morning. So did the cats that owned Dennis. They will snuggle, but it is on their terms and their terms only.

No wonder they were thought to be royalty at one time in mankind's long history. Also, because of these same traits, the insanity of the Salem Witch Hunts also had them murdered by the droves.

I have always allowed that the word *mankind* is an oxymoron, But, I have allowed my complicated shrinking brain to go off track. Since it never shuts down—and woe is me when it does—I simply follow for awhile and then rein it in, retrace and get back on track.

Dennis and cats.

I speak of Dennis here because he had such an influence on my last few years, these years when my brain began to obviously shrink, and because we also discussed these things. However, never actually believing it was happening to either of us. Not really. We were aging, but we were not atrophying. Our brains were too active to ever atrophy.

Atrophy: Waste away, degenerate, wither… These terms did not describe our constantly active brains.

The title for the last in the BooCat series, *BooCat Throws a Frisbee,* came from Class of '64, Irvin High School, El Paso, Texas. James "Jim" Perry. Jim is a dear friend so long as we do not talk politics. This BooCat book took a flight of feline fantasy, unlike the first three that were described as inspirational (but not religious) and of course, humorous. Always humorous.

This volume, the epitome of pure Southern fun, introduced Aunty and her young niece and BooCat. Together they solved one crime, unusual event, and odd occurrence after another. What differentiates it from the average book of this genre is that it is told as seen through the eyes of BooCat. I figured if BooCat could write a book, she could throw a Frisbee. And vice-versa.

Dennis was Class of '63, I was Class of '62. What good memories I carry from those years in El Paso. I fell in love with the countryside and I fell in love with Dennis. However, that was short-lived even then. He was a jock (football player) and very handsome, but, he had his agenda and I had mine. We passed in the night, so to speak, and neither of us forgot the other. He remembered a particular skirt I wore that he liked. I remembered spending the night with his sister Pat, and how we smooched (because that's what it was called back then, and that was all it ever amounted to), for a little while after his parents had gone to bed.

Later, he admitted he didn't know what he was doing anymore than I did… and as it was, we did not do anything. Our temperatures rose and our hearts beat fast, but then we said goodnight.

Back to Jim. He made a donation to the Morehouse Humane Society in honor of BooCat, and dear friend Ann (Ruthann Wilson) Hamilton, Class of '62, made one in memory of Mary, one of my old rescue dogs. They do not make people like that anymore. Irvin High School, El Paso, Texas… alumni with hearts.

For fun Dennis and I penned a book together: *Unquenched Thirst: The Crush that Lasted Fifty Years.* He came up with the title. Go figure. He was always reminding me of the crush I had on him in high school. Male ego made him like that very much. The book is an erotic romance, and was a bit of an adventure to write. Neither of us had ever tackled anything like this, so in essence, it simply pulled us closer together, knitting the ties that bind more tightly. Like all the other books I have written, it is available on *amazon.com* and Kindle. Just be warned, it is has several XXX's in its rating. And, I don't mean ex-husbands.

I was almost finished with my psychological thriller, *NORMAL, a Novel,* and had in fact sent the hardcopy draft to Dennis for his editing, when everything went wrong.

⁓

THE MAGICAL KEY

"The key to successful aging is to pay as little attention to it as possible."
(Judith Regan)

EMAIL: HAVE A NICE TIME WITH KELSEY

From: Barbara Sharik
Sent: Friday, November 23, 2012 10:02 PM
To: Dennis Claiborne
Subject: Have a nice time with Kelsey
Hello to Kelsey from me, if you read this before you go.
And please, try to relax and have a nice time. Every day you do get better.
You will be okay, Dennis. Just let it happen.

HOPE SPRINGS ETERNAL FOR ALL ETERNITY

"Old folks live on memory, young folk live on hope."
(Gayla Reid, All the Seas of the World)

EMAIL: HAPPY NEW YEAR

From: Dennis Claiborne
Sent: Monday, December 31, 2012 6:46 AM
To: Barbara Sharik
Subject: Happy New Year
And Good Morning

EMAIL: NEW YEAR'S RESOLUTION

Email

From: Barbara Sharik

Date: January 1, 2013

To: Dennis Claiborne

Subject: New Year's Resolution

Jan 1 2013

Alright, dear friend... sober up.

Make a New Year's Resolution... out with the old and in with the new... the old is the bottle that is dragging you down and down. The new is walking tall, enjoying a more constant contact with Kelsey... smiling, finding joy, no more droopy, so sad feeling, covered over with a pile of shit too heavy to dig out from under... toss those scotch bottles and move forward... healthy, wealthy and wise.

You know how much I care about you and I am not giving up on you because you are such a good soul and you don't toss away good souls.

I don't care what you say when you are in your suds, you are kind, smart and worthy of being my friend. You see, I don't let many folks hold that distinct position. I allow you. You are special. You and Hadley.

Now, Happy New Year.

No more tears. No more frustration. No more shit.

I love you D. Like the best friend you are.

Friends don't let friends down.

Barbara

P.S. Good morning.

BTW: Here's the completed NORMAL

Stay sober so you can read it, 'cause I don't want you reading it drunk.

—

THE BIG BOOM THEORY

Nat: "Maybe you broke something." Midge: "I know. Never fall down, never fall down!"
Nat: "Ah, it's nothing. I fall down every morning. I get up, I have a cup of coffee, I fall down. That's the system. Two years old, you stand up and then BOOM! Seventy years later, you fall down again."
(Herb Gardner, I'm Not Rappaport)

—

EMAIL: SANITY

From: Dennis Claiborne
Sent: Friday, January 04, 2013 2:32 AM
To: Barbara Sharik
Subject: Sanity

There are only two sane people left in this country, one is an animal nut, the other is a drunk.

—

DAMNED DIADEMS

"With age, gone are the forever's of youth. Gone is the willingness to procrastinate, delay, to play the waiting game. Now each day is a treasure beyond compare . . . because there are so few such diadems left."
(Joe L. Wheeler)

EMAIL: CHOPPED LIVER

Email

From: Barbara Sharik

Date: January 5, 2013 8:10 AM

To: Dennis Claiborne

Subject: Chopped liver

By the way, your observation is extremely accurate, and for such, you should be awarded the Nobel Prize... or is that the Noble? Or the No-Bell? Yes. That's it. The No-Bell prize.

There are but two sane people left in this country and the nail has been hit on the head. Me and Thee.

I see by your emails you were up late last night... but at least you were up... when I left you, you were on the floor and I wasn't so happy because I am an arsehole and worry about you.

At least, you were alive around 2 a.m. & your sense of humor (sense of humor is related to "sense" but not necessarily good sense) was intact.

How cool if you were well enough to zip over here for the wkend and meet Tess & Carla... I'm cooking a home-cooked meal complete with homemade banana pudding, the legendary (but original) green bean casserole, old fashioned corn pudding, everybody's favorite fruit salad, baked turkey and the best stuffing you ever let melt in your mouth... and whipped potatoes made from... get this... real potatoes, peeled, boiled, buttered etc. (Say no more. I am not asking you... I am just ruminating... is that the right word?)

Hadley will go crazy when he smells that turkey baking. I've ruined him by allowing him to enjoy tidbits from my plate... he's gracious. He eats tiny bits and waits in line behind TacoBelle and RoseBud. No taking my hand off, however, he has learned to stand up beside me, feet on the counter, as I fill the dog bowls each evening with wet dog food... tail wagging and salivary glands no doubt kicking in... knowing one of those bowls is his and his alone.

Oh, don't forget to watch for a little package... I sent you a Louisiana Road Trips magazine, plus.

Did I say Good morning?

Good morning.

DENNIS: THE BEGINNING OF THE END

When he had not responded to my email, nor call me that Saturday morning by 10, I at first thought perhaps it was because daughter Theresa and Carla were visiting. I did not panic exactly, thinking he was giving us time to visit... but that never stopped him before. Nothing stopped him from calling, day after day, month after month, year after year. Thus, I deemed it highly ireregular—in fact unheard of—so I called him.

He had fallen, driven himself to the emergency room and was at that moment being taken by ambulance to a larger hospital. A rib had punctured his lung and he had bleeding in his brain. He underwent two brain surgeries and an arterial procedure to prevent a blood clot from traveling.

The blood clot on his brain was said to be the size of an open palm. It filled the entire half of his headspace.

He got better and then blood clots started popping up everywhere. The last time we talked he sounded so tired. I said, *I love you, Dennis. You are my best friend. You are going to be alright. We have another book to write, you know.*

He said, *I know. I love you too.*

And he did. He really did. We were soul mates.

Nonetheless, he slipped away, leaving his sister Pat, his daughter Kelsey—and me. He left me. I was a robot for weeks, simply going through the motions. There is another hole in my heart.

Son, Tony.

Lover, Jon.

Best friend, Dennis.

Dennis said, once it was determined we were not in love with each other, although we loved each other dearly, that he never had a *"girl"* for a best friend, but he liked it very much. So did I. His death affected me emotionally much more than I ever anticipated. He left an empty intellectual spot in my shrinking brain. The stimulation provided by our daily conversations ceased, and I stumbled.

So, while we touched on growing old and senility, we never delved into Alzheimer's disease itself, except for him to say his father had developed it. He moved from the Dallas area to Jacksonville, Texas, close to his parents so he could help, and talked unabashedly about how he never dreamed he would find himself washing his father's genitals one day, wiping his chin after a meal, watching him turn inside out and fade away.

It was heart-wrenching. He had the tenderest heart. His soul weeped when someone hurt or suffered.

Dennis Claiborne. He was a good man. He had not so long before, arranged to have his body donated to science. He did not like funerals. His little sister died when she was around four years old. We were friends, school mates and neighbors at that time, and I remembered how sweet little Karen was, and how her death impacted me as a friend of the family.

Dennis never got over it. He was forever sad about Karen's untimely death. Thus, no funeral. Science, take what you want. When he died, his sister, my dear friend Pat, sat sadly at the hospital and waited for them to come for his body.

How lonely that must have been. I wished I could have sat beside her. Kept her company.

Why do I spend so much time talking about Dennis? Because he did become so important in my daily life, and when he died, it was an emotional strain. I kept my upper lip stiff, because that is what I do. But, I cannot help but wonder, when a body is under such stress, such strain, experiencing so much unhappiness, does this not also manifest itself in some way, take its toll? Did my sorrow jump into the weakness in me, in my shrinking brain? Did it enhance, speed up, the process? When a person's resistance is low, they are more susceptible to illness. More prone to fall ill.

Nothing could make a resistance lower than the loss of a dear friend, surely. I am a layman. I do not know. I am only wondering. If a strong wind blew, if a feather reached out, if a steep incline presented itself, I likely would have tottered. I was that bowed over, despite my upright position.

So, again, I ask, how does our emotional health combine with this shrinking brain thing? This advancement of Alzheimer's? Do emotions play a part? Either healthy positives or unhealthy negatives? Can a big emotional event impact the brain in a negative way?

Or in the grand scheme of things—if the scheme is grand after all—does anything matter one way or another? Is life random? I have always leaned toward randomness.

I recall noting back in May, 2012 my thoughts on everything for a reason as versus random acts.

⁓

THE SEVENTH VEIL

There comes a time in every Salome's life when she should
no longer be dropping the last veil."
(Harvey Fierstein, La Cage Aux Follies)

RANDOM ACTS OF KINDNESS SHOULD BE A GIVEN, NOT SOMETHING ACCIDENTAL

Both my dear friends Carolyn and Mona believe there is a "reason" for everything. Most people I know do. I always feel like the odd man out, but it is mostly because of my locale—the deep South—rather than that there are few people who think as I do.

I disagreed with the *everything for a reason theory* and said I think it is *all random*. I believe that more than ever now, now that I know about my shrinking brain. What can be the reason?

Did I stub my toe so I could buy Band-Aids, thus keeping the Band-Aid Company is business?

Did I stub my toe so I would have to limp for a week? I mean, what came of my stubbing my toe? What was the reason?

I do not believe in a lottery system either, where your number is drawn and time is up. That is too much like the "for a reason theory."

We are like a house of cards, each of us. Subject to a random puff of wind blowing us down. Or a careless kid bumping the table leg of where we are sitting high and mighty and happy, in our own world, minding our own business. Or, Hadley's tail wagging so hard with happiness, it swipes the cards. Just be glad he does not stop to chew them up once they are scattered all about the place.

The three of us, such dear and devoted friends, did not go into philosophical detail, but Mona did tell about this really nice guy she knows... he was in an accident and became a paraplegic. Now he has been diagnosed with cancer.

I popped up with... "And the reason for this is what?"

I did not mean to be rude. I am sure I took her by surprise, but what she said was that because of his attitude he has been an inspiration for people around him... *his attitude is so good.*

I stopped. Religion and politics... and core beliefs must not be discussed among friends.

But, I am thinking, *his attitude has been an inspiration for people around him* is a helluva reason to become a paraplegic and then come down with fatal cancer, just so the people around him can garner something inspirational from his "attitude."

Religiosity. If people really listened to what they are saying in an attempt to deal with what I call guano, wanting to make it all okay with the simple *"There is a reason"*... if they thought about it, they surely would realize it is blarney.

I would be praying every day, *Dear God. Do not make me an inspiration for anybody anywhere by striking me down with some horrific ailment. I can cheer them up all by myself. Thank you, Amen.*

Okay. So that sounds harsh. What it is, is making a point. I do not mean to sound angry; it is just a matter of a difference of opinion. Who is right? Who is wrong?

But, still I ask, how can there be a reason for evil? The six-million who died in concentration camps, no reason on earth should have allowed that. Children violated and murdered by someone who professes that god told him to do it—he hears god's voice in his ear, no reason on earth or in heaven should have allowed that.

And the list goes on forever.

It cannot be that there is a reason, because something good comes out of something bad—Phoenix rising from the fire. No. It is human nature to make the best of a bad situation. We react rather than pre-act.

I wrote something for Ann and Larry Hamilton several years ago, based on a war experience Larry had while serving in Vietnam. He swapped places one night with a friend of his. He was supposed to pull guard duty, but his friend took his place. Then, that night the bombs fell from the sky and his friend was killed.

During this sad time, this reckoning, Larry was devastated, confused, and filled with remorse and sadness. At long last he was able to come to peace with the event after he and Ann traveled to California and visited with his friend's family.

We talked about random acts of kindness. To believe in random acts of kindness one must also believe in chance.

I have come to believe this. I cannot accept predestation. If that were the case, we might as well pull up our pants and go home right now. We are all doomed. The sandbox is overflowing.

Chance is an unpredictable thing. We are exposed to chance every waking moment. Careful as we might be, trying to control our destiny, we might climb out of bed, take two steps, trip over a carelessly left slipper and fall.

Certainly the fall could have been avoided if the slipper had been left elsewhere. Tripping over it could also have been avoided if the person who fell had stayed in bed all day. But, life cannot be lived staying in bed all day.

Thus, Larry switching places with his friend Mac was nothing more than a sad happenstance. He was not responsible for his friend's death. They were at war, a terrible war, as all wars are. No one is promised a return ticket when they go to war. In fact, we are not promised one single minute more of life, from one minute to the next, from the beginning to the end.

Thus, shrinking brains resulting in Alzheimer's disease happen. If it is predestined or if it is simply random, it happens. We do not know enough about the disease yet to determine how to prevent it, how to cure it, much less why it happens in the first place.

It has been identified. It is taking its toll. It rages like a California wildfire. The flames reach higher. The smoke still occludes the skies above.

Someday, a light may shine through the darkness. There is always hope. Strides are made.

Polio was a killer and a crippler. Then there was a vaccine.

Smallpox wiped out millions. Then there was a vaccine.

Whooping cough. Measles. Maybe some day there will be a vaccine for Alzheimer's disease.

However, back to the hypotheses, another scenario might well have been the case, had the man not bought the slippers in the first place. The "what ifs" are infinite.

Every moment in life can be questioned with a "what if."

Three men walk side-by-side along the road. One looks down and finds a coin. Another, although walking exactly, pace-for-pace, beside his friend, looks up, sees a bird singing in a tree. The third is oblivious to the coin and the bird. His eyes are straight ahead. All three men are at the very same place at the very same time. Exactly.

One bends down, picks up the coin, smiling. He says it is going to be his lucky day. He just found a quarter.

The other, who just happened to be looking up instead of down, at the very same moment the quarter became visible to whoever happened to be looking down, agreed. He too smiled and said his day was going to be good; seeing and hearing the singing bird made him happy.

The third kept walking. He found no coin, he neither saw nor heard the bird. Yet all three men shared an identical space at exactly the same moment in time in this universe.

Happiness is in the eye of the beholder. Luck is all about chance. Some people are luckier than others. One man could scratch off ten Lotto cards and win nothing; another could win ten times running. Still another, maybe once or twice.

We live in a haphazard universe. To believe something happens for a reason is the choice of some, but not everyone. Some of us believe in random acts of kindness and pure chance. Some believe in luck: both good and bad. Some do not think about it one way or the other. Who is to say which is right, which wrong?

Was there a reason that Larry's friend Mac died the night they switched guard duty in Vietnam? If it was meant to be, it would have happened no matter the switching guard duty that night in that place of killing. If it was just one man finding a quarter and another hearing a bird singing and a third missing both events, then it is what it is.

Larry found the quarter. Mac did not. It was not Larry's fault that he found the coin. It was not his fault that Mac did not. But both men heard the bird singing for a while. Still, stuff happens.

In this case, as in my own life, I advise always remember the positive: Larry and Mac became friends. That was a good thing. Hearing the bird sing, even for a fleeting moment, was a good thing. There is always good mixed with the bad and the sad. We must wrap our hearts around the good and tuck the sad in our back pockets. Do not cry because Mac is gone; rejoice instead for Mac's having been.

Such is life.

On the other hand, it does not make the fear of the unknown, the unavoidable and the inevitable, any less. Knowing that death is a given, once a babe is born, does not make the future any less frightening if one is to think about the variations.

My philosophy? Simply do not dwell. Take care. Be smart. Just do not dwell. Think positive.

When I renewed my driver's license during the month of June, I checked the block to become an organ donor. In Louisiana DL renewal is always due during the month of your birth. Easier to remember. Louisiana driver's licenses are good for four years. Not quite as easy to remember which year, but still doable. Pull out your wallet at the beginning of your birth month and give it a quick check.

Daughter Theresa has always checked the organ donor block as well. She also donates blood regularly. I always thought Dennis and Theresa would meet someday and that they would like each other very much. She is always posting humorous statements on her Facebook page, and while Dennis did not do fb (except for those three magic days when fate—fate?—let me reconnect with him), he liked very much when I shared her humor with him. He said over and over, what a brilliant mind she has. I always responded that I took after her.

In any case, I never thought about my shrinking brain being anything of import when Dr Shelat first advised me. Part of life. Like hair turning gray and skin wrinkling.

Perhaps his assurance kept my fears at bay before fear ever really blossomed. Stashed on the back burner. Nothing to fear. After all, Dennis said not to worry, and he was very smart.

There is much in life to fear and logically, we cannot enjoy life if we stay frightened of things that may not ever transpire. Living in a state of fear would overshadow everything beautiful.

Put the scissors on the high up shelf and do not run in the house. Even still, there will always be things that go bump in the night, but there will also always be sunrises, flowers blooming, kitty cats meowing, puppy dogs wagging their tails, children watching and learning, smiling and laughing as they grow.

Good and bad are like parallel lives. You cannot have one without the other. There may be a cushion of airspace between the two, but they are always present, streaming like a movie played on your computer from Netflix, and steaming like a pressure cooker awaiting the lid to be removed. Jump back so the steam does not burn your face and make you bang into the wall behind you. It is a war zone out there. Every day. Duck. Jump. Swerve. But, it is just what it is.

It is also a ray of sunshine and a glitter like diamonds with every raindrop; rainbows peeking from behind dark clouds. Parallel lives and parallel happenstances. A leader is powerful to the degree he empowers others. Likewise, life.

Day in and day out, just another fluke in a world of flukes and endless mayhem. Like the air that we breathe, the tears that we cry, good and bad is part of being alive.

My prayer: *Lord, please. A steady breeze.*

EXERCISE CLASS

I feel like my body is totally out of shape, so I asked my doctor if I could join a fitness club. With his permission, I decided to take an aerobics class for seniors. I bent, twisted, gyrated, jumped up and down, and perspired for an hour. Phew! But, by the time I got my leotards on, the class was over.

AN AFTER THOUGHT

In the above chapter about *Random Acts of Kindness*, I mentioned that my friends Carolyn and Mona believe there is a reason for everything. I got a little snippy and retorted that I would be praying every day, *Dear God. Do not make me an inspiration for anybody anywhere by striking me down with some horrific ailment. I can cheer them up all by myself. Thank you, Amen.*

And what happens? I am diagnosed with early onset Alzheimer's disease and the first thing I am moved to do is to put together a book discussing this frightful deadly ailment as seen through the eyes of someone who is standing on the precipice… me.

I also elected to invite others to comment, from their own individual experiences, dealing with this disease.

Why? Well, of course, to help others.

Mona, honey, if you are reading this, I know you also read the part where I reported what you said about this really nice guy you know who was in an accident, became a paraplegic, and then was diagnosed with cancer… Remember my reaction? "And the reason for this is what?"

I was rude to question Mona's core beliefs simply because they were so at odds with my own. My attitude was insufferable. Haughty. Rude. I did not recognize it at that moment, but I certainly can see clearly now upon reflection. Not all my neurons are misfiring. I still know right from wrong and can recall to mind this particular incident when I was so very wrong.

Not what I believe, but how I reacted. It is a wonder I was not turned into a pillar of salt. Had god and Moses had their way, I would have been.

Mona graciously explained that she believed because of his attitude, he has been an inspiration for people around him.

Well, by the time she is reading this, she knows the rest of what I said and what I believed… and now, now I am eating my words. (Pass the *Tums* please. Twice digested words can be a little rough on the innards as well as the heart and soul).

Yes, Mona is laughing at me… ah, but laughing with a heart of love. Good friends can do that.

Here I am, determined to put my diagnoses out there in the hopes that it will help someone who might come after me. Too late for me, on one hand, although writing this is good for me as well. So, it is a two-way street.

Mona, I love you, girlfriend. Since it had to happen, whether randomly or for a reason, at least, let the end results be good. I am not acknowledging that you are right nor insisting that I am. No, I am simply admitting that occasionally some good comes from a bad situation. It happens all the time.

Randomly.

The Biggest Bolder

Photo by: Ann Hamilton,
Monument Valley, Utah, May 2013

The big huge rock is part of <u>Monument Valley</u>*, many movies have been made there, particularly John Wayne movies. It is also the Home of the Navajos and many WWII code talkers. -Ann Hamilton.*

Mostly we are okay. People of faith proclaim god never gives them a burden they cannot handle. However, the weight can be overwhelming at times and some pray *Dear God, help me withstand;* others pray *Dear God, let me die because they cannot go a minute more.*

The more pragmatic, non-religious, plod along carrying the weight of the world, bending a little lower and moving a little slower as time passes; not stopping until... god, fate or the unknown erects the final barrier: HALT!

It is then that the bolder crushes your physical body even as your soul rises to heaven or simply moves to another dimension where it is either here or there. How can we ever know? How. Can. We. Ever. Know?

BRAIN SHRINKAGE, LIKE DEATH AND TAXES, IS INEVITABLE

As I start reading and begin researching lightly, it appears there is no cure for the shrinking brain and Alzheimer's disease. These healthy diets now being touted by one section are not supported by the other portion.

I mean, healthy diets are always good but for the most part they are not believed by the whole medical community to be the cure-all. So far, best I can determine, the medical community does not believe there is a cure-all yet available for the ravishing disease.

What should we do? What should I do? The breeze is not so steady if I allow myself to dwell. Thus, now that Alzheimer's has my attention, I am thinking if the bunch of believers that push healthy diets and exercise as the answer to help slow the progression and help me to deal, what can I lose by giving it a whirl?

Eat healthy!

Admittedly, with this diagnoses I am drawn to articles on the subject. I do not search them out, but it is good to read a positive and lately there have been numerous articles written about fish-rich diets and foods with high levels of vitamins B, C and E being associated with increased cognitive performance. With increased cognitive performance comes decreased risk of brain shrinkage…, which equals Alzheimer's disease.

Is it a pipe dream? Is this simply more of the *Vitamins and minerals cures everything* hype? More of the, *You are what you eat* propaganda?

Can it be so simple?

If it is so simple why is it so serious? Because, Alzheimer's is serious. It is dead serious.

Dead as in D.E.A.D.

So, the straws are groped for. If researchers have found that when either vitamin B12 status or folic acid status is increased, one or the other appears to reduce the rate of atrophy, than I would be foolish not to take these vitamins regularly. Right?

Which is most important? Vitamin B12 or folic acid.

From what little I have read, it has not yet been determined which of these two vitamins is the most important. However, somebody is working on it. At least, I hope they are working on it because Dr Shelat has pre-scribed B12 injections and folic acid pills.

Additionally, do diets aid in slowing this scary process?

Can we stop our brains from shrinking; keep them sharp simply by changing our diets?

I do not know.

Obviously, based on some of what is being written some scientists and doctors do believe this might be the case. Maybe not stopping all brain shrinkage, but at least, keeping brains sharp and focused throughout the portion of our life known as *old age.*

Keep senility at bay.

Keep incoherency from taking over.

Keep the nuts and bolts tightened, the screws oiled and the links from one section to the other, connected.

What can it hurt to eat healthy? Nothing, right? Therefore, logically, I should be nodding and asking what do I have to lose?

What, indeed.

Just my mind. My precious mind.

However, while I am not in denial—I am too smart for that—still I have *not* made a conscious effort to take the eating-healthy step. I still eat cookies for breakfast because accompanying instructions advise that some of my pills should be taken with food and I do not have time or appetite for breakfast.

Swallow my pills. Drink my morning coffee. Eat a couple plain-Jane cookies. Biscotti. Chessman. Vanilla wafers. No chocolate for breakfast. At least, that. Surely, that is a plus. No chocolate for breakfast.

How do I talk myself into eating the healthy diets recommended? I know I am going to die, that is a given. However, the assurance I want to be assured of is not death itself, but that I die with dignity.

Dying with dignity.

No dreams of going out with a bang, rather, simply to go out with grace. When I lie down the night before I do not wake up, let me lie down with a good book, read myself to sleep as I have done for most my life. For many years. Another day. Another night. Then, no more days. No more nights.

It is the end. A serene end, but with the night before still filled with coherency. I want to have been, in spite of everything, lucid. This is how I want it to end. Lucidity and coherency still mine as I read myself to sleep.

Let me be found with my book marked midway through as though when I closed the covers and set it aside, I might awaken to read another chapter… and then another the next night. Peacefully passing in the night. With the grace of modern medicine, determination and never giving up, this is how I hope it will be.

Give my hope wings and I will fly to the other shore during the night one night, leaving behind the shell that once housed this body and the ever shrinking brain.

FUN-FUN-FUN

"Aging can be fun if you lay back and enjoy it'"
(Clint Eastwood)

THINGS THAT GO BUMP IN THE NIGHT

Seriously, because as much as I make my way through life finding humor there are moments when seriousness is called for. This is one. I mean, it is serious and even though I will deal with it in a mostly humorous manner—being my main way of coping—I will accept that being diagnosed with Alzheimer's disease is indeed serious.

People with loved ones already stricken might interpret that I seem to make light; that I am too flip. They will be offended, angry even.

It is not funny; they will want to scream at me.

I will respond, *Alzheimer's is not funny, no, but dealing with humor, with lightheartedness, looking for the good amongst the evil, is not a bad thing.*

I *know* Alzheimer's is a progressive disease.

I *know* it destroys memory.

It destroys many vital mental functions. *I know this.*

It confused me at one time. What came first, dementia or Alzheimer's? Are they one in the same? I heard about dementia long before Alzheimer's came along. I remember a frightful Grade B movie, maybe from the late 1950s, titled *Dementia*.

Well, I have since learned, now that I have a horse in this race, that Alzheimer's is the most common cause of dementia. Dementia and Alzheimer's, wrecks our social skills, kills off our intellect. With time, our day-to-day functions will be affected. With enough time, our day-to-day functions will be nonexistent.

My shrinking brain, now diagnosed with Alzheimer's disease, is degenerating. The brain cells are dying.

There is no cure for Alzheimer's disease.

Diagnoses: Death by degeneration of the brain… beginning with a continual wane of memory and an eventual complete disintegration of mental function.

I remember when Dennis told me that when he worked for a couple years as a prison guard while going through a major transition period in his life; he thought the cruelest thing was to see someone in solitary confinement. He worked in a psych ward of a prison in east Texas, and he was too tenderhearted, it hurt his soul working there.

He needed a job quick and the prison always needed bodies to put in guard uniforms.

Solitary confinement is what happens to a person's mind when it is overtaken by Alzheimer's disease. It gets sealed up in solitary confinement. A light may burn twenty-four hours a day, there may be no sheets on the bed, and food might be slipped under the door… everything to punish the guilty. But, there is no human contact. In solitary confinement it is a punishment. What is it in life? Alzheimer's disease. Punishment for what?

Again, this is why I cannot allow myself to think there is a reason for everything. I do not want to believe I am being punished for something I was not even aware I did wrong, or did not do right.

I am guilty of nothing, why is my brain going to be sentenced to solitary confinement one day? Days and nights will become one long expanse of nothingness. Food will mean nothing. Sheets? What will they matter? Likely, I will not even know what a sheet is.

This is something to look forward to? I remember someone asking "Is this all there is?" *Is. This. All. There. Is?*

Aw, no. Hell no! Whatever life doles out, I will partake. Remember, I'm the crazy old lady who is dancing as fast as she can.

IT'S ALL ABOUT ACCEPTING

"Over the last few years, my comfort level with how I look has improved. My age has helped. You get used to yourself and accept yourself."
(Lynn Redgrave)

WHEN THEIR EYES GLAZE OVER, YOU KNOW YOU ARE REPEATING YOURSELF

Here's the thing that may be confusing… you can remember something that transpired years ago, but not five minutes previously. This is actually the first symptom, the alert… however, it is difficult to recognize in one's self.

A little forgetfulness can be blamed on having too much on your mind. A bit of mild confusion, maybe you are tired. Except, with time, it is more difficult to recall the most recent memories.

Why?

Everyone has memory lapses. We all know that. I have mislaid my keys. I have forgotten someone's name. I did these things when I was young. So, surely this is normal, natural, a part of everyday overload. Just because I misplace my keys, does this indicate I have Alzheimer's?

Except, from memory lapses, comes repeating yourself.

Stop me if I already told you this.

Polite listeners may simply let you ramble and say nothing. After all, everybody knows that old people repeat themselves.

Setting something down without paying attention usually is remedied by simply backtracking. Nevertheless, when we start putting items in abnormal places—the ice cream in the microwave—then that is most assuredly the beginning of a problem.

I have always written down my appointments; then I check the calendar each day. This has been my means of keeping track without getting bogged down. I am always involved in multiple endeavors, so this works for me. I purposely put things out of my mind.

However, forgetting appointments or events—and then not recalling them later—this is a symptom. It is part of the progression.

People with Alzheimer's will eventually forget not just the name of someone they rarely see, but people they see regularly… even family members.

Another symptom that eventually manifests itself is forgetting what day it is. I do not forget what day it is, but over weekends I might have to refresh myself as to the exact numerical date. Especially when writing a newspaper column that will not run immediately. I have to figure out the date of when it will run in the paper… but first, I have to figure out today's date.

I have two wrist watches and both have calendars (one needs a new battery… I have had it in my purse for several weeks. I must remember to go by the jeweler next week).

Again, I have allowed myself to be lazy, use props, even before the thought of losing track forever ever entered my mind. Props are not necessarily crutches. They are simply, in my opinion, a smart way to keep an overly full mind from shorting out from overload.

My mind.

Eventually, people suffering with Alzheimer's disease forget what time of the year it is. Summer. Winter. Fall. Spring. These slip away along with the unstoppable dwindling memory.

The most basic things. Gone. What a cruel disease, this Alzheimer's.

This phase causes people afflicted to lose themselves even in familiar places. This dread disease disrupts the ability to properly interpret what the eyes see. You might have been someplace a million times, and suddenly, you are lost. You have no recognition, no idea of where you are.

Oh god.

Can it get any worse?

Yes. It can. Reading is a passion. Writing, my salvation. My shrinking brain will be able to read and interpret less. I will find myself searching for the right word. I have owned a Thesaurus for as long as I can remember. Dictionaries, a set of encyclopedias and a Thesaurus are the tools of a writer. With the advent of the computer, I do not have to turn to my Roget's Thesaurus. I can find the word I want under *Tools* in my Microsoft Works Word Processor.

I do not want to be a sitting duck for dementia. I do not want to wind up a mangle of metal… a train wreck already happened. Derailed. Exploded. Shattered and smattered and scattered from here to Sunday.

But, there will come a time when I will not know what word I want, and thus, will be unable to find a synonym. I am screaming inside. This is something I do not think I will be able to stand.

Difficulty concentrating, thinking, reasoning. All in danger. Also, making decisions and having good judgment. Will I be able to prepare a pan of homemade lasagna when Theresa comes to visit? Was the last pan I made my last lasagna?

I cannot imagine the changes in personality many Alzheimer's sufferer's experience: depression, mood swings, irritability, distrusting people around me, becoming aggressive, wandering around aimlessly, losing my inhibitions, and delusions.

When everything stops being funny, I will be done. I will turn in my house key and move on down the road. *The long and winding road.* You will know me by the fist being shaken toward the heavens and the tears streaming down my wrinkled cheeks. You will know me even when I no longer know myself.

⌒

THE PROBLEM WITH AGING

"The problem with aging is not that it's one damn thing after another—
it's every damn thing, all at once, all the time."
(John Scalzi)

⌒

THE SIGN SAID: ALZHEIMER'S MEETING CANCELLED.
NO ONE REMEMBERED

Like a computer compresses files to make room for more downloads,
Perhaps the brain compresses or deletes memories to make room for more.
Tammi Carroll Garner 07/02/13

Tammi Garner said, "I'll go anywhere with you, except crazy."

Now, that is a good friend.

She adds that she remembers seeing someone wearing a badge that read: *Don't remember my name? Don't worry. Sometimes I don't either.*

I work with Tammi, but I first met her through Jon several years before she came to work with me at Bonita where she serves as the water and court clerk.

Tammi has a wicked sense of humor, which immediately drew me to her. Also, she has a heart as big as Texas.

When we started talking about my doctor's early diagnoses, she told me about a man she knows whose mother is suffering from Alzheimer's disease. She said he complained that when he called her on the telephone she didn't know who he was.

Likewise, he said that the last time he visited her, she didn't know him.

Devastation.

Heartbreak.

Tammi said he told her that it hurt him so badly; he does not call or visit his mother any more.

"I hate to call him selfish, but that is all I can think of," she said.

You know, this is where it gets complicated. To see someone you love drift away, how do you cope? Because it hurts so much, do you do like this man did, just stay away, thinking, *Oh well, she won't know me anyway?*

Maybe this is his form of self survival. However, I also understand why Tammi thinks it is selfish. He is not thinking of his mother, he is thinking of himself.

Yet, on the other hand, perhaps at this point, self survival is more important than sitting in front of an oncoming train with its whistle blowing; *I'm so lonesome I could cry...*

Tammi said, "I can only imagine what it would be like to not even know your own name, then to be totally alone. To sit in a room with blank spaces in your mind, looking at pictures of people you once loved more than life itself, and not know them anymore."

She grows quiet. Silence fills the air.

I'm so lonesome I could cry...

After a moment she says, "Then he says it just hurts him too bad..." She shakes her head in sadness.

Tammi lost both her parents within the past couple years; her heart has a huge hole in it, yet it beats with love and sweet caring. She is a good person. What to do when this dread disease strikes and carries its victim far away, so far away? Her solution is not to run and hide. No, she says, "If mom or dad can't remember you as their child, how about becoming their friend now?"

The sadness of the moment leaves and a smile fills her pretty face as she thinks about another friend whose mother also suffers from Alzheimer's disease.

She said, "My friend surrounded her mother's room with pictures. She made a scrapbook of places, events, family reunions and grandbabies. People with Alzheimer's forget. They repeat themselves. They are just as unhappy about it as you are sad about it."

Tammi understands that people have to learn to handle and understand Alzheimer's. Learning to handle and understand is a coping mechanism. No one promises it will be easy.

"People with Alzheimer's will forget. They will even come to the point they forget they have a disease. They will not remember asking, telling, what is what or where is where. You have to learn patience. You have to understand and you cannot get aggravated or upset because they are repeating themselves over and over," she said.

Now, I ask you, how can I ask for a dearer friend? She understands. She cares. I know that she will be there when I begin to deteriorate. And, I suppose I will deteriorate. I do not want to. I hope it does not happen. But, wishful thinking is a lot like living in fantasy land. Neither is real.

Tammi has advice for someone afflicted with this debilitating disease. She came up with a unique tip that might help someone in the early developmental stages, not yet completely progressed. She suggests the person wear a bracelet with Reminder Charms.

Reminder Charms? I ask.

She said, "Yes. Charms of a cell phone, a purse, a key, a pet—cat or dog—day-to-day things that a sufferer doesn't want to forget while going out for a couple hours."

Tammi explained that before leaving home the wearer can finger the bracelet and be reminded: *I need to get my cell phone and put it in my pocket. I must not forget my purse. Let me take a moment to feed the cat or dog and let me be sure I have my keys…*

"Also," she adds, "This will not bring to light your disease if you are self-conscious about it when out in public. It is a unique and quiet reminder."

Tammi, dear Tammi. She is thinking about me and how for the second day in a row my cell phone got *lost*.

Yesterday, I thought I left it at home, but instead, I simply had not searched my big old purse thoroughly enough. It was stashed in there beneath the notary seal, wallet, camera, flashlight, an apple, the hand cream Mona gave me for my birthday, and other things I deem necessary to tote each day.

Today, the day she suggested the charm bracelet, I *did* leave my cell phone at home. I unplugged it from its charger, carried it out into the living room, told myself explicitly, *I am setting my cell phone right here, and I will not forget where it is.*

Location fixed in my head; then I went out onto the patio and fed the new little Musk Turtle, StinkiePooPoo. Back inside I made my way to the kitchen where I put on a pot of coffee, fed BooCat, TacoBelle and Rosie. Hadley was already outside for his morning potty-run.

I poured a cup of coffee, came into my home office, sat down and checked my email before adding a chapter to this book.

Soon, my coffee was gone; I called Hadley inside, gathered up my purse and lunch, walked out the door telling the furbies, *I'll be back. Mama loves you.*

I slid into the car, started the motor, backed out from under the carport, and drove up the driveway, listening to the latest news on the local PBS radio station.

Ten minutes later I arrived at work.

Inside, I turned on the computer and that is when I thought about my cell phone.

It was not in my purse. However, I did not panic. I had an unmistakable mental image of where it was. My mind's eye pictured it clearly. I left it exactly where I said I would not forget leaving it.

I did not forget. And, that is precisely what I told Chuck when I called, *"I know just where my cell phone is…"*

I could hear the laughter in Chuck's voice when he asked, "Where?"

He agreed to retrieve it and bring it to me.

Is this two steps back and one step forward?

This incident, the second in two days, is what prompted Tammi to suggest her unique idea, *Reminder Charm Bracelet.* She also pointed out that many people wear ID bracelets, "Just engrave the phone number and address on the back," adding that this might help if an Alzheimer's sufferer becomes disoriented or lost.

I smile when I think about Tammi and how wonderfully understanding she is. Coupled with a rip-roaring sense of humor, she is one in a million.

No matter how this disease ravages my shrinking brain, I know… I just know… I will never forget her.

◦⊸

"MEMORIES ARE MADE OF THIS"*

*(Recorded by Dean Martin)
My memory's not as sharp as it used to be.
Also, my memory's not as sharp as it used to be.

◦⊸

Too Many Mountains to Climb

Photo by: Ann Hamilton,

Mt. McKinley aka Mt. Denali, August 2013

This snowcapped mountain is <u>Denali or Mt. McKinley.</u> It is actually named both. The locals want to officially change the name to Denali. It was named after President McKinley and it is the tallest mountain in the US. I took this shot when we were flying over in the small plane, then landed up there on a glacier. It was last August with my sister, Bobby, Larry, and me. A fantastic and unforgettable adventure. -Ann Hamilton

There are so many mountains to climb in life. There are stumbling blocks, bigger rocks, and tall barriers constantly falling in our paths. A shrinking brain is the biggest mountain... starting as a few pebbles, building into boulders and cliffs and finally, a mountain. Mountains have been scaled. They have been crossed. Does there remain a single mountain that has not been climbed?

Never quite give up hope. Yesterday's despair becomes today's aspirations, dreams and expectations. Cling to optimism. This is how it should be, how it must be, and this is how it will be.

~

THE UPSIDE OF THE DOWNSIDE

Right now I compartmentalize and departmentalize. I make lists and then put whatever I have written down on paper out of my mind; a habit both healthy and helpful.

I have not had to label drawers and I have not put the butter in the microwave but occasionally words leave me and I have to fight harder to find them. As I write this I searched for the term *Phoenix Rising*. It eventually surfaced, but I wonder why I had to lose it in the first place.

Then I remember. *Alzheimer's disease.*

Now, have I said this before already?

Likely I have. This is what happens to the shrinking brain. Repeating one's self.

Have I already mentioned backtracking? The secret to avoid a lot of backtracking is set things down in the same place, and try not to get sidetracked, reacting without paying attention. Maybe this is where the labeling begins for some.

Keys. You know to put your keys there and then when you need them again, you also know to go to the drawer labeled *Keys.*

Put them there and they will stay there until you need them again.

Backtracking. The upside of the downside of forgetting where I leave something requires that I go back—backtrack—making maybe six trips, so I get plenty of exercise. The forgetting is the downside. The extra exercise is the upside.

Likely, you figured that out already.

Sometimes I get more exercise than I want. At work this morning, I looked around for my cell phone. I went blank. I did not recall when I had last seen it. I felt around in my carryall purse. I really dislike large purses, but I generally carry something large to work because I need my notary public seal, wallet, tissues and Chapstick, a book to read during lunchtime, a pen and notebook, my camera and flashlight, hand cream and business cards.

My cell phone normally gets dropped in as I walk out the door. However, I did not feel it down in the bag. In search of my phone, I pushed stuff aside, felt in the cracks and crevices and then determined I must have left it still charging beside the bed.

I searched my mind's eye. I could not picture where I might have set it down. Will this shrinking brain affect my ability to picture things in my head, my mind? I have counted on mental pictures for as long as I can recall.

Recall.

God, will I still be able to use words like recall, remember, recollect, summon, and bring to mind… once this disease shrouds my brain?

I drove back to the house, went to the bedroom and the cell phone was not there. It was not in either bathroom. It was not on the kitchen table. It was nowhere.

I asked Chuck to call me. I would track the phone by its ringing.

I never heard a sound.

I decided to try calling from my portable house phone letting it ring while I made my way around the house. About then, Tammi answered.

She advised she heard the ringing from inside my oversized purse. It was in there all along.

I took a deep breath. Told myself, *Self, do not beat yourself up over this incident. It could have happened to anyone. Even someone with an unshrunk brain.*

So, how do we determine when something is a simple mistake or innocent forgetfulness, as opposed to the onset of Alzheimer's disease? Where is the fine line? And is the line so fine after all? Is it based on age alone? What about a busy brain instead of a shrinking brain? Overload. Surplus circuitry sparking.

I refuse to pick at the scab because I do not want a scar. I stand strong; do not want to give into any weakness. I did that once a very long time ago. I fell apart emotionally when my husband of twenty years fell in love with another woman, leaving the children and me spinning like precarious tops about to run out of momentum. We teetered and tottered and we all fell down. He never looked back.

I determined never again would I put all my eggs into one basket; let my heart be held by another completely. I will give my heart but I will hold my council. I will give my heart but not my soul.

On the other hand, truth be known, there is no one breaking down my door for either. Easy to talk tough when standing all alone with no love words threatening to loosen the ties that bind up my self-pledges.

I am realistic if I am nothing else. However, I am never lonely because I do not let myself dwell. I stay busy, keeping active physically and mentally.

I never want to wind up *"Wastin' away again in margaritaville, searchin' for my lost shaker of salt…"**

(*Jimmy Buffett).

~

THE HEARING AID

I was telling Tammi that I just bought a new hearing aid. I said, "It cost me two-thousand dollars but it's state of the art. It's perfect." "Really," said Tammi. "What kind is it?" "Twelve-thirty," I answered.

WISHING ON A STAR

I remind myself that a single aspirin can halt a headache that would otherwise render a person painfully useless for the most part. Putting it in the simplest of terms there are things that work.

By the way, for a very long time I suffered from an aching in one particular portion of my head. Me, who never has headaches. I mentioned it to my doctor. Whether he found it significant or not, he did not say. Eventually, the pain that still comes and goes, in the very same location, is bearable… and even could be said to have subsided for the most part, so I ignore it. Now, I wonder, is this part of the shrinking process? It makes my head hurt because it is actually in motion?

Forget the side effects that come with everything we put into our bodies, including something so accepted as the common but miraculous aspirin. Just recognize that it does not have to be complicated to be successful, to work.

Then there is the other side of the coin. There is this thing called faith. Believing. If you want something bad enough, have faith enough, it shall come to pass.

There are people who put their faith in their faith. I understand clinging to any lifeboat within reach. It is human nature.

Can believing make it so? I wish. Oh god, how I wish.

Unfortunately, wishing and hoping, believing, wanting so bad that it hurts… well, none of this, in my humble opinion, is even close to being factual. If it were, my son would not be dead. Period.

And, following that one main thing—my son still alive and not killed in a horrible traffic accident—my personal list is long and full of wishes.

If horses were wishes, we would all ride.

On the other hand, if frogs had wings, they wouldn't bump their butts every time they jump. Or should that be "leap," as in Leap Frog?

Jump and bump rhyme. I will leave it at that.

Dennis was right, my brain is too full.

Ann Hamilton told me about someone she knows who suffers from dementia or Alzheimer's… a beloved aunt.

Wait! Have you ever noticed we use the term *suffering from* in connection to any ailment?

We have it, thus we are suffering from it. Although the degree of suffering differs from person to person and disease to disease but since the disease under discussion is Alzheimer's, the term *suffering from* is accurate. And it is a monster.

The Troll that takes its Toll.

Ann related that she "has dementia and refuses to acknowledge it, and she's at the point now that her world has become for the moment.

"She doesn't remember anything recent and not too much of the past, and it is progressing.

"It's been about five years. She has never taken medication but guess what? She drives the car. Her husband, who is legally blind, tells her where to turn… and away they go.

"Yikes! We hold our breath for them since she thinks nothing is wrong. And, of course that's what she thinks. She lost the ability to think. That's what happens with this disease.

"Their kids have tried to get them to go to assisted living and her husband is willing and ready… but not her."

Ann asked a doctor one time about the difference between dementia and Alzheimer's and she understood him to say it all pretty much falls under the Alzheimer's category.

"Either way" she said, "the symptoms are pretty much the same, he told me."

Speaking again of this woman, her aunt, Ann said that she "never forgot a birthday and this year she has forgotten several of people that are close to her, including Larry's in June. She was always the first to call on the birthday day and sing 'happy birthday.'

"That has been taken away now. I think if she underwent tests, as you have, they would probably find the shrinking brain. But, she won't allow it. We usually meet them for a quick dinner at the local Mexican restaurant. She doesn't remember anymore what she usually gets. We have to help her with that. But, she wants to meet at 4 pm so they can get home before dark… it gets dark at 8 pm and they live 5 minutes away. She's driving."

CAN IT GET MUCH WORSE?
IS A BLUE BIRD BLUE.

Several days after Ann related the above information, she again shared another more recent incident about this same woman and how her dementia affects not only her and her husband's lives, but the lives of others who care about them.

Ann said, "Yesterday was my uncles birthday. On Friday my aunt called us and asked if we wanted to help celebrate his birthday.

"I said of course, ask him where he wants to go."

Ann said she asked and he said he wanted to go to Red Lobster—his favorite place.

"So I told her we would meet them there Saturday at 11:30. I told her to write that down on her calendar. She said she wrote it down—*Saturday at 11:30, Red Lobster.*

"So we go over there yesterday. My sister came too. We got there at 11:15 because they are usually early. We waited, and waited, and waited. They never came."

Upset now, Ann said, "Of course we knew something terrible must have happened, they're never late."

She said they started making phone calls. She said the couple does not carry a cell phone because they could never figure it out. Ann called their kids in Dallas, getting additional phone numbers of people they may know.

After waiting an hour, Ann and Larry started back tracking. She said they live in a town about 15 miles out so they drove down the freeway in that direction but saw nothing.

Ann reminds me, "Remember, she is still driving with her dementia, and refuses to go to an assisted living place, and says sometimes her brain doesn't work just right."

Ann and Larry ended up at their house. Her granddaughter and great grandson had been notified. They were there and were trying to get into the house. It was locked up tight.

Ann said that the garage door has curtains on the window so they couldn't see inside to see if their car was there. Seeing no alternative, they broke the window and looked inside the garage.

The car was gone.

"Where are they… She who has dementia and is still driving," lamented Ann.

She said they decided to go take another drive around and, "Lo and behold, I saw their car driving toward their house. We followed them, got to the house and they told us they had been to the hairdresser, then to another restaurant. She had written down *Sunday at Red Lobster*."

Ann said that it is apparent from talking to her she did not remember from the time she hung up the phone to the time she wrote on her calendar, the day.

"She only remembers at the exact moment. My uncle said, 'Well, that's what she said, Sunday, not Saturday.'"

Ann said, "This situation is getting bad and all of us feel helpless. Her granddaughter said their kids need to do something. They don't realize how bad things are because they don't live here."

The exasperation coupled with sadness, is in Ann's words, "It's bad. She's into about year five of this disease, no medication. Won't take it, never has."

And so, what next?

Well, for now, Ann and Larry and her aunt and uncle are going to try again today… 11:30 at Red Lobster.

Ann added, "Barb, I think the saddest thing of all is my aunt was stone-faced and had absolutely no idea how much she had us all worried. She did start singing *Happy Birthday* to my uncle. But it is so sad that she wasn't even aware."

The ending? Ann smiled sadly and said, "I guess I better give my aunt a call and make sure they are going today. Sure don't want another day like yesterday."

No. Yesterdays like that are not so good. The only problem is, tomorrow never comes. All we have is today, one day at a time.

From on minute to the next.

This instant.

Right now.

Did you hear the one about the guy who spent all his time talking to himself?
Nope. Never heard a thing. Guess he wasn't talking to me. *
(*Barbara Sharik)

TALKING TO YOURSELF BEATS A BLANK

Carol Holston, long time friend jokingly reminded me, there is only so much you can talk to yourself about before you run out of things to talk about.

I countered, *Well, that won't happen when you have Alzheimer's. You can keep right on talking because there's a good chance you won't remember what you just said, so you keep repeating… And the conversation, even with yourself, continues.*

We discussed additives in foodstuff that are not healthy, artificial colors, artificial sweeteners. I recalled climbing on a super high bandwagon when my children were little after reading of the possibility that hyperactivity in children was caused by certain additives. My Tony suffered a degree of hyperactivity.

From there, my thirst for more kept me reading and learning. I subscribed to *Consumer's Union*, adored Ralph Nader and everything he stood for, and trembled like a lone Maple leaf on a tree at the end of fall.

Unfortunately, here, where I live, I was preaching to people who looked at me like I was a spider under a microscope. A weird outsider with wild ideas. Still, I loved the people; they could not help that they thought I was off the wall. They had never met anyone quite like me.

On one hand I was out of my element, but then again, I had no element. This was my home by choice, and so, I carved my niche and I stayed. At least the people are goodhearted and accepted me even if they couldn't convert me—I was a quirky strange pet, but I was their quirky strange pet.

DON'T BE A SITTING DUCK FOR DEMENTIA

On the other hand, I have always been intelligent and am well read. I live to learn. I paint. I write. I thrive undertaking all things mental. Word games, challenging crossword puzzles, acrostics… these things feed my brain.

When I want to unwind, relax, I play *Boggle* on my computer. This is the game where you make words from randomly placed letters. Words. I love words. Mental challenges make my day. Would eating healthier trump a lifetime of mental activities? I ask because I have always used my brain, kept it active, but I have not always eaten healthy. Off and on, yes. But more off than on.

I gained weight so what did I do? I said, *Grandmothers are supposed to be fluffy.* I said, *I'm not fat, I'm fluffy.* I said, *I can warm you in the winter and shade you in the summer. Now can a skinny woman do that?*

Now, it is time to be serious. No jokes for a few minutes. I remember when I was married to Chuck, he once asked me, *Can't you ever be serious?*

I guess not. We are long divorced, but we are the best of friends. He can be a grump and I can be a fool because in the end, we each live where we live and that is not with each other.

So now, I have to ask, which works best for this alien ailment? Mental activities since my brain is affected, or a healthy diet because we all know, junk food and food with additives and artificial coloring, these do damage brains.

What about exercise. I wear a little pedometer some days and find I do anywhere from three to six miles a day at work. My job is a sit-down job. At my desk, at the computer. But, when I am in my healthy mode, I try to make extra trips. If I have to make copies of three things, I will make three trips. Of course, I can only do that when I am not swamped.

Mostly, I am swamped.

You see, my lifestyle allows me to take a walk around the yard with the dogs… but it gets so hot, I have to do it in the early morning—which is my favorite time anyway.

Then, there are the mosquitoes. I heard on the news that some mosquito larva in Ouachita Parish have tested positive for West Nile. Already, it is beginning. It is a crap shoot out there, every day of our lives.

However, that does not negate my current problem. Alzheimer's and trying to do the best by myself while I can still do so.

Exercise. Eating healthier. I already do the brain exercising. I just have to work on the eating healthy and exercising. Excuses are like checks on a piece of gingham… they are plentiful but unless you want to be stuffed in the bag of used clothes and carted down to the Goodwill… well, you get the picture.

My choice. My responsibility. Making up my mind. Doing it. I might get hit by a meteor tomorrow night while gazing at the stars, but today, I should be locking the cookie jar and slicing a nice fresh tomato out of Chuck's garden.

Hope springs eternal.

Healthy diets and exercise. Thinking positive. Praying. Having faith. Concentration. Mind over matter. Desire. Wanting something so bad it just has to happen.

Santa please bring me a baby doll that cries real tears and wets her diaper.
Santa, bring me a six shooter and a horse just like Trigger.

Ah, the innocent days when little girls played with dolls and little boys played cowboys and Indians. We never gave the term "Politically Correct" a thought, nor did we give senility a thought. Grandmothers might call us by the wrong name, but they gave us kisses and candy. Grandfathers might have been hard of hearing and talked too much, but they gave us pennies and nickels. Sometimes, even a dime.

A kinder, gentler time.

We never heard the words: *Alzheimer's Disease*. If we had, we would have paid no attention. That was then, this is now. I am all grown up and I am weighing all the pros and cons, the things I think I know; the things I never knew and things I should know, want to know. Must know.

Perhaps, it would be the added touch now in my time of need to find that the combination of using my brain and eating healthy coupled with taking specific vitamins would slow the process because, admittedly, to learn my brain is shrinking and that I am developing Alzheimer's disease does thrust me into a time of need.

I expect if I did the study I would find most researchers very likely agree that to combine healthy diets and utilizing the brain to full capacity combined with the magic of good genes would be the best available tools to fight Alzheimer's disease.

I am rambling. Groping for straws, still so unsure what to do. With my quest for knowledge, I know I will have to do research. I must. It would be foolish not to do so. I was never one to say something could not happen to me, however, I never thought Alzheimer's would happen. I simply never thought about it.

I have never broken a bone. I do not anticipate breaking one now. So, why should I have anticipated Alzheimer's disease rearing its ugly head?

However, on the other hand, there is a crude saying: "Shit happens." I generally change it to "Guano happens." Either way, the fan is being hit.

By the way, I received a hand addressed postcard last month from "The Arbor & Terrace" an assisted living retirement community. It has a *"special memory care unit."* The motto is *"Assistance when needed. Service when required."*

I am invited to *"live life your way"* because they *"offer gracious residential living in a home-like setting with dedicated, knowledgeable staff, available 24 hours a day to meet the personal requirements and needs of residents. The*

Terrace, our memory care community, provides a secure supportive environment for those with memory-related disorders."

They advised *"We have an apartment available!"*

Me and my big mouth.

Nevertheless, it is good to know, here in my rural parish in northeast Louisiana, someone heard my cry in the dark and sent a lifeline if I wish to catch hold.

EXCUSE ME?

An elderly gentleman, maybe in his mid-nineties, very well dressed, hair well groomed, expensive looking suit, flower in his lapel, smelling slightly of a good after-shave, presenting a well looked-after image, walks into an upscale cocktail lounge. Seated at the bar is an elderly lady, about mid-eighties. The gentleman walks over, sits on the stool next to her, orders a drink, takes a sip. He turns to her and says, "So tell me, do I come here very often?"

"BABY'S GOT HER BLUE JEANS ON"*
(*Mel McDaniel)

Genes. Another country, another voice, heard from. We are often at the mercy of our genes. Heredity. It has long been accepted that heredity plays a major roll in each of our lives.

Was my grandmother verging on senility when she called everyone by the wrong name before she hit on the right one? Was my mother beginning to fade because she occasionally lost a thought?

Honestly, I was more concerned when listing diseases known in my family tree on medical questionnaires, fearful on some level that I might be inclined to develop something known to skip a generation.

But, it is not my fault to think this way. The forms request patients to list particular ailments. I checked *yes*, my grandfather died of Tuberculosis. *Yes*, my mother had breast cancer.

These are two of the hereditary questions I believed vital to my makeup. Obviously, the medical field finds them important as well, otherwise, they would not be standard queries on standard questionnaires required every time I visit a physician's office for the first time.

We have come a long way, baby. We really have. But, not far enough. Will we ever come far enough? Just when we reach the end, somebody ties a knot in our rope and it gets shorter. You have seen the poster of the cute little kitten hanging on. I feel like that kitten hanging onto the knotted up shortened rope.

Now I ask, because the times are changing and we are spreading our microscopes farther a field, was there any dementia in my family tree?

I answer that I do not believe so and if there was, it was before my time. A generation unknown to me personally. Nothing I ever picked up on with my ever listening ears and constantly craving mind. However, remember, I never lived around my relatives; dad was a serviceman and we moved all around the country. We only visited aunts, uncles, cousins, grandparents, on wonderful, but relatively rare occasions.

My mother's mother died of a stroke, best I recall. I know she stayed with us for a period of time and I remember mom being her caretaker... but even though my brain was young then I cannot recall much more than that. There was a dreadful incident where my mom, Phyllis Geoghan Sharik, was helping my grandmother to the bathroom and she had an accident along the way. She was so very, very embarrassed. I remember the pain of her embarrassment. I felt it. I empathized even as a mostly centrally-focused youth at that time. I felt the horror, but I was not cut from the cloth that rushed to help my mother clean up the mess made by an illness that took away my grandmother's dignity.

Always so proper, she was horrified. She was emotionally devastated. And now, now I know how she felt. I remember how I felt at that time but now I know how *she* felt.

I have experienced an embarrassing moment very similar since this ailment has begun progressing. I now live in fear of a repeat. I clench my jaws, almost grinding my teeth, I clench my sphincter muscles. I am so at the control of my weaknesses for moments at a time. All my stoic stable strength blinks on me… Like a poor heart monitor reading… Beat. Beat. Beat. Skip. Beat. Beat.

Irritable Bowel Syndrome? IBS. Everything has initials. Rearrange them to ISB: Incredible Shrinking Brain. Maybe that should be Irritable Shrinking Brain. My brain, once incredible, is now irritable. My brain, my bowels. For just a moment, I feel so scared, The fear melts into sadness. Then, I take control and I am okay. For now, I am okay.

But, tomorrow?

Next week?

I dare not even consider next year. One day at a time, live life to its fullest, accomplish, live, love. Each day. Yesterday is gone. Tomorrow is not promised. Live now.

I wrote a poem so many years ago about taking the tomorrow train down a one way track. It is not necessarily good poetry, but it makes a point, reveals my philosophy even back then… when we had a rural route delivery address, instead of a 911-address. That is how long ago it was. That is how long my mind has been bent in this direction.

THE TOMORROW TRAIN

Nothing is accomplished by looking back.

Better to ride the tomorrow train

down a one-way track.

Shedding tears over a phantom past
makes bitter water for flowers
that can never last.

Yesterday is forever out of reach
like sifting, shifting sands
on a wind-swept beach.

Foolish to waste the precious present
for today is only borrowed
and tomorrow barely lent.

Forget the web that yesterday weaves.
Empty the shallow china cup,
tossing out the used tealeaves.

Yesterday was temporary and can't come back.
Better to ride the tomorrow train
down a one-way track.

Some of the things I grew up thinking that I knew I later learned were not necessarily exactly as I understood them to be. Instead, some were a child's misunderstanding—something overheard and left stuck somewhere in my brain before it began shrinking.

I was sure I remembered *this*, but it turns out it was *that*. So, I have no specific facts regarding anything more than the TB and breast cancer. Oh, yes, and my father had five heart attacks before a sixth laid him low. He came through each heart event with flying colors; so he had good genes, which means I must also have good genes. I do not recall picking up on any dementia the times I was around him when visiting over the years.

Hereditary. Genes. Blood.

Some scientists, from what I have ascertained, do believe that for most people Alzheimer's disease does result from a combination of genetics, lifestyle and even environment.

What is the percentage that Alzheimer's will be caused by specific genetic changes? I have no idea and although I am not a scientist, even I know these things play a role in our makeup. Naturally, these factors affect our brains over time.

It has to be a given. A fact of life... *and death*.

By the way, BooCat seems particularly affected by my affliction. She is more clinging, more protective. Is she one of these death-sniffing animals I have read about? She is intuitive, smart (after all, she helped me write the BooCat series), but there is something new going on. She has not left my side when I am home for several months.

This is an aside from hereditary, genes and blood. It is animal intuition. Animals have it. Instincts. What vibe is she picking up from me of late?

Dennis always said of his one cat, *He knows when I am in angst.*

BooCat knows also. Simple as that. She knows.

But, back to the genes. I remember visiting my Uncle John and his family in New Jersey after I was grown and married. I was immediately aware of his mannerism, his speech pattern. He was my father made over. Family resemblance yes. But, I am talking about the way he moved, the way he stood, the way his eyes twinkled, even. Everything.

My father had not lived around his brother, my uncle, for many years. Dad left home at age 17, joined the Army, met and married my mother and then went off to fight in the Battle of the Bulge in World War Two. He returned as a well decorated Ranger having survived Hill 400 where many went up, and few came down, a battle worth looking up if someone is interested in such things. With the advent of the Internet, there is much to be read about this particular battle, including an impressive headline from the New York Times.

A man who fought side-by-side with Dad wrote a story about that particular battle and quoted him talking about his new daughter, Penny. That was his nickname for me.

Back to my uncle… you might note that while it seems I ramble, and one thought reminds me of something else, it is simply because I have so much in my head—Dennis was right—sometimes it just needs to spill out.

While it still can.

In any case, I recall marveling at the identical gesticulations, movements… between that of my uncle John and my father, Michael.

Somewhere in the grand scheme of things, there is a DNA connection that cannot be denied.

Still, not every ailment is hereditary.

Therefore, taking hereditary traits off the table is not a given because not every scientist is putting them on the table in the first place. Shrouded in misconceptions, mystery and misunderstanding. How do you clear the air, see a uniform picture when there are differing opinions being offered by equally qualified scientists? They all know Alzheimer's disease is real. What causes it, how to treat it… these are the things that are being worked on, on different levels and different scales.

Removing genetics from the page, I sum up that even though someone may have a heart attack in the middle of a workout, I cannot condemn the belief that exercise and proper nutrition decreases the possibility of heart disease.

Genes may or may not contribute. So much is still so unknown. Dr Salk is not around to create a vaccine. He beat Polio. The world is awaiting a Dr Salk to come along and beat Alzheimer's disease.

SURPRISE ME

"The afternoon knows what the morning never suspected."
(Robert Frost)

Rocky Horizon
Photo by: Ann Hamilton,
Monument Valley, Utah, May 2013

We are born into a world with rocky horizons surrounding us. How we meet these rocky barriers is up to each individual. Nobody is promised a rose garden. Even while smelling the flowers, we face the possibility of getting bee-stung. Such is life.

You rise each morning, go about your business, do the best you can. You do not give up. This is the secret to true success. Always think positive. Never let a little beesting make you cry for very long.

Tears cleanse the eyes, optimism cleanses the soul. Someday, someone will find a cure for Alzheimer's disease. While I know I cannot live forever, I would like very much if that breakthrough were announced tomorrow. Or, even the next day.

ONE BLT–CUT THE MAYO

One proper-eating, constantly-exercising, individual still falling dead should not throw up a red flag negating the good that adopting healthy behavior does substantiate. Likely, he could just as easily have fallen dead as he slept in his recliner after a heavy meal. Or, slipped away in the night, peacefully.

So, back to the question will a proper diet and exercise delay Alzheimer's disease? It has helped in many other ailments that befall mankind. Diabetics must adhere to strict diets. People with certain food allergies must eat with care. People wanting to lose weight follow another sort of diet.

Eating healthy cannot be ruled out of the picture. Is it the cure-all? On one hand, we can hope. Also, it cannot hurt. Most importantly, *it cannot hurt.*

What is the phrase physicians promise when taking their Hippocratic Oath? Something about doing no harm. Eating healthy can do no harm. So much that humanity undertakes can and does, but certainly not eating healthy. First I will attempt the healthy eating, then I will consider the exercise…

Even such simple activities as taking a daily 30-minute walk can help improve an individual's mood, not to mention can be vital in maintaining the health of joints, muscles and our hearts. Regular exercise has shown to benefit heart health so it makes sense that it may also play a role in preventing, maybe even reversing, cognitive decline. This is one of those *It cannot hurt* sort of things. Do it even though you do not know if it will prevent or reverse; just know that it can do no harm.

Do I sound like a commercial? An ad? On the other hand, maybe I am trying to talk my own self into committing to what makes sense as well.

Eat healthy. Exercise. Keep the body and the mind active and healthy.

Just as there are scientists that differ in opinions regarding the cause of Alzheimer's disease, there are physicians that differ on treatment.

There are those in the medical field that swear by eating diets rich in whole grains, fruits, vegetables, and nuts, and diets low in meats and fats. Some health-advocates believe diets low in carbohydrates, especially sugars and high fructose corn syrup can make a difference. Such a diet is thought to reduce brain inflammation.

Brain inflammation.

Others believe there is the possibility that smoking, diabetes and high cholesterol levels raise the risk of Alzheimer's disease.

Believing, but not actually proving. So much makes sense but so much is unproven. Common sense, yes. Curing, no proof yet.

Smoking.

Diabetes.

High cholesterol levels.

Healthy eating.

Exercise.

Positive thinking.

However, beware of charlatans with dollar signs in their eyes. When certain nutritional supplements are marketed specifically to treat Alzheimer's disease, understand the Food and Drug Administration (FDA) does *not* approve products marketed as *Medical Foods*.

Medical Foods.

How lovely if it were so, but to date there is no definitive data showing that any of these supplements are actually beneficial or in fact, even safe, according to the Mayo Clinic.

According to the National Institutes of Health (NIH) the herbal mixtures, vitamins and other supplements promoted to support cognitive health, and perhaps even prevent or delay Alzheimer's disease has not found this to be so. It may sound good, and it may make sense, but testing has not verified these claims. This would include taking extra vitamin B, vitamin C, vitamin E, folic acid or beta carotene.

Can it be detrimental to take these vitamins on the off chance they might be beneficial? Well, as an aside, everything I have read from reliable sources strongly advise that no one should take vitamin E except under a doctor's supervision. Research has shown an increased risk of death associated with taking vitamin E. Scary stuff.

Still there are physicians and naturalists who advise to take folic acid, eat spinach, and exercise the brain and the body. Some advise not to drink alcohol, despite others advising a glass of wine is healthy. Who is right and who is wrong?

Another thing to bear in mind—supplements promoted for cognitive health might interact with medications being taken for any health condition, including Alzheimer's.

Exercise the brain. Healthy diets and healthy lifestyle habits cannot hurt no matter if it is a cure-all or a preventive. Sometimes we have to grope and grab for the gusto based on common sense in order to protect ourselves from our own bad habits.

However, on the other hand, the NIH panel *did* conclude in a study, that there may be some evidence that omega-3 fatty acids in fish oil *might* help prevent cognitive decline. Thus, the run on everybody eating salmon. Broiled or baked, of course. We are still being warned about ingesting too much fried foods.

The NIH also did an extensive study on the possible benefits of Gingko. Just a few years ago I kept hearing everybody talking about Gingko. Well, it turns out that this plant extract containing several substances at first thought to be beneficial is now believed to have no effect in preventing or delaying Alzheimer's disease after all.

One day it is on the hit parade. The next, it is bumped into oblivion. What do we know? How do we know? Three ways:

1. Common sense.

2. Trust your physician.

3. Common sense.

Oh, I believe I already said that. However, I cannot say it enough: *Use your common sense.*

Although there is no lifestyle factor that has conclusively shown to reduce the risk of Alzheimer's, proper rest coupled with healthy physical and mental exercise to stimulate the neurons have been declared not to be detrimental. They cannot hurt. We still have such a long way to go to know, to really know. In the meantime, even if taking care of ourselves does not completely curtail or prevent Alzheimer's disease, it will not hurt. In fact, it may help prevent our coming down with some other nasty ailment.

Do no harm. Oh yeah, and use your common sense.

It cannot hurt.

My diagnoses? It seems from all I have recently read, there is more that cannot hurt, rather than any one thing being declared a cure-all. There is no cure-all at this time but we do know some things that will hurt, are hazardous to our health, so we go with the next best thing. We do what cannot hurt.

It cannot hurt to take care of ourselves, be consciously aware of what we are putting into our bodies and what we are doing to our bodies… Our brains are a major part of our bodies. Bodies and brains must be in sync.

Your body is the jug that carries your brain. If the jug gets a crack in it, the leakage might affect your mental wellbeing as well as the physical aspect. Keep everything in sync as best as possible.

My convoluted mind reread: *as best as*. It jumped to asbestos. An English teacher just turned over in his/her grave. God, I will miss my brain when it is gone.

Important to report that some studies have indicated an association between lifelong involvement in both mental and socially stimulating activities, possibly reducing the risk.

Do not withdraw and omit socially stimulating activities from your lifestyle.

Also, there is the *possibility* that the more education, the more stimulating the job, the better.

Work that brain.

I stuff mine so full, it never stops soaking up and accumulating. Whether this will help me in the long run, in the end, I cannot say. However, it stimulates me now. It provides me a fulfillment that is satisfying. I will never know it all, but I want to know as much as I can.

Pay no attention to the folks who warn a little knowledge is a dangerous thing. In my opinion, a *little* knowledge is better than *no* knowledge. Now, that, *that* is a dangerous thing. Exercise your brain. Think. Think. Think. Never stop thinking. Never stop flexing and stretching your mental muscles.

Back to what is written about what helps and what does not. Read this, read that. Which is right? Which is wrong? There is so much hit and miss, but how else will we reach the end of the line and come to the light at the end of the tunnel? That brilliant light. *Shine on.*

Star light, star bright.
I wish I may, I wish I might.
I wish my dream will come true tonight.
What goes up the chimney?
Smoke.
May your wish and my wish,
never be broke.

~

IRONY

"I want to grow old without facelifts... I want to have the courage to be loyal to the face I've made. Sometimes I think it would be easier to avoid old age, to die young, but then you'd never complete your life, would you? You'd never wholly know you."
(Marilyn Monroe)

~

In the Mist

Photo by: Ann Hamilton,

Sunset at Monument Valley, Utah, May 2013

Brains shrink and we become shrouded in a mist. This is the sunset of our lives. It is inevitable to a degree. What is not always inevitable is the onset of Alzheimer's disease. Why do some shrinking brains develop this frightening ailment while others do not? Why are some of us wafted off into the misty moonlight while others sit eyes wide open in the bright shining sun?

If somebody knows, they haven't told me yet.

However, I am listening for the answer. I am attentive. I know the answer will be found someday. I have to believe this or hope would be nothing more than a thing with wings.

~~

YOUR GUESS IS AS GOOD AS MINE: CARING FOR THE INCURABLE

While there is no specific test available at this time to confirm Alzheimer's disease on a living individual a good physician can make a judgment based on the variety of symptoms, information provided by the patient, plus the assortment of tests that when combined gives a pretty valid picture.

Believe it or not… and this is damned scary, Alzheimer's disease can be diagnosed with complete accuracy *only after death*.

It is the autopsy that will reveal characteristic plaques and tangles. Plaques are clumps of a protein called beta-amyloid. They damage and destroy brain cells by interfering with cell-to-cell communication.

Threads of tau protein twist into abnormal tangles inside the brain cells, which foul up the transport system that brain cells depend on to carry essential materials and nutrients… and with the transport system all tangled up; there is a strong implication in the decline and death of brain cells.

With the advent of plaques and tangles doing their damage, the disease progresses.

Dr. Shelat always checks my reflexes, muscle tone and strength, balance, coordination, walking and standing, my sense of touch, sight and hearing. He is an astute observer.

He also runs periodic blood tests to rule out as much as to determine, what is going on. Thyroid disorders and various vitamin deficiencies are potential causes of memory loss and confusion. Just because someone suffers memory loss from time to time does not automatically mean they are suffering from Alzheimer's disease.

He did a spinal tap, which provides measurement of biomarkers, key protein patterns in blood and spinal fluid.

My generation remembers a movie titled "*This is Spinal Tap*," an American 1984 rock music mockumentary directed by Rob Reiner about the fictional heavy metal music band *Spinal Tap*.

However, in the medical world, a spinal tap (lumbar puncture) is a serious and important medical procedure to collect and look at the fluid (cerebrospinal fluid, or CSF) surrounding the brain and spinal cord.

A needle is carefully inserted into the spinal canal low in the lumbar area and samples of CSF are collected. These samples are studied for color, blood cell counts, protein, glucose, and other substances. These samples can be put into special culture cups to check for bacterial or fungal infections. The pressure of the CSF is also measured during the procedure.

My late son, Tony, had a spinal tap. He had spinal meningitis at age 11-months. There are important diagnoses obtained from a lumbar puncture: cancer, multiple sclerosis, Guillain-Barr syndrome and even to detect bleeding in the area around the brain or spinal cord.

I had several milograms done in relation to my back surgeries. In this case, a dye is put in the CSF to make the spinal cord and fluid clearer on X-rays. These reveal bulging or ruptured discs as well as cancer.

Dr Shelat conducts brief mental tests to assess my memory and thinking skills. Mostly, I believe I pass these tests except when I have to subtract in my head; I fail. He does not know, but I have never been good with figures in my head. I knew mathematical tricks, counted slash marks and my fingers so I managed to pass my math tests in school. This weakness in me has nothing to do with a shrinking brain.

The adding machine and calculator saved my life; allowing me to become a crackerjack bookkeeper. Not to mention, having worked in a couple banks for about eighteen years. So, even though I cannot subtract backwards, I can keep your books and everything will balance to the proverbial T.

Brain imaging is paramount in his testing. These tests allowed him to pinpoint changes.

There was the Computerized tomography (CT scan), the Magnetic resonance imaging (MRI) and Position emission tomography (PET).

There have been other tests that have obviously been helpful for his diagnoses of early stage Alzheimer's disease. He has been thorough but he has not abused the testing. He did an initial MRI followed with a second a year later. He said there is no reason at this time to do another, three years later. He is a rare bird that does not test just for testing sake.

His testing monitors my progression.

I do not actually know how fast my diagnosis of Alzheimer's disease is progressing. I do know that I am aware of little things, changes in my abilities. What is most frightening is that as Alzheimer's disease progresses, as the brain shrinks, I know these changes will eventually affect physical functions.

Remember, I read. And I encourage people to be aware and to read. Do not read and then become fearful. Read to become proactive.

1. Swallowing.

2. Balance.

3. Bowel and bladder control.

4. Falling.

I have read that as Alzheimer's progresses, someone afflicted will experience a mixture of emotions that include anger, frustration, confusion and uncertainty, fear, grief and depression.

So far, I am upbeat, rarely feel anger or frustration and only of late have noticed a tad of confusion. I have no fear, grief or depression. I have always felt impatient with people who suffered from depression. I did not understand the full impact of the disease; as I believe it is now considered to be.

I knew that I would never allow myself to feel so sad I would pull the cover up over my head and wallow. I did not understand why everyone could not be this forceful. Take charge of their own lives. There is so much we cannot control, but we should be able to rein in our emotions and function. This is what I believed.

Then I met Dennis. He suffered all his life from some degree or another of depression. We discussed the subject thoroughly.

I have read there is a chemical called serotonin that is considered by some to be responsible for binge eating and certain depressions. I am not going there. I do not know enough to speak with any authority or real knowledge. Likely, since I first read about serotonin, a million other chemicals have come to light.

In the end, even if it is a real thing, my staunch belief is that no one should give in to it. No one should pull those covers over their heads and vegetate whilst feeling so sad and sorry for themselves.

It hurts. God, yes it hurts. But, nobody can make it stop hurting except me, me and me. My son was killed in a traffic accident. I cried in the shower, tears blending with the water cascading down my body. Once out of the shower I went to work. I worked long into the night. I was doing the water billing for our local water system and we were not computerized at that time. I did them by hand. Bless this busy work. It had to be done and I knew it had to be done thus I could not shrivel up and become silly putty in the hands of the gods who dole out disease, despair and damage to our bodies, souls and hearts.

I shook my fist at the god who let my son be here one second, giving me a hug, saying *"I love you,"* and thirty seconds later a mangled body in a mangled truck on a highway of hell. An accident I could see from my house. The corner I must drive every single day of my life.

I already felt betrayed when my marriage went south so when my son was taken away the period was put at the end of that sentence. Random acts rein blows down upon mankind just as snow falls and smoke rises. It happens. *It happens.*

Therefore, I can only assume my shrinking brain is a random thing due to any possible number of happenstances from genes, eating the wrong foods, being in the wrong place at the wrong time… *It happens.*

If we do not know the cure, how can we know the cause? Or vice-versa. Bless the men of science for they have worked many a miracle. We are still in need of more miracles that come not from divinity, but from the brains of brilliant men and women.

Do not even begin to tell me that there is a god that provides these brains; because I will counter, then who provides these devastating diseases and disasters?

Six-thousand people died during the Holocaust. What was god doing then? Taking his forty-winks?

Oh wait, that was Rip Van Winkle… but it might as well have been god.

No. I do not believe in a god, nor do I believe in the theory that there is a reason for everything. I am more of a random believer. However, even that belief has pitfalls. People. Brains. So much is random, yes, but much is also preventable.

Brains.

There we are again.

Brains and me. The incredible shrinking brain. ISB.

When a person—me—reaches the final stages, I wonder what will become of me. Over and over, I say that I want to live long enough to die of something besides Alzheimer's disease. I do not want to be a burden. I do not want to become a vegetable.

Do not get me wrong. I have no desire to check out early, so I am counting on Doc to do me right... keep me upright and in prime condition as long as is feasible.

Will I know the turning point? Will my brain function to the point where I know I am failing? What is the thin line between lucidity and senility? Forgetfulness is only the beginning. Slight to marginal to complete forgetfulness.

These declarations send a flitter of something through my shrinking brain: I recall seeing listings in the classifieds in the newspaper for support groups for the caretakers of people suffering from various afflictions; including Alzheimer's patients.

Caretakers must create a safe and supportive environment, adapting the living conditions and situation to the afflicted person. My home from years of being a collector along with normal accumulation over a lifetime, is so cluttered. It is not Alzheimer's friendly at all. According to everything I have read, excess furniture should be removed. All clutter needs to be cut down, eliminated if possible.

Throw rugs can be the cause of tripping. This can be true in reverse. I stepped out of the shower a couple months ago, missed the rug and instead, my wet foot slipped out from under me on the bare floor. The rug would have prevented that slippery-footed slide. Of course, had I taken time to make sure my feet were dry before stepping out of the shower that would have been a good thing also.

No. It was not preordained that I slip and fall. No. The devil did not make me do it either. Stuff just happens. I tell you, stuff just happens.

Handicap accessible… even a home bathroom and stairways will eventually need handrails. Sturdy handrails.

Slippers and shoes need good traction, along with comfort.

I have a couple office chairs with wheels. I just started to sit down; my hips hovered over the chair seat when Rosie the Doxie showed up with a runny nose. She suffers from a severe sinus condition. I leaned down to wipe her nose and the chair rolled right out from under me. This was less than a month ago. My tailbone is only just now feeling sit-able. Tailbones are slow to heal but it could have been so much worse. I did not hit my head or break any bones. Most my backside is fairly well padded. (Bright side speaking up).

I am a tough nut to crack. I have had many surgeries but no broken bones. I have had many setbacks but nothing I could not overcome. There have been roadblocks, but they were maneuverable.

Sometimes I have to think which is the left and which is the right… my heart is on the left. I cross my heart. Thus, this is my right (the hand that crosses) and this is the left, where the heart is. But, I have been playing that mind game ever since I was a child. It has nothing to do with diseased brain cells. It has to do with a crutch I discovered early on and still rely on occasionally, unconsciously yet intentionally.

People with Alzheimer's disease forget to eat. First, they do not feel like preparing meals, then they are incapable of doing so. Even without such a diagnosis I do not feel like cooking for one. My pills say *Take with food.* I eat a couple cookies.

I recognize that not eating a healthy combination of food is detrimental, with or without Alzheimer's. Living alone, not bothering, even without a shrinking brain, it is a problem. Nonetheless, it is one more thing that happens when someone slowly dwindles away mentally because of Alzheimer's disease.

Living alone is complicated in this way. Therefore, even though we live separately and apart, Chuck and I often share meals. No. We do not sit down and dine together; we just fix enough so we each have a plate, thus a more hearty meal than one-on-one cooking for one-on-one. I used to be a good cook. Chuck still is. We like different things, but it works out for the most part.

I have never been a big drinker of any sort of liquid. I can make one can of soda last two days. With that in mind, now I must make a conscious effort to hydrate. Besides dehydration, I recently read that constipation can become a problem.

I shudder. I have been troubled with this malady of late. I did not know of the connection of not enough fluid intake. Right now, as I write this, I am running a dreadful race without a finish line in sight. It started with a bad virus. I spent so much time in the bathroom that when I did start eating, the condition my condition was in was not normal.

Next thing I know, I was constipated. Then, without having managed to get on a schedule, my stomach again became *upset*. I barely made it to the bathroom.

Then, again, I was bombarded with loose bowels, only bouncing back to another bout of constipation. Next, another urge to evacuate, and an accident. I did not make it to the bathroom quickly enough. The sphincter muscle failed.

Devastation. Humiliation. Indignities.

Will this dreadful cycle never end? Is it due to Alzheimer's or just an irritable bowel? Irritable Bowel Syndrome. IBS. Whatever it is, I am scared. I live in fear of not making it to the bathroom in time again, yet I cannot seem to manage to regulate myself.

Do I dare socialize, get far from home? When will it strike again and if it does, will I soil myself?

On top of that, I probably already mentioned this distressful situation. Repeating myself again.

Damned dementia.

TALK ABOUT TROUBLES!

Floyd is walking through the park when he notices an old lady sitting on a bench crying her eyes out. Always the gentleman, he stops to ask her what's wrong. She sobs, "I have a gorgeous 24-year old husband at home. Every morning, he makes passionate love to me, and then gets up and brings me breakfast in bed." Puzzled, Floyd says, "That sounds great, so why are you crying?" Wiping tears off her old wrinkled cheeks, she replies, "For lunch, he makes me my favorite homemade tomato soup and a grilled cheese sandwich and then he makes love to me all afternoon long." Still confused, Floyd says again, "That sounds wonderful, so why are you so sad?" Between gasps for air, tears streaming down her cheeks, she replies, "For dinner he takes me out to the finest restaurants, pays for everything, and then takes me home to a night of unbelievable lovemaking." Exasperated, Floyd asks, "Well then, why on earth are you crying?" With a look of utter despair, the old woman bawls, "I can't remember where I live!"

Staying Balanced

Photo by: Ann Hamilton,

Balanced Rock, Canyonlands, Utah, May 2013

It is important each individual stay balanced, focused... so we do not topple. We can withstand both monumental metaphorical and significant tangible weight and still stay upright. Keep on keeping on. An answer will come someday. Polio was licked. Small pox wiped out. Measles almost unheard of now. It will happen. Alzheimer's disease will one day be overcome and eliminated.

"ENROLL IN AUTO-REFILL NOW!"*
*STRAIGHT TALK

Removing mirrors may be necessary because sufferers of Alzheimer's sometimes find images in mirrors either confusing, or frightening, caregivers have found.

Can you imagine looking into a mirror and not knowing what or who you are looking at? Yet, this is what I just read can be the state of affairs in some cases. It takes my breath away in sheer horror. Imagine fading so far from reality you do not recognize your own self.

What kind of disease is this? Cut off my leg; do not cut off my head. I can hobble, but I cannot become a vegetable.

Alzheimer's disease is like falling into a horror movie. Something Alfred Hitchcock might have written. We thought *The Birds* and *North by Northwest* were frightening movies. Imagine living in a horror film that never ends. The reel keeps looping from reel to reel, round and round, over and over. Until the film snaps. Then it is all over. But how long until the film snaps? How long?

Sharing what a caretaker goes through with others experiencing the same thing, is the goal of support groups I used to occasionally see listed in the classifieds; helping each other cope. Out of curiosity, I looked in our local paper since I learned of my impending predicament. I have seen no listings advertised. Either everyone is well or no one has time to do the support group thing. Obviously, there is some other reason for there being no listings. Maybe there is another network, like contacting local nursing homes or senior citizen organizations.

Now, with this thought in mind, I can only imagine that caring for someone with advanced Alzheimer's disease can be both physically and emotionally debilitating, demanding, daunting even.

No!

I cannot imagine.

I cannot imagine. I misspoke. I *know* it must be both physically and emotionally debilitating, demanding and daunting. Most of all, it must be damning.

You see, this again brings faith to mind. Or my lack thereof. Do not give me the lecture on good and evil. Why would any god allow such devastation to reek and ruin with no rhyme or reason?

I will bow to the sun. I will float on the breeze. I will count the stars above. I will find funny faces in the clouds. I will care for our world ecologically. I will support the animal rights activists and do my part keeping species of furry, feathery and scaly creatures alive and well. But, I cannot thank an unknown entity for allowing such mass and sundry death and destruction to keep repeating itself over and over.

Imagine a reel to reel of tape winding and rewinding, over and over and over. A never-ending loop.

But, that is just me. It has nothing to do with Alzheimer's disease. In other words, even if I believed in a supreme being, I doubt I could pray away my shrinking brain. It is a fact of my life.

Please, do not hate me for having become a nonbeliever. I do not condemn someone who does find solace in their faith. It is a good thing; I just cannot understand the illogic of believing so blindly. Have I belabored this point? Perhaps it is because I did believe blindly for all my life and now I am having withdrawal symptoms.

Give me black. Give me white. Give me life. Give me death. Give me a seed. Water. A flower. Let the sun shine. Down comes the rain. Beware lightning strikes.

I felt the strike of lightning a couple times. Did that electricity shooting through my body from head to toe damage my brain, add to its shrinkage?

The sound you do not hear is me shrugging my shoulders and shaking my head, indicating that I have no idea.

If I were to become a Christian once again, I would do it for selfish reasons. I know this. I would pray I could find my lost keys. I would pray I would not forget how to get to and from work. I would pray that I do not soil my underwear. I would pray that I will recognize everyone who comes before me. I would pray for a miracle. I would pray that I will not become a vegetable.

But, it is too late for that.

I cannot turn to religion for convenience. Even, brought to my knees, I cannot do it. It would be hypocritical.

Does that make you laugh? Hypocrites have always been associated with religion. They are the charlatans and the frauds.

In the eyes of a believer I may be lost, beyond redemption, but I cannot compromise just for my own wellbeing.

If there were a god, he would see me as a person praying far too selfishly to be a good member of the flock. So, then, to reconcile this, would I have to begin tithing?

It is so complicated. It is so confusing. Can I blame it on the shrinkage? Can I be forgiven because I do not know what I am doing?

Caregivers are saints. They are sewed from far stouter cloth than me. However, they need to take care of themselves. They need a break on occasion, spending time with friends. Ask for help if needed. Do not be a hero and try to do it all alone. A martyr does more harm than good in the long run.

Next, I wonder about the adverts I used to see. Were any of these groups for the patients themselves to gather and share personal experiences, including what works and what does not, before they lose all comprehension?

I was not interested until it happened to me, so I do not know.

On the other hand, considering what happens as our brains shrink, we might not remember why we are at a meeting, once we are there.

I came. *I do not know why.*

I saw. *I have no idea what I am looking at.*

I want to be here. *But, what am I doing here?*

I am here. *How did I get here?*

Is it time to go home yet? *Where do I live?*

I want to go home. *But I am lost.*

You know, it would be like going into a room and wondering why. *What did I come into the bedroom for?*

Right now, I can stop and think. I can even back up and retrace my steps until something spurs my memory.

What happens when backtracking no longer works?

What happens when nothing goads my memory, and I find myself standing in the bedroom, looking around, asking, *What am I doing here?*

Still worst will be wondering and not knowing, *How did I get here?*

Worst of all will be when I ask, *Where am I?*

No. No.

There is still something even worse than that. Oh yes, much worse. So much worse… When the brain shrinks so drastically that I become so insular I can no longer ask *what, why* or *how.*

This would be worse, when the vegetative state becomes my life. I do not want to become a turnip. I am not blocking. I know it is inevitable. Unless, I happen to be fortunate enough to die from something else before that happens.

When I am well on my way into the world of Alzheimer's oblivion, let the old heart just stop its beating. Bury me with a smile of comprehension on my face, not one of complete confusion.

Let me add *Amen* just to cover all my basis, okay?

SEXUAL RELATIONS

An elderly couple was sitting together watching television. During a commercial, the husband asked his wife, "Whatever happened to our sexual relations?" After a long thoughtful silence and during the next commercial, the wife replied, "You know, I don't know. I don't even think we got a Christmas card from them this year."

—

"LISTING" IS MORE THAN A NAUTICAL TERM

I make lists. I have always made lists. What I learned early on is that by writing down what needs doing, I can put that particular task out of my mind until such time I am ready to tackle whatever it might be.

This is my way of keeping my mind from becoming boggled and over-loaded. I do not keep worrying about having to do something that needs doing, because I have it written down, so I will not forget. I will do it when I come to it. Writing it down lightens the mental load. When your mind is always in full swing, as mine is, it is good to be able to compartmentalize some of the stuff that is swirling around up there.

Last Saturday's list looked something like this (admittedly, I have added more detail when recreating the original list for the sake of clarity):

Change sheets
Wash clothes
Shake and wash throw rugs
Vacuum/ Mop
Write Bastrop Daily Enterprise newspaper humor column
Write Louisiana Road Trips humor column
Wash dishes
Feed fish
Change BooCat's kitty litter/ Change puppy pads
Feed wild birds/ inside birds

Answer Cousin Mike's letter

Paint Hawaiian surf scene pix for Ann and Larry

Paint metal rooster and hen for Scoopie

Dust

Write Almost Normal

Write Hadley book

Write BooCat: Letters from Jackson

Water outside potted plants

Feed turtle

Color hair

Hang Hadley pix painted and sent by Ron

Hang sun catchers made and sent by Jim

Arrange Moab Utah rocks in Argosy Garden, sent by Ann

Paint new Wits End Comedy Club & Zoo sign

Program replacement Bluetooth (Hadley ate the old one)

I do not have to write down *make a pot of coffee* and *take my meds*, or add *check email* and *visit facebook*. These are givens.

Actually, I probably should not bother writing *Dust,* because it is rarely worked into the weekend schedule anyway. Some things must be done; some are still on the list the next weekend. Some things are ongoing, like writing chapters in my novels and books in progress. Some things, like most women's work, are never done; or if done, than need doing all over again shortly thereafter.

Like dishes. Vacuuming. Mopping. Washing clothes.

I do not write down that I will play *Boggle* while watching *The Voice* or *American Idol*. Nor do I write down that I will *feed the dogs and BooCat*. These things are a given. Some of the other things ought to be under that same heading but because of time and energy, are no longer so important.

Priorities. It is all about priorities when you reach a certain age. Especially when you are the sole proprietor.

You do it, or it does not get done. If it does not get done, who will even know, except you and the cat, and the cat does not care.

―

IT'S A GIVEN

"When I was younger, I could remember anything, whether it had happened or not; but my faculties are decaying now and soon I shall be so I cannot remember any but the things that never happened. It is sad to go to pieces like this but we all have to do it."

(Mark Twain)

―

"WELL THE RACE IS ON AND HERE COMES PRIDE IN THE BACKSTRETCH"*
(*George Jones)

I am not so old, nor has my brain shrunk so much that I do not remember when plates had to be washed the minute they were emptied. However, now, with just me it does not bother me to stack them for a day or so. This is not a sign of senility. It is prioritizing. I cannot work a fulltime job, pen books and novels, weekly newspaper and monthly magazine humor columns, paint pictures, commune with nature in my Argosy garden, and spend hours cleaning house too.

I live alone. I do what needs doing or it does not get done. There is just one me. Some things are put off. I cannot take a clean house with me when

I die, but I can be remembered as the woman who wrote all those funny newspaper columns and great books. Mostly, I would rather write than eat. Although, I manage to do both.

Oh, so you noticed, did you?

Harrumph. This is what I say if anyone notices I am fluffier than I used to be: Nobody loves a bone but a dog, and he buries it.

And, if I had a man in my life, I would tell him in a New Orleans Minute (which is far better than a New York Minute), that I can warm him in the winter, and shade him in the summer.

I can. And I will. For just as long as I can. There is that ever circling cycle. I can. I will. So long as I can. Can. Will. Can.

Our lives are built upon cycles. I am in the final cycle. And, let me point out, it is strange how as I age, with or without a shrinking brain, my priorities changed.

I must write. I am driven to write. I am not driven to vacuum and mop more than once a week. Does the dust pile up thick enough to pick it up by hand? Perhaps in some corners of the house it does. Will I get to it? Eventually. Eventually, but not right now. Right now, I am writing a book.

BEATING THE ODDS

"There is a fountain of youth: it is your mind, your talents, the creativity you bring to your life and the lives of people you love. When you learn to tap this source, you will truly have defeated age."
(Sophia Loren)

DOES BEING CALLED A B-BRAIN INDICATE A BRAIN THE SIZE OF A BEE OR IS IT SHORT FOR BARBARA'S BRAIN?

My brothers used to call me B-Brain. It was not meant as a compliment. They were typical brothers, and teasing one another is what kids do. Mostly, they gave as good as they got. How many years ago that was. So much water under every bridge I ever crossed. Some raging rivers, some gentle streams. Some dried-up creek beds.

Now, I approach my 69th birthday (and will surpass it before this book is finished, even though I am dancing as fast as I can). As a wanna-be-hippy back in the early '60s, but with too much staidness and solemnity and not enough nerve to let it all hang out I did what was expected of me. I crossed my foolish dreams from my life's list and I did not live in New York City with my cat. I did not dress in all black and paint pictures and write poetry in pure beatnik style. I talked my young husband into visiting a coffee house once but he was so uncomfortable, so out of his element, even as I was yearning and feeling stifled… so I closed my eyes and heart to this dream. Girls grow up and get married and have children… they are happy homemakers.

Other braver females may have traveled the path I yearned to travel. I picture Joan Baez clutching the arm of Bob Dylan on a cover of one of my favorite albums. They dared. I did not. I yearned, but I stayed true to what was expected of me; and am not sorry for the most part. I lacked the ambition to go against the grain. I settled, yes, but settling is not a bad thing when good things fill your life.

Still, I wrote poems no one read. I penned short stories that never saw the light of day. I did not lament, even though there was a constant yearning ache like a lover left unsatisfied. Instead, I got married, had two beautiful children, loved and adored my husband, respected my elders, taught Sunday school and talked about children, casseroles and church.

I raised a garden, learned the art of canning, baked cakes from scratch, joined various civic organizations, was a 4-H Leader and became well known and respected in my community. I am still a moving force within my community. I have name recognition, although I attribute much of it to being a big fish in a little pond.

What good are blue ribbons from the county fair if there is no one who really cares? What good is doing good when inside you are drying up? Even though you smile all the time, no one knows you are tethered and will never gallop as you once dreamed.

Wild Horses*

Childhood living is easy to do
The things you wanted I bought them for you
Graceless lady you know who I am
You know I can't let you slide through my hands
Wild horses couldn't drag me away
Wild, wild horses, couldn't drag me away
I watched you suffer a dull aching pain
Now you decided to show me the same
No sweeping exits or offstage lines
Could make me feel bitter or treat you unkind
Wild horses couldn't drag me away
Wild, wild horses, couldn't drag me away
I know I dreamed you a sin and a lie
I have my freedom but I don't have much time
Faith has been broken, tears must be cried
Let's do some living after we die
Wild horses couldn't drag me away
Wild, wild horses, we'll ride them some day
Wild horses couldn't drag me away

Wild, wild horses, we'll ride them some day.

*(Mick Jagger and Keith Richards, The Rolling Stones, 1971. Rolling Stone rated it at #334 in its '500 Greatest Songs of All Times' 2004).

To contradict settling—and I am not necessarily unhappy that I did not do more with my life—I find humor almost everywhere, almost all the time. It drives me and it stills me. I jest. I smile. I laugh. Humor, coupled with some deep driving force keeps me from covering my head up and with-drawing when the world becomes a large mushroom cloud enveloping my every move, sucking out my every breath.

It keeps me from dreaming about wild horses long gone.

I am a survivor but I am not strong. I do not venture into the unknown. Perhaps there is something in the horoscopes that have me locked in as a Cancer. I have all the traits, both positive and negative. I scuttle backward, rather than plunge forward, just like my starshine-sunsign, the crab. Crabs retreat.

Had I been a stinging scorpion, perhaps I would now be running my own business.

Wait. I am running my own business. I named it *It's Barbara's Business!* and years ago I even obtained a tax ID number. What is Barbara's Business? It is miscellany. I am a notary public on wheels. I kept books for many and various businesses over the years. I did income taxes for pay and free for the elderly… before I myself became elderly.

I painted signs for businesses. I painted pictures for people. I edited people's books. People needed forms filled out, letters written, reports done, and I did these things.

However, my business head was not as strong as my non-business heart. I did these things for people because I care about people and I wanted to, for the most part. Cut rates or favors. Of course, I was popular.

People called for advice.

In fact, all my life, strangers are drawn to me and they unload. What magnetism is emitted from my being that lets them speak freely and openly to me? For as long as I can remember, people with problems seek me out whether knowingly or not. I believe I have an aura surrounding me. There can be no other explanation.

Also, it is because I really do care. I offer empathy. I let them unload. I do not offer advice, nor do I judge. I listen. People need people to simply listen.

Also, weird people are attracted to me.

I shrug my shoulders even as I type this. It is what it is, even if I do not know what that might be.

Back to running my own business, I was referring to a real business, a money-making business, a profitable business.

In the end, I use a tired expression, *it is what it is.* I am what I am.

Although I have dealt with more pain than is fair, I cannot blame my lack of ambition on that. After all, what in life is fair? My beautiful son, Tony, killed in a traffic accident, but in his stead, he left behind a wonderful daughter-in-law, Cindy, and beautiful granddaughter, Alisha.

Not to mention, I have a most loving and caring daughter. My Theresa makes me proud every moment of every day. She has a lovely partner, Carla; and together, they fill my life with love. What is life if empty of love? Is it a life at all?

On the sadder side, my wonderful daughter-in-law developed a brain tumor. She was hospitalized and diagnosed the same time I was hospitalized and being diagnosed with having seizures.

Our brains were communing in a most dreadful way. Coincidences should be good. This was not.

Cindy was not expected to live more than several months when her brain tumor was first discovered. They told her, *Three months, maybe.*

Then, suddenly it stopped growing. It is inoperable and it is still there, and it has caused damage and physical functional problems, however, it has not killed her yet.

This is where religious people lose me. They say, *Thank god, the tumor has stopped growing.*

I want to stand up and shout, *Hey god! How come you let my wonderful daughter-in-law develop a brain tumor in the first place?*

My thoughts on religion have become convoluted over the years. I went from believing blindly to one day putting logic to the test, and the test failed and I fell away from the grip of god. Any god. All gods.

Logic overruled and I decided to worship the universe all around me; the tangibles... the sun, the sky, the trees, grass, flowers. Mother Nature became my god. My goddess.

The evil that men do negated anything godly that I once accepted wholly. I found myself asking over and over, *If there is a god, then why...* Not to mention, everybody has god on their side, no matter which side they are on.

It turned out in my new way of reckoning that god is *not* love after all. There is too much evil for that to be the case. Logistics took over my brain and I turned off the god-button.

Should I suddenly find religion? If I started praying to this god who spends every Friday night flipping a coin to see which football team's prayers he will answer under the lights, would I become one of his miracles?

Friday Night Lights.

Would I be cured?

Too late. So many millions needed curing. Not me. I have lived my life. The six-million murdered in the German concentration camps, now they should have been saved.

Apparently, the god of love was busy elsewhere and failed to notice the Nazis at work.

But, I rant. Blame it on my shrinking brain.

My brain. A shooting star. Lighting up the night sky. Then falling into darkness. Disappearing from view. Burned out. Gone forever.

As more and more brain cells die, the more the brain shrinks. This is Alzheimer's disease at its worst. Yet, it is also Alzheimer's disease at its most norm.

Cindy's mother died shortly after our Tony was killed. How much sadness can one person stand and still remain standing? An amazing woman, my Cindy, I am blessed to have her as part of my life all these many years. Even though we live miles apart, rarely a month goes by that we do not speak by phone. I am her mother. She is my daughter. We both have brains that are in trouble. We both cope. We deal.

God appears to be looking the other way again.

=~

TIME IN A BOTTLE

"The wisest are the most annoyed at the loss of time."
(Dante Alighieri)

=~

"THEY CALL THE WIND MARIAH"*
(*Soundtrack: Paint Your Wagon")

After moving to Louisiana, in between becoming involved with civic affairs, doing the Susie-Homemaker thing, being so very happy with life in general and in particular, I worked. In fact, I was working at a bank located right next door to the grocery store my husband I bought as an investment, when my world first fell apart.

An expression: *My world fell apart.* And, it fell so hard, there should have been a clanging heard 'round the world. Surely, my wailing could have been heard if anyone listened. Likely, they thought, it is only the wind howling. Just the wind.

The father of my children, my husband of twenty-years, was a cotton farmer, having taken over his father's cotton farm after he got out of the service.

You see, my father was in the Army, so I was an Army Brat. Lacking roots allowed me something so much more important for the first part of my life: living and learning and experiencing. Thankful for my constant thirst for knowledge, even more thankful for the opportunity to quench that thirst.

Dad was stationed at the Pentagon in Arlington, Virginia and we lived on base at Fort Myer, Virginia. My father, my mother, two brothers and a little sister: Michael and Phyllis Sharik. Michael James "Jimmy" and David. Janet. And me, the big sister, Barbara.

It was an amazing childhood because I had this constant thirst to do and to learn. I took myself to Sunday school, church and Vacation Bible School regularly. I joined the Girl Scouts; earned every badge I could and was awarded Best Scout of the Year with the opportunity to go to Girl Scout Camp free. However, we moved that year to Maryland and I did not get to go. Dad was stationed to Turkey, so we moved to mom's hometown.

However, while at Ft Myer, I rode the same horses that drew the presidential Caissons. I wandered from one end of that Army base to the other. One end was the Pentagon, the other the logistical part of the base with the Arlington Cemetery in the middle.

Living just across the street from the Arlington Cemetery was amazing, and an education in itself. We lived in walking distance to the Lee's

Mansion and the Tomb of the Unknown Soldier. There was not a monument or public building I did not visit in and around DC and Virginia. History wrapped me its arms and I snuggled deeply, completely in love with my country. Hearing Taps played every evening, as men in uniform stopped and saluted, built patriotism into my very soul.

There are so many individual memories… too numerous to relate, but they all aided in shaping and molding me, bringing me to this time in my life, where even to see a military convoy traveling down the Interstate brings patriotic tears to my old eyes.

I watched the fireworks blossoming in air over the Washington Monument every Fourth of July. I ate chestnuts that had been roasted over open fires on the streets of our nation's capital, as we stood muffled and mittened watching the lighting of the Christmas tree on the Whitehouse lawn.

Class trips took me to historic Roanoke, to the home of our first president George Washington, to the Thomas Jefferson homeplace Monticello, and even for a memorable visit to the farm of Wesley Dennis, illustrator of all the Marguerite Henry horse books… books I grew up reading like eating chocolate.

My best friend was an only child, her father a Major and most memorable was the time her father's niece was selected as Miss Philippines, competing in the Miss Universe contest, and we had supper at the Philippine's Embassy in DC.

I ordered steak. There were four of us kids in my family. Pricilla was an only child. She ordered a hamburger. She had plenty of steaks while I had had plenty of hamburgers.

I did my first oil painting at age 10. I went on to win many awards in the field of art. I dreamed of going to art school… but that was before I did what girls did during my time in life… graduated from high school and got married.

Dad brought home an old manual typewriter and I claimed it for my own, writing my first long story after reading *The Call of the Wild* by Jack London. No doubt, I plagiarized big time because my characters all spoke in similar French Canadian dialogue, but what it did was, it awakened a need to write.

Next I wrote about a black stallion with a white ring around its eye I called Dare Devil. I strived for and achieved much because of the hunger of a wild child wanting something more. But, I was of the wrong era, and I was not strong enough to reach for the stars. I traveled Easy Street.

I have been writing ever since that first story about a dog and the second story about a horse, to some degree or another. As a newspaper reporter and columnist, overly sentimental poetry, short stories, long stories, books and novels. I smile with pleasure knowing I have finally been published and have name recognition. What else is there in life, if not to earn a little recognition? It is a good thing because, even after having conquered my shyness, for much of my life I felt more like an honorable mention than a blue ribbon. My self-esteem was lower than it should have been. I know that now. I settled. Most my life, I settled.

Blasted negative side of my horoscope. It has me pinned. *No pun intended.*

〜

THIS IS NOT A PUN

An old man, enjoying chatting with a delightful, attractive young lady, asks, "How old do you think I am?" She answers, "You're 85." Startled, he asks, "How do you know that?" She answers, "You told me yesterday."

〜

A LUST FOR LEARNING

From Virginia, as I said, we moved to Maryland where Mom was from, where we had cousins, aunts and uncles, and where memorable things continued to fill my life.

A friend, who lived across the street from me, another only child, invited me to supper with her and her parents by way of her father piloting a small plane one evening. We traveled high above in the night sky, looking down at the lights of Maryland, Virginia and DC. My first plane ride.

The first covered mall east of the Mississippi River, the Harundale Mall, had its grand opening in 1958, and I was there. So was then Senator John F. Kennedy.

I went swimming in the Chesapeake Bay and the Atlantic Ocean, wandered around the cobblestoned streets of Annapolis and the Naval Academy, was awed by the tall ships in the Baltimore Harbor where the *Star Spangled Banner* was penned, and loved visiting the zoo at Rock Creek Park. Glen Burnie had one of the few Rolls Royce dealerships way back then.

I fell in and out of love dozens of times during these formative years, when I was actually too young to be dating, but I did it anyway.

Steeped in history and wrapped in the beauty that is the east coast. I love *Maryland, My Maryland*. Virginia is beautiful, but Maryland is special forever.

Next, we moved to El Paso, Texas where I graduated from high school, met, and married my husband, who was fresh off the farm in Louisiana, not long graduated himself. He joined the Army and was stationed at Ft Bliss, Texas where we were living. It was only natural to meet nice young Privates at the swimming pool on post, a favorite place to hang out during the summer. I worked on my tan and I worked on my love life.

El Paso, to me and my nature-loving nature, had a beauty all its own. Mountains and rocks, horned toads and tarantulas, rattle snakes and sand storms and tumbling tumbleweeds. A mixture of good and bad, and I loved it. To stand atop a mountain with a warm breeze wrapping itself around my young body was an indescribably delicious awakening into adolescence. My body stirred with the caressing of the winds, even as it ignited with the caressing of the gentle hands of the young soldier boy I married the day after I turned 18, a month after I graduated high school.

Daughter Theresa was born in El Paso and shortly thereafter, we were stationed to Colorado Springs where we lived at the foot of Pikes Peak, a short drive from the Garden of the Gods and the Royal Gorge. Everything about Colorado and its quaking aspens, including the snowstorms, was good, except for one thing.

I discovered I never again will drive a stick shift vehicle in snowy mountains; automatic transmissions forever hereafter. Imagine, pulling up to a stop sign on a steep mountainside and having to change gears without rolling backward into the cars behind you. I tensed up every time. It was also in Colorado Springs where I did my first wheelie. Fresh snow had fallen and when I approached a stop sign, applied my brakes, the car kept going and the car with me at the wheel made a sliding circle in the middle of the road.

I turned around… no, let me correct that. I was already turned around, so I drove back to the house. Wherever I was headed, I did not need to go there.

Actually, I do recall where I was headed that morning. I was going to work. I had taken a part time job as a hostess at the NCO Club. I was also the president of the NCO Wives Club on base. That was not my first induction into the life of the club woman, however. Shortly after getting married, I was invited to become a member of Beta Sigma Phi International Sorority. In fact, in March of 2013, I received a letter of congratulations of a very special milestone in my membership. I have been a member for 50 years.

Imagine. Fifty-years. I started a chapter when I moved to Louisiana, and it thrived for many years, but alas, is no more. Now, I am a member-at-large. For whatever that is worth. Things that meant much to me are no longer so important.

This is not the social withdrawal that often accompanies Alzheimer's. No. This is just an old lady who never slowed down for her entire life, constantly waxing, but now, is gradually unwinding, aware of the pull of the moon as it wanes. Yes. I am waning, but I have not yet withered away.

From Colorado, we moved to Bavaria, West Germany where we lived for three years. The first six months were spent in Stuttgart, and the next two and a half years, in Ulm, where my son Anthony (Tony) was born.

From first labor pain until his birth, a mere two hours and twenty minutes passed. We never made it to the hospital. To top off the anxiety of having a baby born on a cot in a dispensary by a doctor who had never delivered a baby before, I had a bad experience, an allergic reaction to Demerol used when stitching my episiotomy. My blood pressure bottomed out. The physician later used the term, *"Hairy."* He said, *Things got hairy for a while.*

At eleven months, Tony got very ill. His fever was 104-degrees and would not break. We rushed him to the dispensary where the physician on duty got his temperature down to 101-degrees after putting him in a bath of ice, and sent us home. Within an hour, we were back.

Tony was diagnosed with bacterial meningitis.

I cannot even begin to describe the fear. Far from home, in a foreign country, with a baby so ill the doctors went on record that he was not expected to live.

But he did. Bless his little heart, he did. His ankles were scarred from vein cut-downs done for IV feeding, but he lived. He was pale, his hair (he was born with a mop of hair and he still had every strand plus more), stood on end, but holding him in my arms and taking him home had me thanking the god I believed in at that time in my life, for letting him live.

However, before the night was through, his temperature shot sky-high once again. He had developed pneumonia. It was touch and go for another ten days. He barely made it. But, he did make it. He made it and life was once again very good.

Both my brother and my father were stationed in Germany the same time we were, so we spent Tony's first Christmas with them. It was wonderful being together after having made it through such a tumultuous time the month before. Little Theresa loved having her grandfather and Uncle Jimmy visit. What a happy family we were.

Unfortunately, I had no idea my father had just recently met a German woman and with his wife and children far away, his heart took flight. Everybody flying almost anywhere has a layover in Atlanta. Flights of fancy have no layovers. They have consequences and heartbreak, but no layovers in Atlanta.

Eventually, Dad returned to the states, advised he wanted a divorce. I recall writing him a letter, admonishing him for his horrible action. Mom had done nothing but love him for all these years. She gave him four children and spent most her life raising them by herself because duty kept calling.

Stuff happens.

Eventually, a divorce was decreed. In Maryland at that time, it took two years. When final, and in the meantime, sometime in between, a child was born—my littlest sister, Michele. Her mother, the woman my father met in Germany, came to the states with this new child and they married.

Mom struggled on alone with the love and respect for all us children. Dad started his new life with the love of his new wife and little girl. My brother David fought in Viet Nam. His marriage worked. Bravo. One out of the rest of us is not necessarily good odds, but any positive is just that: a positive.

However, the rest of us Sharik children were not meant to have luck in love and romance. My sister Jan married and had two beautiful baby boys, who grew into fine young men. Unfortunately, her husband had a wild hair and could not be satisfied with just one woman, so eventually they divorced.

Jan, like mom, sacrificed and provided for her sons, both who have grown up into fine young successful men. Let me inject, that since then, Jan got snowed in with a fellow she was on a date with, and apparently cabin fever did not eventuate—or maybe it did—they wound up marrying. She and Kevin have been happily married for many years.

Brother Jimmy married a German lady, had a baby girl they named after me; but once settled in the states, his wife became homesick and wanted to go home for a visit. She never came back. Many years later my brother and his daughter (who was named after me) were reunited. And, lucky me, I have come to know her as well, and thanks to facebook we are in continual communication.

Jimmy went many years without remarrying. Finally, he met a woman, they married, but several years ago, she passed away. So, he is once again alone, except for the joy of finally getting to know his long-lost daughter.

Typical American families experiencing typical events. Bad interspersed with the good. Everywhere you cast your eyes, open your ears, you will see and hear this constant combination of sheer joy interspersed with the depths of despair.

That's life. Precious life.

TRICKY

An old woman commissions to have her portrait painted. She tells the artist, "I want to be painted with a diamond necklace, diamond earrings, emerald bracelets, a ruby broach and a gold watch." The artist looks at her and tells her, "But, you're not wearing any of those expensive things." "I know," she tells him, "But when I die my husband will probably remarry. I want his new wife to go nuts looking for the jewelry."

"TAKE ME HOME, COUNTRY ROADS"*
(*John Denver)

Returning to the states, we were stationed to Ft Hood, Texas where fellow military friends and neighbors warned me to shake out my shoes before putting them on because scorpions loved dark places and often took up residence in the toe of a shoe.

It was at this time my husband's father called to say he wanted to retire, asking my husband if he would like to take over the cotton farm. Wow! I never had roots and suddenly here was the opportunity to sink some.

He got out of the service on an early-out, and because he had only three months left, when his name came down to go to Viet Nam, he did not have to go. We moved to Louisiana, built a house and lived a fairytale life.

Until the Wicked Witch of the West moved into the picture and my husband, the father of my children, fell under her poisonous spell. I often wondered why he could not simply have had an affair and been done with it, come back home and continued being the father and husband I loved for half my life.

It was not to be, but I elected to stay here in Louisiana. You see, for the first time in my life, I had a real home, real roots. The children had a place to call home. They would not have to be uprooted for all their formative years. While I thrived on the nomadic life, living to learn, I saw this as a different sort of opportunity for them. It was one thing to suck up everything out there my own self, but suddenly, it seemed so important that my children have a place to call their own. They needed a home and a hometown. Otherwise, at the end of the day, where would they come to lay their head?

I was made of a different cloth, and as I said, I never minded being uprooted because I was a restless child and craved learning and doing. I know for a fact, with my personality, I would have stagnated if I had been stuck in rural Louisiana as a child and teen. However, as an adult, it was where I wanted to be. I made friends. I dug in. I became a big fish in my little pond.

And now, my brain is shrinking much like a silk garment meant to be dry cleaned only, but instead is accidentally dropped into a washer full of hot, soapy water.

The silk garment is ruined. There is no redemption. The trash bin for what was once a lovely piece of clothing, a favorite. There is no need to save it for posterity. It is rendered useless. Colors all run together and it is now too small to ever wear again.

But, my brain? What about my shrinking brain? Must it be tossed into the trash bin without any hope of ever being of use again?

I am diagnosing, probing, trying to figure out what has happened, when and if it might have been preventable.

Was it something I ate? A defect just waiting to surface? Something caught by association, contamination, pollution?

What do we know? Why are some stricken, others not? Why are some vulnerable to disease while others remain healthy? Is it really all prewritten in somebody's big book? Preordained? What about reincarnation? If it can be thought, man will think it.

Is mankind nothing more than ants on a larger scale bustling busily about their anthill, taking care of business until the big foot comes down, smashing, crushing, obliterating? Man, like many animals, according to certain scientific studies, continually evolves.

Is there another dimension? Are we but one, while simultaneously another mimics and repeats over and over?

How can we figure out what causes our brains to shrink when we do not even know if there is a Supreme Being or if we are all the result of the Big Bang Theory?

It muddles the brain, the ever shrinking brain. The poor shrinking brain.

Twinkle, twinkle little star…

≈

THE INCREDIBLE SHRINKING BRAIN

"As you get older; you've probably noticed that you tend to forget things. You'll be talking with somebody at a party, and you'll know that you know this person, but no matter how hard you try, you can't remember his or her name. This can be very embarrassing, especially if he or she turns out to be your spouse."

(Dave Barry)

≈

Wilson Arch

Photo by: Ann Hamilton,

Arches National Park, Utah, May 2013

Wilson Arch, named after Joe Wilson, a local pioneer who had a cabin nearby in Dry Valley, is a formation known as Entrada Sandstone. Over time the superficial cracks, joints, and folds of these layers were saturated with water. Ice formed in the fissures, melted under extreme desert heat, and winds cleaned out the loose particles. A series of free standing fins remained. Wind and water attached these fins until, in some, the cementing material gave way and chunks of rock tumbled out. Many damaged fins collapsed. Others with the right degree of hardness survived despite their missing middles like Wilson Arch. (Historical information provided by Ann Hamilton).

Such is life... Each individual is a sustaining sandstone formation that eventually develops superficial cracks, giving way under varying degrees of living life to eventual collapse over time. However, if the right winds blow, although eroded and going from ashes to ashes, dust to dust... the legacy of some will forever remain as an arch even with the middle missing.

THE BEGINNING OF THE END

It all seemed to start, best I can determine, when I was at work at the newspaper one Thursday. I worked at the Village of Bonita three days a week and at the Bastrop Daily Enterprise twice a week. I started feeling odd, but went to lunch unsure what to do. I was not sick. Nothing hurt. The newspaper is located just down the block from the hospital and the hospital has a cafeteria. I decided I would eat lunch there. Something guided me and made me stay close to finding help if it came to that.

Nothing changed. I do not even remember what I ate. I only know, I continued to feel odd. I made my way to the Emergency Room and was immediately admitted. I have never seen my records, only pieced together after the fact, that it was believed I had suffered a stroke. It was attributed to a possible reaction to *Mobic*, the prescription form of Motrin. I had recently developed a bad pain in my ankle, visited an orthopedic physician who prescribed the pills for the inflammation.

Six months earlier I had reconstructive female surgery I jokingly called *Retail Surgery*, because the doc redid my "tail," so to speak. Actually, according to the physician, it is a type surgery many women who have bore children eventually need. I had a hysterectomy when I was 27, and have undergone a handful of operations over the years.

The hysterectomy was fine. The uterus had dropped and was boggy and causing much discomfort. However, the physician left my ovaries, because they were functioning properly and to remove them would have plunged me into immediate menopause.

About ten years later, the same physician determined my ovaries needed now to come out. I underwent what was to be a simple enough operation; the only detriment being I would have to start taking hormones.

Following the surgery, he said things went well. He found polyps, something else or another, and took care of them.

The ovaries?

Whoops!

He forgot.

Three weeks later, they came out as intended. I started a very long period of using a hormone patch that seemed to work just as it was intended. No hot flashes. No beard growing on my chin. Sexuality still in place. Plus, the original removal of the uterus rendered me sterile. No unwanted pregnancies. I had two beautiful children and I was good to go.

Previous to this, I had a blood clot removed from the vein in my inner elbow, first thought to be a tumor, until the orthopedic doctor opened my arm. I had been sent to an orthopedic specialist because of an original misdiagnosis by my general practitioner (GP). However, it was a reasonable assumption.

Then there was the cataract surgery needed sooner than it would have been otherwise because of a long battle with Uveitis that required numerous steroid drops and injections. A couple years later, the other eye required cataract surgery, coupled with repair surgery on eye number one. I was tired, but I still churned out my weekly humor newspaper column and monthly humor magazine column.

There was non-cancerous surgery, resulting in the removal of one nipple. Later, a cyst was excised from my other breast. The records said "... *it is a firm piece of gray white tissue with some attached fat. It measures 0.8 x 1 x 1.6 cm in greatest dimensions. The specimen is bread-loafed and the firm white tissue shows a small duct less than 0/1 dm in greatest dimension.*"

It continued, "*Diagnosis: Fibro adipose tissue, left chest showing fat necrosis, foreign body glaucomatous inflammation and acute and chronic inflammation.*"

But it was not breast cancer.

My mother eventually had breast cancer. She had a mastectomy. Will someday it be like mother, like daughter? I foolishly seldom check myself, although every couple years or so, I do get a mammogram. So much has gone wrong, I wonder why I am not concerned about this? I have no idea, but I am not.

A TRUISM

"It's paradoxical that the idea of living a long life appeals to everyone, but the idea of getting old doesn't appeal to anyone."
(Andy Rooney)

"THE LONG AND WINDING ROAD"*
(*The Beatles)

The treatment, and finally surgery for Meniere's disease at Shea Ear Clinic in Memphis, Tennessee, included the removal of a benign tumor on the bone directly behind the ear. That ear is now rendered deaf, and is left with a hole the size of my thumb where the bone used to be. Meniere's disease has to be one of the most debilitating ailments ever.

Jon Darlin' took me back and forth; I could never have managed on my own. I do so much on my own, but this would have been impossible. The Emergency Room physician I first went to, when I suggested Meniere's Disease—then called Syndrome rather than disease—negated this immediately, saying it is too rare. Only one case in ten years, had he ever seen.

Rare indeed. My nearest neighbor was diagnosed with Meniere's around the same time.

Meniere's is a disabling disease. The off and on bouts of dizziness since I was a teenager, did cause me to look through medical books over the years. I had a hunch. But that day, when it struck with such a fury, Jon and I were sitting at the table, eating peanut butter on toast.

It struck so suddenly. No warning. I told him I felt dizzy. Within minutes I began throwing up. I could not stop. He called an ambulance. It took a wrong turn and he had to drive after them and bring them back. Jon was so frightened. Admittedly, I was also.

I could not open my eyes. The world spun. My equilibrium was completely slammed.

At the emergency room I was administered something that eventually quelled the dizziness. The ER doctor advised I go to my GP, Dr. Wyatt Webb, the next day. I did.

He immediately suspected Meniere's also. Doing online research, he located the Shay Ear Clinic in Memphis, Tennessee. The rest is history. It took a long time and a number of trips, but eventually, my Meniere's was quelled. For many years afterward, I never went anywhere without a bottle of Meclazine pills in my purse. I lived in fear of becoming dizzy and being so sick again.

Every time we went, the place was packed full of people with their heads down, suffering miserably from dizziness and the nausea it brings.

I still have Tinnitus and my ears ring constantly, but the Meniere's is gone. I still have one ear left… please, do not tell the God of Ears. Gods have a way of wanting to show their power and omnipotence by throwing lightning bolts about.

Not everything I contracted required surgery, but usually, what developed was relatively rare and often had to do with my immune system like Lichen Sclerosis. It is said to result from an overactive immune system. Fortunately my bouts with psoriasis, another immune related ailment, have never been debilitating, but have stayed with me (originally diagnosed as eczema) for most my life.

I am also of the generation that came down with what was quite common—considered a childhood disease all children eventually came down with—a case of chicken pox, leaving behind the opportunity to revisit as shingles. Which, of course happened, however, I did not have a severe case, just a long lasting one. My longtime friend, and fellow high school graduate, Ann Hamilton (Ruthann Wilson), said, *Now we are the old shingle people instead of the young chicken pox kids."*

So it would seem.

One unusual ailment after another. I mention Ann because she is the only other person I know who has experienced as many weird ailments as I have. We are sisters under the skin, in more ways than one. In high school we both had a crush on the same guy. While I dated him, he did take Ann out more often than me. However, we soon learned he was a player and likely he liked us competing for his affections. I would like to say because Ann was the prettiest girl in the school the odds were in her favor, but she had more than beauty on her side. She was, and still is, one of the nicest people in the world. It is heartwarming for both of us that our friendship has spanned the years and the miles.

I endured a painful bout of plantar faceitis, developed a cyst inside the backside of my knee, and even dislocated my little finger playing basketball.

The military physician who treated my poor little finger warned me if I continued playing basketball—because he treated many WACS with sports injuries—I would also endure many more similar bumps and bruises.

That was my first experience with physical therapy. Speaking of which, what a long way that has come. The therapy basically consisted of my hand with injured little finger, immersed in warm swirling water for awhile.

With the development of inflammation in my left shoulder and hip about six months ago, I had good results from physical therapy. This time, all these years later, PT is a lot different from the original basketball injury. Whereas, I doubt any specific healing came from the swirling warm water, I did find relief and repair this time around.

Why did my left side start hurting, I asked. Dr Shelat suggested because of the stroke affecting my right side, the left side had to overcompensate.

When he tests my walking, even I notice that my right arm does not swing. It hangs there. It used to swing. I assume when walking briskly, swinging arms is a normal thing.

Nonetheless, I am still upright. I am still standing. I hope I can say that next year. And the next.

BREAKING A BAD HABIT

Two elderly women were talking about their husbands. One said, "I wish Roy would stop biting his fingernails, it annoys me." "Bob used to do that," said Linda. "But, I quickly stopped him." "How?" asked Paulette. "I hid his teeth," said Linda.

CROSSROADS

The first back surgery went alright, considering it was back surgery in the 1970's. The second scheduled surgery some years later, with a different physician—the first had retired by this time—was a little different. This specialist affirmed it was necessary and I agreed, however, he showed me charts and talked about a great advancement in this field, using some little back brace box-like things…

They looked complicated. They looked invasive. A back brace on the outside is one thing; internal braces left me slightly fearful.

However, the literature he provided sounded innovative and the results positive. I put on my big girl pants and headed to the hospital.

As I was being prepped it hit me. What hit me? A feeling. An uneasy feeling. An intuitive warning.

I am not someone who travels by instincts alone. If I did I would probably be dead by now, because my instincts lack intelligence for the most part. I talk to strangers. I never look around when walking alone, even in dark parking lots. I am so trusting. I would not hurt anyone; I do not expect someone to hurt me.

I am naive. I know this. My son Tony was the same way. We would talk to anybody about anything anytime, anywhere. We never meet a stranger. Even strange people become less strange because we reach out with our hearts instead of our brains.

Tony was mugged when he was living with his grandparents in Ohio, one Friday after work. Payday, he had money in his pocket. He knew the attackers, and having grown up in rural Louisiana where everybody knows everybody, he never learned about the necessary shield when out in the real world, in big cities.

The muggers left for him for dead and he wound up with over one-hundred stitches in his face and head. The police photos curdled my soul. Married to Chuck at the time, we immediately made the long trip to Ohio, bringing him home.

The culprits were caught, of course. After all, they knew Tony. He thought he knew them also.

But, back to my pending back surgery. The anesthesiologist visited me as I was being hooked up to the IV, and began explaining how blood would be taken from an artery in my neck and held. *Just in case.* Standard procedure.

Was it? No one had told me that they were going to do this. To the best of my knowledge, it was never done in any of my previous surgeries. I mean, they know what my blood type is, but to draw my own blood in advance, while sounding good on one hand, visualizing it being drained from my neck, apparently scared the hell out of me.

I am not queasy about blood but this was different. This scared the sugar right out of me.

Already lying on a cot with my hospital gown on, I turned to one of the nurses who was hooking up the I.V. and asked, *Is it too late to change my mind?*

To this day, I believe I saw relief sweep across her face. She assured me it was not. I got up, got dressed and left.

The blues song, *Something is wrong with my baby, something is wrong with me...* ran through my head. Something is wrong... wrong... something.

Six months later I wound up having the back surgery with a different physician in Shreveport, and it was very successful. No complicated back cages were needed. No blood drained from the artery in my neck *just in case.*

My back has been good ever since.

MORTALITY

"The curse of mortality. You spend the first portion of your
life learning, growing stronger, more capable. And then, through no fault
of your own, your body begins to fail. You regress. Strong limbs become
feeble, keen senses grow dull, hardy constitutions deteriorate. Beauty

withers. Organs quit. You remember yourself in your prime, and wonder where that person went. As your wisdom and experience are peaking, your traitorous body becomes a prison."

(Brandon Mull, <u>Fablehaven</u>)

SWEET YOU ARE

For awhile my life was really good. In fact, I met Jon just a couple nights before the successful back surgery. Jon loved me as I have never been loved before or since.

Sadly, so sadly, after 711 days of living on top of the mountain, I was cast back into the valley. Jon passed away in 2002 of a massive heart attack. He was much too young, ten years my junior.

I once asked him, *Where have you been all my life?* He quipped, *In grade school.*

Once, shortly before his untimely death he handed me a bouquet of wildflowers, saying, *Barbara, I am your biggest fan.*

You see, before I turned in my religious card, I believed God sent an angel to look after me. He was big, strong and good. He gave his love freely, touching my hand, my heart; made me smile every single day.

He loved me blindly, every minute of every day was a song. He would touch his lips to mine, saying, *Now we are one*, as he breathed in my breath.

With one plate, one spoon, he would feed each of us one bite, then another. He held my hand without a second thought. He filled my life, made our house a home. Twenty-four hours were never enough, we needed more. Being with Jon, every day was an adventure. He opened every locked door, dismantling the wall I had built around my heart.

We went camping, sleeping under the stars, watching comets streak across the sky, making wishes on every falling star. If we were not walking in the early morning light, communing with nature, we would fish. He loved to fish.

He also liked to drive, to explore. We traveled for miles, visited cemeteries and ancient sites. Like me, he had this constant quest for knowledge. We did crossword puzzles together. His mind was filled with trivia and silly nonsensical stuff. He told jokes and made everything fun. He laughed all the time, and so did I.

He also spoke love. Not to sound gushy, too poetic, but when he came into my life, I willingly served up my soul ala-carte. He brought me so much joy and he never even have to try.

For all his gaiety, I heard his silent cries. I recall the time he spoke of his mother's death and his eyes filled with tears. He was so tenderhearted.

And, sentimental. He wrote me notes all the time. I would find them stuck to the bathroom mirror, the refrigerator, inside the cabinet door, in the refrigerator, between the pages of a book I was reading... everywhere all the time. I saved every note. I do not reread them because I cannot bear to put myself in pain's way caused by the unbearable lightness of his passing. Still, I treasure them.

Jon would sing, *You Are So Beautiful,* while holding me in his arms late at night. He sang, *You Are Always on My Mind,* adding *I love you, Barbara* every time. He did that so often, because we used to go to the Moose Lodge on Karaoke Night, that one time when he finished the song, dear friend and co-worker Tammi piped up, *I love you, Barbara... Well, he was going to say it anyway!*

Everyone laughed. You had to laugh when Jon was in the room.

Yes, he sang to me, songs of the heart. And, he told me he would love me forever, that we would never part. He gave me love, like none I had ever before known. He said he would love me until the day he died. And he did.

Angels are only lent. I will forever miss my angel, Jon Haskell McNeil. God sent him to me November 10, 2000, and then God called him home October 22, 2002. October 22. The birth date of my son Tony. The death date of Jon.

Everybody deserves this type love at least once in their lives.

⚊

LAUGHTER

"You don't stop laughing when you grow old,
you grow old when you stop laughing."
(George Bernard Shaw)

⚊

ISB AKA "INCREDIBLE SHRINKING BRAIN"

I would have to get out my list to see if I have managed to list and mention all the various surgeries and peculiar medical experiences that have plagued me most my life. Likely there are a few oddities I have since forgotten. Like having to list what medicines you are taking, each time you visit a new doctor, most physicians want to know what surgeries you had. My list is long. Too long.

Now, with the ISB I am wondering, how many times in a lifetime, can someone undergo anesthetics before the brain is affected? A layman's query.

Does being put to sleep—under anesthesia—damage brain cells? And what about the event with the bradycardia? Also, the stroke itself.

It is all so confounding, so I put each happenstance out of my mind, as each healed and went away. I do not worry. Not worrying is my self-help to self-survival. I shut it out. Blocking. I am not an Ostrich with my head buried in the sand, however, I simply do not dwell.

Again, my Retail Surgery went well, but about four or five months later, I was diagnosed with Odynophagia. My esophagus had eroded due to reflux, and ten days later, I developed hip bursitis and tendonitis in my right ankle and foot. I was falling apart, but nothing too serious. I still felt fine and dandy, overall. These particular infirmities (and even that is too strong a word), were bothersome, but not much different than a fly buzzing around; a swat and it is shooed away.

I continued on my road to recovery until the third day taking Meloxicam prescribed by the Orthopedic surgeon, something went wrong. That is when I felt strange enough to have the good sense to eventually take myself to the Emergency Room.

Being a layman, and being in distress at the time, I believe I heard the ER doctor saying I had a reaction to Mobic… so I can only assume that is the same thing as Meloxicam. It is difficult to know for certain. I was, after all, in distress, moved to the Intensive Care Unit where I stayed for several serious days. Not to mention, for the longest time they were quite baffled as well. They knew my vital signs were very poor, but it seemed they were groping for medical straws for a diagnosis.

As I lay in the little room in the intensive care unit, when the hospital physician visited, he talked about a pacemaker; my heart rate was so slow. He used the term Bradycardia. I have since read that someone suffering from bradycardia, their brains and other organs may not get the supply of oxygen needed.

Eventually, the beating returned to normal and the blood pressure rose to a proper place. However, as a result, I started seeing a heart specialist. I was mostly well, but because I came out of the incident with palsy in my left hand, he sent me to see a neurologist.

Parkinson's was suspected. The tremors were that severe, but, best I was able to discern, it must have been a residue from the stroke. In between, the heart doctor had me tested for Sleep Apnea and it was found I stopped breathing many, many times during the night. I was set up with a Cpap machine.

I am still using my Cpap machine religiously. Both the heart doctor and the neurologist believe they save lives. Actually, the neurologist prefers the BiPap rather than the Cpap.

He explains that the BiPap allows a person to breath in, with an intake of airflow that keeps the throat open; but when breathing out, the pressure changes and lessens, reducing any pressure that might cause a strain on the heart. He made a drastic statement about dying using a Cpap, because of this constant straight-line wind being pumped into the offending throat.

It made sense to me. So, I switched to the BiPap machine. Unfortunately, just recently it stopped heating the water in the humidifier which caused my throat to become sore and my nasal passages irritated.

Consequently, I dug out the Cpap. I must look into getting the BiPap repaired when time allows. In the meantime, I must keep getting a good night's sleep.

Several sleep studies were done, verifying there is a problem. When a person is continuously being brought to the surface of awakening, they never obtain the deep, peaceful, healthful, sleep required.

So many times, almost as soon as I got behind the wheel I would began to feel my eyelids closing, especially when driving any distance. Before being diagnosed with Sleep Apnea and undergoing and undertaking the only treatment available to date, it was all I could do to get home safely far too many times over the years. I would close one eye, than the other… trying to ward off falling completely asleep and likely running off the road, killing myself, or worse, someone else.

Ah yes, then there was the wreck that permanently damaged both knees. A man pulling a trailer full of scrap iron and metal, jackknifed when he came up on a slow moving tractor. That sent him directly into the path of my car. I could not go to the left, because the tractor was there. To turn right, would have run me directly into the truck… and while I did turn my wheel that way as a natural reaction, I slammed into the trailer full of heavy metal. Very heavy metal with nothing to do with bands and music.

It was like running into a solid brick wall at 60-miles per hour and of course my airbags deployed; I credit them for saving my life. When I came to, someone had stopped, called the police.

The State Trooper who worked my wreck later became the sheriff for our parish. What a small wonderful world I live in, even though strewn with dreadful things. The good. The bad. Life.

The orthopedic surgeon wanted to operate on both knees immediately. I held off, saying, so long as I could walk… and I could, even if painfully… I would wait. I had enough operations. I was too damaged emotionally to voluntarily submit to having both knees operated on.

To this day, I cannot put any weight on either knee, but I did not undergo surgery. No crawling around on the floor for me.

The thing I recall going through my mind and even though everything happened within seconds, I remember thinking, *This is April. Tony was killed in April. Now, I am going to die in April also.*

I did not die.

CRACKS & CREVICES

"The older I get, the more I see there are these crevices in life where things fall in and you just can't reach them to pull them back out. So you

can sit next to them and weep or you can get up and move forward. You have
to stop worrying about who's not here and start worrying about who is."
(Alex Witchel, The Spare Wife)

"OUT DAMNED SPOT!"*

(*Macbeth Act 5 Scene 1 - Lady Macbeth's sleepwalking scene - Shakespeare)

Six months later, I again felt strange. My blood pressure began bottoming out once again. This time it was suggested, between the hospital doctor and the neurologist, it was likely the result of a seizure, or seizures.

Once out of Intensive Care, the testing began. The MRI revealed a spot on my left frontal lobe. A very, very tiny spot. A brain scan showed activity where it should not have been. Shrinkage showed up when a comparison MRI was done a year later. The spot was not mentioned, but the definitive shrinking was paramount.

Dr Vipul Shelat, my neurologist, started me on seizure meds and vitamin B12 injections the first year. After the second MRI revealed the shrinkage, he started me on memory medicine... medicine used in the treatment of Alzheimer's.

I recently found a sticky pad note in the bottom of a little used purse, with the words: *Brain cells damaged.*

Beneath, I had written *Namenda. Alzheimer's meds.* This was March 2012. However, Dr Shelat did not use the term *Alzheimer's disease* with me at this time. He monitored me closely. He monitors me still. But, he did not say *Alzheimer's disease.*

Just because he did not say it aloud, does not mean it was not happening. Because, apparently, it was. It is. It just never crossed my mind, despite what the meds were prescribed for. Remember, these descriptions also add something about "or for what the physician determines," or words to that effect.

Several months ago, he asked if I had anyone living close, or at home. I advised my daughter Theresa lives in Gulfport, Mississippi. He said he would like to see her when she next comes to visit.

Generally, Theresa and Carla come on a Friday night after work, spend all day Saturday and then, head back home on Sunday. It is a five-hour drive each way.

When Dr Shelat asked a second time about seeing Theresa, I called her. She called him. She made a point of coming with me for my next appointment. She drove up on Sunday, April 21st and we went for my doctor appointment together on Monday.

Theresa has the same wicked sense of humor that I suffer from (or is that, makes me insufferable?), however, as I jest, I tell her I inherited my sense of humor from her.

So, when I said I wondered what he wanted to talk to her about, she popped off that likely he wanted to tell her that what I had was hereditary.

We laughed together.

Inside, I wondered, but sloughed it off as just his individual personal care he gives as a physician. He does not operate the typical medical office. And trust me, there are typical offices everywhere. His receptionist is his wife. He does not have a half dozen rooms where a nurse herds one patient after another, taking temps and blood pressure and noting them on your chart, and often jotting down the reason for your visit.

No, he does this himself. This is part of his examination. He examines each patient individually. When you tell him why you are there, what you need, it is not like playing the child's whisper game… where you tell one person one thing and by the time it reaches the end of the line, it may come out completely different. You speak directly to him. From your mouth to his ear.

He has one patient room but there are never a lot of people sitting around in the waiting room because he allows thirty minutes for each patient.

Most doctor's offices I have visited over the years, more than one person is given the same time slot. Sometimes many more than one.

I have never felt rushed. He takes as much time as he deems necessary to evaluate my condition.

The month before this special visit, I underwent a brain scan and blood tests. The results would be available at this upcoming visit. The timing would be good. Results presented while Theresa is present.

And so it was, when she and I visited Dr Shelat, he had reached his conclusion.

The results of the brain scan and blood tests provided confirmation of what he had been suspecting and actually treating.

Obviously, based on the medications prescribed, he had already made a tentative diagnosis. He simply had not come out and said to me: *Barbara, you are developing Alzheimer's Disease.*

But, now, he did.

Do you come down with it? You come down with the flu. Interesting question. I have no idea what the answer is.

SWEET NOTHINGS

An elderly man, having dinner with an old friend, was impressed by the way his host preceded every request to his wife with such endearing terms as Dear, Precious, Love, Sweetness, Honey, Darling, Sweetheart…He was amazed. Obviously, even though they had been married for over 60 years, his friend was still hopelessly in love with his wife.

While the wife was in the kitchen, the man leaned over to his friend and whispered, "It is just wonderful how, after all these years you are still so polite and courteous to your wife." His dear friend shook his head sadly and said, "I have to tell you the truth, I forgot her name 20 years ago."

"THREE STRIKES AND YOU'RE OUT!"*
(Baseball - idiom)

I recently read about something the National Institute of Health calls *"silent strokes."* I did not make note of who or what, but because I am constantly reading, I do recall the subject.

Silent strokes.

Having possibly, more than likely in fact, had at least one stroke, I was interested, so I read more.

According to the article, there are small spots of dead brain cells and memory loss in elderly persons. These have been tied to memory loss. There are so many tests ongoing, and some indicate one thing, others indicate something else. Dr Shelat said it is best not to look things up on the Internet, advising, not everything posted is accurate.

However, there is one fact posted on the Internet, and appearing more often in articles, that is not disputed: Alzheimer's is a disease that causes memory problems.

Another statistic not disputed is that Alzheimer's is said to be the sixth leading cause of death in the United States according to the Alzheimer's Association.

Still another statistic not disputed: There is no cure.

No cure.

Another: There is no preventive means.

The fact is, so far, it is iffy whether or not any of the approved medicines actually slow the progression.

I know that sounds confusing… *the fact is… iffy… whether or not…*

Why is so little known? Why is there not a better understanding? This ailment, disease, death-sentence, has been coming to light for what would seem to a layman like myself, for a very long time.

However, as with various cancers, although there is constant ongoing research, breakthroughs are so slim, to the point of being none for the most part.

Slim to none.

Still, today, we know so much more than when I first read about the strange white substance found in the brains of certain, but not all, deceased elderly people.

Connecting the dots on paper is one thing. In reality, it is quite another. Especially when the dots often do not connect.

Dot, dot, dot, dash. Disconnect.

There are two types of drugs currently being used to treat cognitive symptoms.

I am taking <u>Namenda (Mematine)</u>, said to be one of few drugs approved in the past ten years, that may possibly slow down the progression. This drug works in another brain cell communication network and slows the progression of symptoms with moderate to severe Alzherimer's disease.

Magic words: *May possibly slow down the progression.*

Even the word: *May* is encouraging. *May* is better than a negative. It is not a one-hundred per cent assurance, but it is positive. A positive trumps a negative in every game I have ever played.

The printout provided by the pharmacy lists common uses: *This medicine is a NMDA-receptor antagonist used to treat moderate to severe Alzheimer's-type dementia. This medicine blocks excess activity of a substance in the brain called glutamate. Blocking glutamate may reduce the symptoms associated with Alzheimer's disease. This medicine is not a cure for Alzheimer's disease. This medicine may be used to treat other conditions as determined by your doctor.*

The other type drug currently used to treat cognitive symptoms is the *Cholinesterase inhibitors.* Donepezil HCL, the other drug Dr Shelat has prescribed, works by boosting levels of cell-to-cell communication chemical depleted in the brain by Alzheimer's disease.

There are several other Cholinesterase Inhibitors available. Unfortunately, it is reported that less than half of the people taking these drugs can expect any actual improvement. Still, taking these drugs, I am hoping to keep the symptoms at bay for awhile. Maybe I am baying at the moon, but, what choice do I have?

The pharmaceutical printout says about Donepezil HCL: *This medicine is a cholinesterase inhibitor used to treat dementia (e.g. Impairment of memory, judgment, and abstract thinking; changes in personality) in patients with Alzheimer's disease.*

Donepezil is also known as Aricept. Another printout says: *This drug improves function of nerve cells in the brain. It works by preventing the breakdown of a chemical called acetylcholine. People with dementia usually have lower levels of this chemical, which is important in the processes of memory, thinking and reasoning. It is used to treat mild to moderate dementia caused by Alzheimer's disease.*

For my seizures, and I have experienced them off and on—flashing lights in the night—sometimes bright purple, other times like a white flashlight being shined around the room—a loud bang, yellow splotches filling the pages of my books yet that I can see through and around, feeling weird and being unable to speak aloud what I want to say—Dr Shelat has prescribed:

Levetiracetam. (Keppra) The printout says: *This medicine is an anticonvulsant usually used with other medicines to treat certain types of seizures.*

Also Primidone. The printout says: *This medicine is an anticonvulsant used to treat or prevent epileptic seizures.*

Thrown in for good measure, and likely to help me cope…and maybe this is exactly why I do cope so well, is Trazodone. The printout says: *This medicine is an antidepressant used to treat depression. It may also be used for relief of an anxiety disorder (e.g., sleeplessness, tension), chronic pain or to treat other conditions as determined by your doctor.*

I have never needed an antidepressant, but then, I never had Alzheimer's before. So, surely, it cannot hurt and just in case I find myself wanting to stop making jokes about everything, and feel sad and sorry, perhaps the Trazodone will kick in. Then I will be good to go.

Additionally, there is Pravastatin prescribed originally by my heart doctor. The printout advises: *This medicine is an HMG-CoA reductase inhibitor (also known as a "statin") used in combination with a low-cholesterol and low-fat diet to lower cholesterol and triglyceride levels and to raise good cholesterol (HDL) levels in your blood. This medicine may also be used in certain patients to reduce the risk of heart attack, blood vessel blockage, stroke, or death due to heart disease.*
Simvastatin is my current statin.

Also prescribed by my heart doctor, Lisinopril. The printout reads: *This medicine is an angioensin converting enzyme (ACE) inhibitor used to treate high blood pressure. It may also be used with other medicine to treat congestive heart disease or to improve survival in some patients after a heart attack.*

Many of our politicians are old. Many elderly people continue as part of the workforce. Singers I listened to as a teen, are still singing. Being old does not mean pulling up your pants and going home because not everyone who gets old becomes senile and useless. I am keeping my marbles in the circle.

Humans experience old age in a unique way as opposed to the life span of other mammals because human brains shrink while the brains of other creatures experiencing longevity, do not.

I am not a turtle, I am a human creature, and my brain is shrinking. Some researchers attribute shrinkage of our brains to the fact that our lives extend into the 80's. When humans were dying at 30, 40, 50 even, some centuries ago, the opportunity for this shrinkage did not happen.

Now, since I am well into old age, I am bound and determined to stave off what is going on inside this old gray head as long as possible.

Mind over matter. Not exactly. Instead it is because of knowledge. Knowing stuff. Knowledge has always armed an individual for the various skirmishes faced each and every day. Alzheimer's is but one more skirmish to be faced, tackled, and perhaps even defeated.

Together, between the care and great knowledge of my neurologist and my own determination, I will slow this shrinkage. I will *"will"* it to cease and desist. I am not your typical grandmother. In fact, I have never been typical anything. No need to start now.

In other words, I am not down for the count. Not yet. In my ballgame, three strikes do not make an out. They simply send me to the bench for a breather, and then I am back. Still standing after all these years, and I hope for many more.

But, only if lucidity remains. I would sadly hate to think I might one day slip into a slumber of uselessness, locked inside my nonfunctioning brain.

A prison sentence. That is what Alzheimer's has heretofore been considered. A prison sentence. I want a reprieve. Sweet and simple, I want a reprieve.

Here's your Get Out of Jail Free card.

~

A POEM

"I grow old ... I grow old ...
I shall wear the bottoms of my trousers rolled."
(T.S Eliot, The Love Song of J. Alfred Prufrock and Other Poems)

~

ATROPHY IS ANOTHER WORD FOR SHRINKAGE

Our brains are the center of our nervous systems. Healthy brains are paramount to our wellbeing. I mean, we can live without a digit, a toe, an arm, even a leg. But, we cannot live without a brain. It is our most precious organ.

Think about it… there I go, even such a simple statement as *think about it* would be impossible without a brain. Although I have a copy of "Gray's Anatomy" I really do not know anything more than the average person about our internal workings. Nothing more than I might have retained when taught many moons ago, or read in an article since then.

Still, even I know the brain affects, one way or another, everything we see, hear, taste, smell… all our basic senses. Cognition. While the equilibrium has to do with the ears, the brain also is instrumental in keeping us upright, balanced.

The emotions we experience, these come from within our brains. Everything starts within our brains to some degree. The death of these precious brains cells is not a good thing. Death… shrinkage.

Loss of brain cells leads to brain shrinkage. Brain shrinkage is also referred to as brain atrophy. Atrophy affects our memory… and loss thereof.

The older we get, the more significant this shrinkage becomes which equals a cognitive decline. We begin to lose touch.

While atrophy happens to some degree in everyone (referred to as mild cognitive impairment), it is much more advanced in people diagnosed with Alzheimer's disease. Apparently, the development of Alzheimer's disease speeds up this atrophy.

Can a cause be found? Can the rate of shrinkage be slowed? Can Alzheimer's disease be stayed?

Can I simply remain slightly forgetful or must I become a vegetable? I do not know. Already I am in a state of acceptance even as I deny. I just ate a plate of homemade lasagna and a bowl of vanilla ice cream. I should be eating healthy.

Common sense is being trumped. Give me time. Just give me a little time.

BANG!

An elderly man advised his son that if he wants to live a long life, simply sprinkle a little gunpowder on his breakfast every morning. The young fellow did this his entire life and died at the incredible age of 98. When they came to dispose of his body, he blew a 3-meter wide hole in the crematorium wall.

THREE BLUETOOTHS AND COUNTING (OR SHOULD THAT BE "BLUETEETH"?)

I left my Bluetooth lying on the kitchen table within Hadley's reach. Hadley is an adopted dog, found with his brother in a rain-filled ditch on the corner of Hadley Street and Garrett Road in Monroe, La. July 12, 2012 and rushed to the vets. He was not expected to make it through the night. He weighed a mere four pounds. He is approximately a year old as I am penning this little book. He weighs a good 60-70 pounds now. He amazes me with his cheerful attitude. He is perpetually happy.

Hadley chewed up my Bluetooth. I expect it tasted like me and he loves me. Likewise, my shoes. A book I was almost finished reading and now will never know who dunnit. The Yellow Book. More shoes. A Styrofoam lid. A pillow. Shoes.

But he means no harm. He chews with a smile on his face and his tail is wagging like a metronome. I love this dog.

I will likely never find where I have stashed everything in an attempt to keep it out of harm's way. However, the joy he bequeaths is worth a few pair of shoes and a Bluetooth.

I purchased two new pairs of sandals, so I am good to go. I also ordered a replacement Bluetooth.

I actually considered whether or not to do so. Since Dennis died, I seldom spend much time on the phone. We used to talk three-four hours a day, every day. He would get in from work and call. I would answer to his, *Lucy, I'm home.*

However, once you have used a Bluetooth, it is difficult to go back to having to hold a cell phone up to your ear. There is so much freedom using a Bluetooth.

So, I did it. I ordered another. Just like the one Hadley had eaten. It came last week.

Then the following Thursday I went to see Dr Shelat in Monroe. Without thinking, I had my cell phone in my pocket and the Bluetooth in my ear. I knew he has signs advising *No cell phones.*

So, I removed the device from my ear, slipped it into its carrying case that was attached to the zipper fob of my wallet. I dislike carrying purses.

As I age, I have bought smaller and smaller purses, until many days, I carry only my wallet.

Dr Shelat did his exam and sent me over to the hospital for some blood work. I left his office, went to the parking lot where Chuck was waiting for me. As usual he had offered to drive me. We often share trips to and from stores in an effort to save gas. The romance is long gone, but the friendship remains wholeheartedly.

I returned to the medical building where Dr Shelat has his office, got on the elevator and made my way to the breezeway that connects his office building to the hospital.

Making my way to admissions, I left my Medicare card with the receptionist and sat with my book reading until I was called to another room where I signed papers galore. I was then taken to the lab where I sat again.

When I was called to have blood drawn, the lab tech turned out to be a reader and we wound up discussing the books I have written. She made a note of all the titles, finished up with my test and once again, I made my way back to the elevator, then walked across the crosswalk, down another elevator and out onto the parking lot.

We headed to a small restaurant famous for its homemade pies and sandwiches and had a light lunch. Well, it would have been light except for the large slice of homemade coconut pie. I could not help myself. I ate the whole thing.

Next we drove back to the city of Bastrop, went to the grocery store to pick up a few things.

Daughter Theresa, her partner Carla and Carla's eight-month-old grandson, Ray were coming to visit for the weekend. I needed ingredients. I planned to make lasagna. It has long been a favorite of Theresa's.

I never thought about my Bluetooth until that night when I got ready for bed. I picked up the Bluetooth carrying case, carried it and the phone into the bedroom where I plugged the phone into the charger. I opened the Bluetooth carrying case and it was empty.

Turns out this was the original carrying case; the case that *used* to hold the first Bluetooth, the one Hadley chewed up.

I went back to where I had left my wallet sitting on the counter. The zipper fob was broken. The Bluetooth had fallen off when it broke, apparently. I thought back. When did I last see my Bluetooth? When was I last aware of having it?

At the doctor's office, yes. When I hooked it onto my wallet. After that I was oblivious. I could not for the life of me recall when it might have fallen. Where I had lost it, with so many steps taken, so many different places visited, there is no way to know.

Should I call the hospital lost and found? Should I call the restaurant? Should I call the grocery store?

I became static. It was overwhelming. I was so disturbed by my lapse of memory, my lack of recall, that I did nothing. I did not call anywhere. I told myself I would call Monday.

Monday came, and what I did instead was go into amazon.com and order one more Bluetooth.

I was overwhelmed and tired. But, I also made a vow that I will pay attention to everything I do from now on. No more acting or reacting without thinking. I will think. I will pay attention.

The saga of the Bluetooth is a test. Only a test. I will receive an A+ on the next portion of the Bluetooth test. I have to. I cannot let something so basic, so simple, so foolish, whip me.

I ordered the third Bluetooth. Everybody knows three times is a charm. Oh yeah, I am planning to wear it on a lanyard around my neck when it is not in my ear.

PHILOSOPHY

"As long as I am breathing, in my eyes, I am just beginning."
(Criss Jami)

~

THE EX OF THE EX-MOSTEST

My first marriage went haywire because the ex developed a Bimbo Brain Tumor. It was fatal. He married her. Well, then I met and married a handsome blue-eyed man named Charles "Chuck" Babb.

We were more than compatible for twelve years. We waged our own battles. He had a drinking problem that was leftover from his troubled past, that finally was shut down after three years of marriage. He made up his mind, no more, and no more it was. Bravo.

My hang-ups stemmed from a terrorizing ex delivering enough torment that some thirty years later I penned *NORMAL, A Novel,* a psychological thriller and based what the book's heroine suffered on nine-out-of-ten things that actually transpired. It made a great thriller. It made me a quivering lump of whipped jelly for a long time.

Finally, Chuck was okay and I was okay and eventually we settled into a comfortable old-soft-shoe pattern. Then, after twelve years, we decided to part, letting each other see if there might be more out there. He hopped on a motorcycle and toured these United States with his son and a friend. I remarried—a blunder because he turned out to be a philanderer. I helped him get his son raised and then we too parted.

After awhile, Chuck worked his way back to Louisiana. He lived several places, and in the end, we hit upon a good arrangement. He moved his travel trailer on my little oasis I jokingly first called *Wits End…* because when you are here, you are there; and then added *Comedy Club*, because it is a laugh a minute around here.

Our arrangement was, keep the yard up, because he loves being out-doors more than anywhere else, and stay as long as he wants. Then one day, his old camper's wiring went bad and burned up, so he cleaned out my unused game room. I sold the pool table, and he moved in there. It has a separate entrance, besides the sliding glass doors into my portion of the house. He painted the glass doors, for permanent privacy and created a perfect little studio apartment. It has a bathroom, kitchen and bar area; also a lovely alcove surrounded by stained glass windows.

He pays half the electricity and water, and we are good to go. He is my constant companion, when I need one. He drives me to and from the doctor when needed. He fixes things that break. We respect each other's privacy and are content just knowing the other is near in time of need. I know I get on his nerves as he does on mine if we hang around together too long at a time. But, he built a patio, my screened-in porch, plants a small garden each spring, and lets Hadley outside around 4:30 if I am late getting home from work.

I sleep better at night, not that I had trouble before. Still, it is a good thing knowing there is someone nearby, because otherwise, I live in the middle of nowhere—which is what my dogs and I prefer.

He never intrudes but he keeps an eye on me, this I know. Already, he asked when I go to the orthopedic doctor about my arthritic thumb; offer-ing to drive me. I negated this offer. I will save my cards for when I really need to play them.

He drove with me when I took my Impala in for a re-repair from two weeks earlier. While waiting, I wandered out into the showroom. When I did not come back, he came in grinning.

Which one are you buying? he asked.

I pointed to the little sunshine yellow 2013 Chevy Spark.

He shook his head. He remembers the time I traded in the yellow Cadillac and came home with a shiny red Pontiac Fiero. Also, the time I went to get new tires and came back with a new Buick, and when I went to get the Saturn's backseat window repaired (it kept creeping down), and returned with the Impala. He says there were other times as well.

Maybe so. I can be impetuous. I believe I am well-grounded and for the most part, think things out. Then, suddenly, there are these moments when something simply seems to be what needs doing at that particular moment in time.

Impetuous? Occasionally. But, only if I can afford it. I know when I can and when I cannot. Which reminds me, I do not window shop. People are always saying it doesn't hurt to look. But, it does if you cannot afford to buy what you want when you see it.

Spending a Sunday afternoon wandering around a Mall without money would kill my soul. I do not do malls. Take me to the park. Let me sit under the shade of the trees. Let me commune. Let me look up at the blue sky and sigh with the peace that surrounds me. But, do not take me to a mall for entertainment.

Not unless I have money burning a hole in my pocket.

So, Chuck. What? A dear friend? Yes. I would say so. In fact, he is my mainstay and my best friend. Everybody needs a best friend.

⌒

OLDSTER'S T-SHIRT

Genuine antique; been there, done that, can't remember.

⌒

Let there be Light

Photo by: Ann Hamilton,

Summer in the Valley, El Paso, Texas, 2012

The clouds may form, they may build and fill the sky. But, behind every cloud there is a shaft of sunshine. This beam is the ray of hope. Never give up hope because with time hope often becomes reality. The reality is... fill in the blank. Someday soon, someone will indeed fill in the blank and Alzheimer's disease will be a thing of the past rather than a bane of the future.

Indeed, let there be light.

WRITINGWRITINGWRITINGWRITING

I am still writing popular and humorous newspaper columns, *Life in the Last Lane,* each and every week. I am still writing my humorous *Louisiana Road Trips* magazine monthly columns I call *Running the Roads.*

Ideas keep flowing. The stream has not dried up yet. The road block has not slowed me down.

I was guest speaker for the local *Optimists Club* last month, and have spoken before numerous groups over the years. I like public speaking but admit, I worried about this last talk. By the time I was invited to speak, I knew about my ISB.

You haven't forgotten what ISB stands for, have you? *Incredible Shrinking Brain.*

Mine.

Incredible but shrinking.

I typed out what I was going to say, read it and reread it, until I was comfortable with my subject. Still, I kept my paper handy, just in case. I believe I did okay. But somewhere within my shrinking brain, I am no longer as confident as I once was.

As an aside, even as I type this, I have been invited to be guest speaker at the Mer Rouge Lion's Club in August. The president invited me to bring copies of my books if I want to.

Of course, I want to. How sweet it is!

Speaking of speaking. I entered the *Jay Leno Comedy Challenge* some years ago. I was one of eight finalists. I did not win, but I went on to do my comedy routine in front of the *American Notary Society* in Washington DC one year, among other groups. That was probably my largest audience. It was the annual convention and the membership was around 20,000. Of course, not near that many attended. But enough, enough so I felt like I was accomplishing something. My sister Jan was with me.

I have been guest speaker at other club meetings and conventions for an assortment of organizations. My brain was working just fine. I did that same basic routine many more times and always, people laughed and I felt confident.

Now, I feel my confidence slipping away and I am trying to hold on with all my might. The song, *Not Fade Away* plays over and over in my shrinking brain even as I reach out, grasping for a life preserver. I am searching for a life jacket to put on, button up and sink deep into the safety it provides. I do not want to drown one day simply because my brain has shrunk up into a nubbin.

I am often asked where I get my ideas. I say I just stop, look and listen. I hear a phrase that strikes my funny bone and a column is born. My newspaper columns usually run 600 words. Writing this precise number of words, there is a permanent place saved for my column each week. It fits.

I have been writing my *Life in the Last Lane* humor newspaper columns for ten plus years. For a long while I was also writing a community column: *News from the northeast corner.*

Prior, when I worked in Arkansas, I wrote community columns for two Arkansas newspapers titled simply *Wilmot News.* Before that, when I was religious, I wrote columns for the denomination I was affiliated with. Prior to that, I wrote columns about Nippon, a porcelain made for a mere 30 year period. I was considered an authority.

Before that, I prepared a *Soil and Water Conservation* newsletter every couple months, because for awhile I worked for that office. Even before that, I was the society editor, when newspapers had such animals, for the *Bastrop Daily Enterprise.* However, son Tony was in the second grade and was having problems, so I decided to stay home and be a fulltime mom. When he and Theresa were old enough to become 4-H members, I became a 4-H leader.

Writing has been a passion of mine for so many years, and because of this, my horizons have been expanded. They continue to expand. I am driven to write.

I also write letters. I have always written letters. I am still in touch with a pen pal in Colorado, our letters started when she was 12 and I was 13. I finally met her when we were stationed to Colorado Springs.

My cousin Mike Sarik and I exchange letters a couple times a month, and have ever since we discovered each other. We are obviously cousin, but have never met. He lives in New York City and I am shrinking away in Jones, Louisiana.

I keep the postal service in service. I remember mailing letters for three-cents. Now they are 46-cents. I also collect postage stamps. Many of the countries no longer exist. Or if they do, they have changed their names several times over.

I have a great stamp collection, started when I was just a child.

I had a letter from President Dwight D. Eisenhower, and kept it until about thirteen years ago, when after the divorce from my ex-husband it turned up missing. But then, so did my copy of *Deep Throat*.

I started collecting books, and reading each and every one when I was about ten years old. Daddy built a bookshelf for me. I have that bookshelf still. Now, though, I have over 6,000 books stacked, piled, shelved, all over my house. People come, they look, they gape and they always ask, *Have you read all these books?*

Yes. Yes, I have. However, for the first time for as long as I can remember, instead of gobbling up a book in one or two days, it is taking me longer. I am busy writing, yes, but when I go to bed to read myself to sleep, I fall asleep far faster than I used to.

I am much more tired than I have ever before been.

Is it psychological because of this diagnoses?

Actually, it started when Dennis died. His death was proof positive that life is a fragile bark and tomorrow is not promised.

I still cannot eat and not read (which is a double negative), but, something is slowing down inside. I am not digesting books at the normal rate. Or, maybe, this is the new normal. (Reversing the double negative: when I eat, I must read).

MIDDLE AGE

"The really frightening thing about middle age is that you know you'll grow out of it."

(Doris Day)

WE KNOW MORE NOW THAN WE USED TO BUT WE STILL DON'T KNOW ENOUGH

Chuck said, "If it can take a man like Leon down—a strong man, strong minded—it can take anyone down."

He is talking about Alzheimer's disease and how he saw Alzheimer's disease "bring a big man down."

He said both this man and his wife were diagnosed; they suffered and died from the disease.

"I saw Leon pick up 500-pounds when he was normal. Before Alzheimer's struck."

The man Chuck is talking about, he and his wife had four children, three daughters and a son. He was active all his life. He went hunting, worked with young kids and the Boy Scouts, worked for Rockwell Standard and later began driving a big rig cross country and locally. He owned a home, raised a family, and was taking care of his wife who started showing signs of dementia before he did. However, what with fate having such a fickle finger, Leon wound up dying from his Alzheimer's before his wife did.

Marilyn, his wife, accused their children of stealing money from them and at first he believed her. He had no reason not to believe her. Her confused accusations pitted father against son and daughters. And then, it all unraveled.

When we live with someone the change may be gradual enough we do not recognize it for what it is. Leon did not see it in Marilyn at first.

Leon's three sisters went to visit him and his wife and upon their return said, "Leon has it too."

They knew by this time that his wife was afflicted, but now they saw their brother also experiencing these same symptoms and behavior. It was horrifying, and so very, very sad.

For awhile the mentally declining couple lived alone. Then a daughter moved in with them, helped care for them. She brought the couple down to visit their family in Louisiana, but by this time both of them were "pretty bad" Chuck said.

"He didn't even remember Linda, our sister, at first." Chuck said.

It was not very long afterward that Leon died.

"I think Leon just gave up," Chuck said.

After Leon's death, the children were forced to admit their mother, Leon's wife, into a nursing facility for her own safety. The children could not handle her. She lived for a few years and then finally, in all her confusion and forgetfulness, passed away.

The term "passed away" is so fitting in this instance. The victim, the sufferer, the patient, simply passes away. Slips away from one oblivion to another.

Chuck also spoke about one of his brother-in-law's mother.

"She used to hide her purse and then claim someone stole it."

Paranoia. Did she hide it on purpose or simply forget where she put it and when she could not find it, assume someone must have stolen it?

This was before Alzheimer's disease was discussed openly, before more and more information has been discovered. The disease is still so complicated and confusing, there have been only a few medications developed during these past ten years appearing to have any sort of a positive affect on memory loss.

Memory loss is Alzheimer's disease in a nutshell.

Nutshell. Crack open a Filbert. It looks a lot like a brain. A tiny brain. And within that tiny brain there are still so many mysteries. Unexplored regions. We wonder about outer space. We also wonder about inner space. It is easier to send rocket ships into outer space than to break down and enter the barriers that divide the inner space of our brains.

"Bob's mother used to say she had to go cook supper for her husband... and he had been dead for 40 years."

He said that in the end, "she laid up there in a nursing home for a long time... in the dementia ward."

You get old and you experience a certain degree of forgetfulness. It is not unusual to drift back into the past, remember things from your childhood, early adulthood. You can do this and not have Alzheimer's disease.

But, when someone is stricken with Alzheimer's disease the first thing to go is short term memory.

Short term memory loss.

The disease destroys current memory. Perhaps this is why so many sufferers do in fact delve into the past... their current memories are gone. Where else can they go? The present is erased almost as soon as it happens.

Eventually, this disease eats even these old memories and the brain of the afflicted vegetates. Hence the expression *becoming a vegetable.*

Carrots cannot think for themselves. If they could they would run for the hills before they get turned into julienne sticks; become part of somebody's slaw.

Chuck said, "I believe it is in the genes." He said he believed his mother was drifting in this direction but she did not die from it. She fell and cracked her neck, dying because of complications from her broken neck that went undetected for too long.

She said her neck hurt but she was just an old lady complaining of many aches and pains. Sometimes we do not listen to what an old person tells us. We write it off… Just one more brick in the wall, one more ache and pain.

Yes. Her neck did hurt. It was broken. And she died.

~

CONCESSION

*"At least wrinkles don't hurt."**
(*Barbara Sharik)

~

THE UP AND DOWN SIDE OF LIVING ALONE

Back in 2009, I penned a column about living alone. This was before the diagnoses of Alzheimer's disease. At that time, this is how I felt about living alone. I did not mind and I still do not mind. I have added a couple dogs since I wrote this, and BooCat. My bed is more crowded and there is more dog and cat fur floating in the sunbeams and settling in the corners.

What will happen to my pets when I become an unknown entity unable to care for them, much less myself? Is this why the Pharos of Egypt often had their pets buried with them? They loved them so much…

I love my furbies so much but I am counting on human intervention. They will miss me when I am gone, but my departure should not include theirs.

You see, there is so much to think about when faced with this dread diagnosis.

Your home. Your pets. Your stuff. Yourself.

I sleep with dogs. Otherwise, I live alone.

On the upside, I stay up as late as I want. I own the remote and watch what I want. Or, I did before this converter box stuff started. Instead of more channels I get less. Analog worked fine ever since TV was invented. Now, with the new and improved digital system my rabbit ears are rendered virtually ineffective. Even the new Flat Screen Hi-Def TVs don't work where I live using rabbit ears like analog did. KNOE's gone altogether and KARD's on its last gamma ray. I need an outside antenna for the wind to blow down.

When it comes to meals the biggest dilemma is determining what to steam, simmer or scorch, but, I eat what and when I want. Except for dogspeak, dinner conversation's lacking. Actually, I prefer to read rather than converse when I eat anyway. Leftovers are a way of life. Three days of the same stuff is my limit. The dogs don't mind. They'd eat it all week if it's people food.

A vending machine, microwave and large trash can would be convenient. Color-coordinated, natch. It's heat it, eat it and toss it. Who needs fine china? My Noritake has served its purpose—no pun intended.

If I don't want to clean house, who is going to notice? Certainly not the pups. They prefer squalor. Mostly we tiptoe around so as not to stir up the dust. I dust when the spirit moves me. However, I can vouch that spiritual movement regarding dusting does not happen with regularity when you live alone.

The most comfy chair in the living room is mine. At shower time, nobody uses all the hot water but me. My toothpaste tube is squeezed in the middle.

I eat the first piece of chocolate in a box of candy. The last one too. Actually, since giving dogs chocolate is a no-no, I get to eat the whole box. Of course, after a chocolate orgy, I stay away from the scales. But, since I'm fluffy, the pups like my lap.

It isn't ladylike to snore, sweat or crack jokes about bodily functions, which is okay. Only the doggies know for sure whether or not I snore and they could care less. On three-dog-nights, like *Three Dog Night*, we snore in harmony.

Factually actually, I could sleep on one side of the bed one week, and on the other side the next, thereby cutting down on laundry. Nobody hogs the covers.

I use only half the number of towels and half as much soap.

I sing Karaoke and TacoBelle, Rosie, and Gizzard are my best audience. They don't boo or howl. Wagging their tails, they are most tolerant and haven't a clue I cannot carry a tune. Dogs love you unconditionally. They really do. And mine are no exception.

On the downside, I have to take my trash to the corner, pay someone to mow my yard, change burned out light bulbs, tote my own groceries into the house and no one sends me flowers anymore. But, I get a lot of liquid sugar kisses from both my inside and outside dogs, and that ain't all bad.

(Bastrop Daily Enterprise, Bastrop, Louisiana)

REALITY

"Just as a woman looks lovely by candlelight, so does a house.
*And, there are times when they both look better in the dark."**
(*Barbara Sharik)

THE GRACELESS ART OF AGING GRACEFULLY

Over the years, I have written many newspaper columns about Life in the Last Lane… Why do I think this one might add a bit of humor and relief from the bad news aging bestows upon us? I don't know. Maybe I felt after all these serious chapters, it is time for a little levity… the next two columns offer just that, levity, lightness and laughter.

Everyone will tell you time heals. True, it may be a great healer but it's also a bad beautician. Age doesn't always bring wisdom, sometimes it comes all by itself. Age that is, not wisdom. Age shows up even if wisdom never arrives.

Brain cells come and they go, but fat cells live forever, especially if you're a nutritional overachiever. Even if you manage to kill off fat cells by dieting, they reincarnate themselves on your thighs with the first bite of chocolate. Me? I could say I over eat to fill out my wrinkles, but my words would fall on deaf ears. Deaf ears? Another part of the aging process.

They used to say, when I was growing up, what goes first is, first your money, then your clothes. But not so. First your arms get too short to hold the newspaper out far enough to read the shrinking words, so you break down and buy reading glasses. It takes several years before vanity allows you to carry them with you on a regular basis. Later, forgetfulness, said to be associated with aging also, has you forgetting them on a regular basis.

Then, as mentioned above, your ears lose some of their sharpness. Someone invites, "Come see me sometime," and you're sitting there wondering why they're asking you to "Come be my Valentine," in November. You smile and say "Yes, about two weeks ago," and you wonder why everyone's looking at you funny. You thought they asked "Did you meet Freddie?" but what they actually asked was, "Did you eat already?"

And then, there's the waistline. For men, there's the old joke about a man becoming a pirate's dream; he has a sunken chest. His chest sinks down and joins his tummy. When women lose their waistlines, they switch to elasticized jeans. Since men rarely wear elasticized jeans, they must let their britches ride down below that pirate's dream.

As Father Time takes us waltzing, we discover bodily imperfections developing. Ever notice women rarely declare, "I don't look good in this dress," but instead say, "This dress doesn't look good on me"? Like it's the fault of the dress.

You begin to care more about comfort than style. After a certain age, high heels hurt. Feet get flatter, wider and longer. Someone said noses do too, but anyway, once you wore size 7, suddenly you're buying 10's. It didn't happen overnight, but it might as well have. There's no reversing the process once it starts. Even if you successfully diet back into smaller clothes sizes, the shoes stay the same. Of course, it's highly likely that shoe manufacturers have changed the sizes of shoes when we weren't looking.

Some men do this comb-over thing with their hair when it starts thinning. Please don't. Just get a shorter haircut and know that bald may not be beautiful, but it ain't bad. Also, men mustn't dye their hair. Unnaturally dark hair and wrinkles clash. Actually, gray hair makes men look distinguished.

Some say life begins at 40. That probably came from someone who had a very boring early life. Actually, what happens at 40 is, that life begins to show. Also, it doesn't get any better at fifty. The aging process has a mind of its own, barring plastic surgery. As you age, you know you've still got it, but nobody wants to see it. You don't even have to do drugs, you get the same effect just standing up fast.

But like taxes, aging is inevitable and that's okay considering the alternative; which is also eventually inevitable. Best advice, is to just let yourself age; let things happen gracefully. Don't try to be somebody you aren't in the name of hanging onto the past. You try to do the new modern dances teens do, you look like a frog in a blender.

So what if your hair thins and turns a little gray? So what if your body parts thicken, shift and sag some? So what if when you go shopping you fill your shopping cart with stuff that says, "For fast relief"? Instead of worrying about getting old, welcome each day with joy, knowing it's one more day that you've beat your own previous record for the number of consecutive days you've stayed alive.

Now that's worth celebrating.

(Bastrop Daily Enterprise, Bastrop, Louisiana)

TIT FOR TAT

"I know I talk too much, but I also smile a lot. So it sort of evens itself out."*
(*Barbara Sharik)

AGE IS ONLY A STATE OF MIND

Please keep smiling. Time enough to get serious again.

I really don't mind getting older, except for a few inconveniences. It hasn't reached the point yet that when I eat out, they make me pay my money up front, but I can't do quite as much as I once did. Fortunately, my memory hasn't gotten so bad that I meet new people every day. In other words, I'm still hanging in there but it's not so much the age as the mileage.

Usually I avoid using the terms old or elderly and stick to calling myself mature. As a mature person my main strength is knowing what my weaknesses are. Actually age is only a state of mind. I consider myself middle aged, provided I live to be 120. Actually, I look as young as my 35 year old neighbor… the one who looks 60.

The last time I got flowers was shortly before Jon Darlin' passed away. He brought me a bouquet of wild flowers. That's okay though because at my age, getting flowers would probably scare me. I'd be wondering what do they know that I don't.

I admit to not getting the exercise I should. It's sorta like a Catch 22. I know I need to exercise, but if I do, I hurt all over. There's no way I can get down on the floor to do some of the old standards because I'd probably never be able to get back up again. That's what I mean about knowing my weaknesses.

I was at the Wal-Mart Super Center the other evening and starting at the milk end, I decided I'd power walk down the nice wide aisle to the other end. Walking is supposed to be healthy. I zipped right past the eggs, the lunch meat, the cheeses, and the seafood and meat products. By the time I got to the bakery end, I'd worked up an appetite. I was forced to buy a box of donuts. The ones with a cream cheese filling since dairy products are good for your bones. I also got some cream puffs. The more dairy the better.

Speaking of a way to get more exercise, someone recommended parking way out on the lot so you'd have to walk farther, thereby getting some extra walking into your day. Me? I try not pulling all the way into my parking space. Works for me.

Actually, housecleaning is sort of like doing exercise. Unfortunately, just thinking about it can send me into spasms of inactivity. I do seem to stay behind with housecleaning. Even if I were to get two weeks done in the next four days, I'd probably still be three weeks behind. My solution?

Defining the problem. I've concluded clutter is just the unstrategic placement of stuff.

And so, being a little on the worn out side of life, I've come to the deduction that when I take a vacation from work I need to take three weeks at a time. One week to rest up. One week on vacation. And one more to rest up.

Let me end by giving the clarifying the meaning of sanity. It's any ideas, attitudes, comments or actions that agree with mine. Have a good day! Don't forget to ask for your senior citizen discount.

(Bastrop Daily Enterprise, Bastrop, Louisiana)

⌐

LEMONADE AGAIN

*My motto is that if life gives you lemons, make a lemon meringue pie...
however, all this meringue is making me fat.* *

(*Barbara Sharik)

⌐

FACING THE FEAR OF AGING

THE COLUMN - JUNE, 2012

Time to get serious again... this column ran in the Bastrop Daily Enterprise in June, 2012 and was probably the most commented upon column I ever published. I write humor. This is not humor.

"Is this Monday?" I hear myself ask. Then I'm frightened by this talking to myself because everyone knows crazy old people talk to themselves.

If someone moved into my head, read my innermost thoughts, they'd find me in a panic trying to remember what day it is, because that split second of being unsure, that split second of not remembering and not knowing, resurrected a fear.

I turned 60. When asked my fears, I never hesitate: Losing my mind and tornadoes.

Now I'm afraid because I turned 60. Dementia, senility, Alzheimer's, scroll through my mind. These fears move in lock, stock and barrel.

Fearful of the mind's ability to fail with age, creating bent old beings dribbling spittle from mouths that forget to close, staining the front of gowns with last night's supper, and not remembering what day it is.

I make lists. The tongue-tip stuff frustrates me.

I worry about searching for things, then not remembering what I'm looking for.

With the age of 60 and the fear, knowing these ailments strike millions a day, I'm determined to develop a plan to facilitate the preservation of normalcy.

I hammer a nail into the wall beside the door. Certain that hanging my keys on the nail the minute I cross the threshold will keep me from giving them a second thought until I need them. Not thinking about keys in between will eradicate excess clutter.

I don't need anything cluttering my mind needlessly, causing me to forget because there's too much to remember.

I don't want to be lost in the '50s. Or lost altogether, fading in and out of lucidity. I want to always remember the songs I sang, to never forget the music, the lyrics, to all the songs that turn my world.

Fugue. So frightening when driving down a highway in familiar surroundings one minute and the next, several miles farther on, wondering how I got there without being conscious of passing time or miles, as though

I slept with eyes wide open. Is fugue another entryway to senility, and having done that, does it mean the door's opening?

The mind operates on automatic, busy behind the scenes, but what happens when the brakes fail, the oil pan runs dry and the windshield wipers no longer work? Will that happen to my brain now that I'm 60?

I stop my silent arguing knowing I shouldn't get in an uproar about something I have no control over. Confused, I worry that confusion is another gateway.

Tangled up in internal struggle, I remember once in all my innocence, before innocence was blown away by the whirlwinds of life-changing events, I believed in rainbows after every shower and moonbeams every night.

I believed too many people died in the name of peace, realizing John Lennon's Flower Power didn't work and neither did his *Give Peace a Chance* because no one will and mankind, which isn't kind after all, keeps killing. Then to compound the confusion, somebody shot John Lennon dead.

Perhaps when I turned 60, I was thinking too much. However, it's a perilous path I travel alone, and if I become mindless, who will save me?

As we age, as circuit breakers flip off one by one, we search for solutions, make excuses and bargains because we never want to forget how to laugh, how to cry. We don't want to disappear.

I've just turned 68. I weathered the fear that wrapped its dark wings around me the day I turned 60. Now, I don't dwell on sagging skin, wrinkles and lessoning physical abilities. Looking back, I see the foolishness of being afraid. Now, I live each day and life is good.

(Bastrop Daily Enterprise, Bastrop, Louisiana)

Wes Helbling said:

I just read your column for this week and it is probably the most moving, and also well written, of all of them. I especially like the quote below. If I was doing it, that would be the breakout quote.

"I want to always remember the songs I sang, to never forget the music, the lyrics, to all the songs that turn my world."

━━

FACING THE FEAR OF AGING

July 3, 2012
The Readers Respond

It all started as a 1,500-word short story written eight years ago. Dennis read it and said this needs to be published. Bringing it down to 600 words was not easy on one hand, yet it was. I needed only to post the barebones. They said it all.

I am talking about last week's column about the fear of growing old and facing the infirmities often accompanying aging. I probably had more responses to this one column than any other. It wasn't my usual humor; it was, instead, peering through the cloudy window we all eventually find ourselves behind. We prop it open as far and wide for as long as possible, fearing the day it closes and the latch slams shut.

Wes told me the column was moving and the best column I'd ever written and Jan said it brought tears to her eyes and reading what I wrote assured her we are not alone—other people are facing the perils of aging too. She said, "Everyone can identify."

"About all we can do is live each day as they come. We all face the inevitable at some time and it does no good to dwell on it," Ann wrote, and Merrilee said, "I agree. Live each day and life is good!"

Jamie wrote, "… this is awesome writing and oh so true. Thank you so much for this. Johnny told me H.J. once said that the things you worry about all your life, most of it doesn't come to pass and in the end, what does it really matter? It matters that you enjoy life to the fullest without worry, without regrets… just enjoy the day you have at hand and everything else will fall into place."

At the checkout counter at Walmart, the checker asked, "Are you the lady who writes for the newspaper? You really hit home with your columns."

Dennis saw people, like his father, with these aging problems and declared, "I'm not going there. I'm simply not. But, as I got there, I figured out not only was I going there but I accepted it too."

He realized that as you age, those things you thought you couldn't accept in your parents and those around you, you now accept.

When his mother was in the hospital and he was sitting alone with his father, knowing he had gone to Vietnam after he had been there, he asked him, "What do you think about Vietnam?" His father had never discussed any of the wars. As a 30-year Army veteran, he'd been in WWII, Korea and Vietnam.

His father quietly responded, "It was different." Dennis said, "I wanted to talk to him because he was a soldier, but the only thing he said to me was that it was different. Having fallen so far into senile dementia by this time, he could remember everything that happened in 1935, but not what happened five minutes ago."

During his father's last year of life, Dennis said he hung his head down and said, "I don't know how I got this way." Dennis vowed that he would never hang his head down like that and yet, now, now, he does. In addition, he also catches himself asking, "How did I get this way?"

Quite simply, although it is never so simple, he said, "I don't know how I got this way, but I am that way now too." And, he accepts.

Minds forget. Hands shake. Comprehension lessens. Yet, accepting with a positive attitude, like a teaspoonful of sugar making hiccups go away, makes the aging process quite tolerable after all.

(Bastrop Daily Enterprise, Bastrop Louisiana)

LIVING LIFE IN THE LAST LANE

I never thought I'd get old. I know the jokes about the alternative not being so good, but, when you're young, you don't think about becoming an old geezer gal. Of course, just 'cause you get elderly doesn't mean you have to get forgetful, deaf and blind, but it helps.
(Barbara Sharik, 2009)

SUBJECT: CARING THOUGHTS FROM WALES

Email
From: Ron Crown
Sent: Sunday, June 16, 2013 5:37 PM
To: Barbara
Subject: Caring thoughts from Wales
My dear Barbara I never touched on the subject Alzheimer's with you as my mother suffered with it for eighteen years. It was terrible to watch a once fit active and beautiful women taken down by this terrible illness.

It took a while before I could even visit my own mother when she was taken into care. But I eventually visited her as often as I could as she was

300 miles from where I lived. No other member of the family wanted to visit her. I eventually talked them all round to visit. It is something that will haunt me always, seeing someone you love trapped as it were.

The point I am making is I feel for you my dear, dear friend and I can understand the emotions this puts you through. I hope they find a cure in time to save everyone from this terrible ordeal that no one should go through. I know it scares the sh*t out of me. Who knows if it is in the genes and has been passed on.

When you do your article on Alzheimer's I would love to read it. 'til then my friend you are believe me a treasure in my thoughts and a very special lady who I am proud to have found as a friend. Hope that does not all sound sloppy. X

⚮

Email
From: Barbara
Date: Sunday, June 16, 2013 7:53 PM
To: Ron Crown
Subject: re: Caring thoughts from Wales

Of course it sounds sloppy... beautifully, caring sloppy. I have tried not to give it much thought... although the thought is always there. At first when the MRI and Brainscan showed a shrinkage, I was not too concerned. I mean everyone knows as we age our brains begin shrinking. And, the doc had not used the words dementia or Alzheimer's back then. I went to him because it was believed I had a stroke... out of the blue.

The ER docs admitted me and the hospital doc talked about putting me on a defibrillator. But eventually, decided that was not needed, but in the meantime, recommended seeing a neurologist. He began his tests. Six months into that, I was back at the ER and this time diagnosed as a seizure.

In between mostly I felt okay. But the neurologist monitored me closely and periodically took an assortment of tests to rule things out, more than anything else. In his mind, everything was pointing to one thing. Thus he began medicating in that direction.

The first MRI indicated something in my brain, that could have been a tumor; however, a year later, whatever it is, it had not grown.

My cognitive skills continued to be good.

However, when I rush into the house, drop my car keys as I go about my business, then in the morning, I had to search... so I have to make a concerted effort to set them in the same place each day, so I won't have to spend time searching in the morning.

Still, if I am on my way to bed, phone in hand, get sidetracked, say remember I haven't fed the fish, set the phone down and go feed the fish, then when I'm done I have to backtrack to find where I left the phone.

I had broken my number one rule, not paying attention to where I sit things down when in the midst of doing something else. So long as I do pay attention, I am good to go... I am not left frustratingly looking for things.

I do not have to label things. I have not put the ice cream in the microwave. I have not put anything in the wrong place. And I have found everything I have looked for...

I only had one incident when I went into a fugue. It was so overcast and so foggy, late at night, driving home from taking the voting stuff (from working at the polls) to the court house and returning home about 10 at night... and suddenly, I looked up... this most beautiful moon emerged and right as I was looking at it, awing to myself, I drove past my turnoff... and a little way down the road I crossed over a canal bridge and knew there were no canal crossings en route to my house. I was lost. I reasoned, I had not turned anywhere, I was still on the road that led to the turnoff to my house... somehow I must have passed it... and if I kept going, the worst that could happen would be that I would come to the river bridge that takes me into the next parish... the road itself I am traveling on from highway to bridge is only about 7 - 10 miles long. I knew I did NOT turn... I was still on that straight road.

Still, I was panicked inside, despite the logic. Because I am asking, how did I miss my turn?

I came to the next road off the left, read the street sign, sighed, turned around and headed back... found my turn and later figured out that the moon had sidetracked my attention right at the place I was supposed to turn.

A fugue had taken over me and I was lost in my thoughts. I live with that fearful moment. Being in a fugue. The fear fighting with the logic. And logic winning.

The doctor asked if he could talk to my daughter, so I told her, she called him, and then she made a point of driving up for the weekend and go with me on a Monday visit a couple months ago. And he advised her to note if when she comes to visit, if she notices anything going on... she assured him, that she has not as yet seen any indication of anything wrong.

I have been back to him once since her visit, and I go again this coming Thursday. This is once a month now, when it had been every 3 months at most. He asks cognitive questions and so far, I am good... I think... except when he asks me to subtract backwards. I never was good with math in my head. He can ask me capitals of states, spell things, etc., and I am good. Then I came across an article about Vit. B12 (I have to have injections because I am depleted) combined with B6 and folic acid, as having been shown to slow down memory loss in Alzheimer's patients. He has me also on folic acid. So, I see, every time I read about what he is prescribing, it is proper and on the nailhead.

So, after Theresa's visit with me and the doctor, the suspicion and the Alzheimer's word was spoken aloud. I have shared all along with my daughter-in-law (the widow of my son), who was diagnosed with a brain tumor, the same time I was in the ER with the seizure... and so, we compare notes on occasion. Her rare tumor is inoperable, but it has ceased growing. She was at first given but 3-6 months to live. It has been 2 years. She's had to have speech therapy and cannot work... which she hates because she has worked all her life and has been a wonderful provider for my granddaughter, all on her own.

This sounds like a soap opera. I just spoke with her today. We talk about once a month. She lives in the state of Pennsylvania... many miles from me.

In the article I read about the inexpensive and amazing good luck that's being had with Vit B12, folic acid and B6 cocktail with Alzheimer's patients, I also learned that in the past 10 years only a couple meds have been approved and shown to slow down the process with Alzheimer's and I am taking two of them... both for memory. One of the two meds is extremely costly... and I think to myself, it is such an important medicine to help so many billions of people, and it costs so much. It seems wrong. But, it is always all about the money, no matter how noble inventors of wonder drugs may be... the bottom line comes down to being expensive and out of reach for so many who are the ones needing the meds the most.

Sometimes, Tammi tells at work, that I said something wrong... she overhears me... I might say something that is almost correct, a sound alike word or something... so far it has only happened about 3 times.

But, it has happened.

I still manage to keep the books and write the checks and do the minutes and everything without anything more than occasionally feeling it takes more effort than it used to when I was so much younger. I blame that on aging and slowing down... not dementia. The doctor says to keep doing mental things... and I always have. Crossword puzzles, reading, writing, bookkeeping... always using my brain.

Recently, after a possible seizure incident (or perhaps it was a mini-stroke), I was left for a whole day where I could not speak what I wanted to say properly... over a weekend, so didn't affect me at work. Since I believed I had indeed suffered something, I told the doc and he advised me not to drive anywhere *"except to church and the grocery store."*

Hah! I laughed to myself... he lives in a heavily populated area where a grocery store is on the corner... I live in the boondocks and I travel 40-miles to get to a grocery store... one way. 65-miles one way to visit him. He did not realize. I simply agreed. No need to complicate the issue with reality.

And so, this is some of what I would like to write about, a human viewpoint of realizing and being diagnosed with something so disabling that just the term itself scares the hell out of everyone everywhere.

Alzheimer's.

Death sentence.

Dreadful death sentence.

Anyway, the last time I was at the doctors I thanked him for his care and proper prescriptions and he immediately told me not look up things on the internet, they can be misleading and they can scare a person... I assured him I would not... He does not know my penchant for learning and that I believe myself to be intelligent and therefore would not be swayed by false hope or taken in by witch doctors.

Anyway, I feel I am in good hands. He has a small office. His wife is his receptionist. He does not have a nurse to come in and take your vital signs, write them down, etc., as many doctors here in America do... he does it all himself. Thus, he knows what is going on first-hand. Plus, amazingly, he schedules one patient every 30 minutes. He gives you the full 30 minutes if warranted. You never have to sit and wait in a crowded waiting room.

Many doctors have 6-8 rooms and patients are headed into each room and the doc goes from one room to the next to the next... with the nurses doing the scud work, taking BP and weight, etc. He is hand's on and it is reassuring. Thank you for caring. I am sorry about your mom. This is a dreadful disease that is only slowly being properly figured out. And then still, there are far too many mysteries.

Forgetfully on occasion yours,

Barbara

⌁

DOWN THROUGH THE AGES

"I've enjoyed every age I've been, and each has had its own individual merit. Every laugh line, every scar, is a badge I wear to show I've been present, the inner rings of my personal tree trunk that I display proudly for all to see. Nowadays, I don't want a "perfect" face and body; I want to wear the life I've lived."

(Pat Benatar, <u>Between a Heart and a Rock Place: A Memoir</u>)

⌁

SUBJECT: ALZHEIMER'S DISEASE

Email

From: Barb Sharik

Date: Sunday, June 16, 2013 8:31 PM

To: Ann Hamilton

Subject: Alzheimer's Disease

Ann,

Just recently I decided to do a short work on my thoughts as I am dealing with it. I have started a folder with thoughts, notes and ideas.

I hope I don't run out of steam before I get it done.

SUBJECT: QUESTION

Email

From: Ann Hamilton

Sent: Monday, June 17, 2013 5:33 PM

To: Barb Sharik

Subject: Question

Larry's dr (VA neurologist) resident, put him on a drug called Buspurone, to go with the other anxiety meds he is taking.

The fourth and fifth night he had some weird stuff happen. It sounded like what u described when u had the flashes of light and the doc said it was a seizure.

When he was describing it to me it sounded familiar like something u had talked about having. It was like a big flash of light and it jolted him. Then it felt like something hit him on the head, and electricity went thru his ears.

He stopped taking the meds and hasn't had it since. I told him it sorta sounded like something u had mentioned having. Does it sound familiar? I think we're all getting brain scary now. He is set up for a brain scan in September at VA. Nothing sooner.

NOTE

Ann and I graduated from Irvin High School in El Paso, Texas together. We both had a crush on the same fellow, Ronnie Lee. Ann figures he played us both. She had more dates with him than I did. I soon got tired of the chase, so I set my sights elsewhere. Ann has become one of my dearest friends in the whole world… she and I seem to meet on a different plane where we are most comfortable.

SUBJECT: MEDS ETC.

Email
From: Barb Sharik
Date: June 17, 2013 7:32 PM.
To: Ann Hamilton
Subject: Meds etc.

I did mention something similar for sure... the flashes of lights and once a loud bang. Didn't feel anything hit me in the head or electricity go through my ears... but the flashing lights lasted long enough and happened often enough that I knew it wasn't normal.

The doc said they were seizures.

I've heard of Buspurone, but haven't taken it.

I think we are getting brain scary now because there is a reason to get brain scary... still, we keep hanging in there.

My doc changed my meds a couple times... but right now, it seems like too much, going from taking nothing to a million pills a day... cells in the brain by preventing the breakdown of a chemical called ascetylcholine. People with dementia usually have lower levels of this chemical, which is important for the process of memory, thinking and reasoning. It is used to treat mild to moderate dementia caused by Alzheimer's.

For the most part, what I am taking seems to be doing good. He changed doses of some, cutting back or increasing. He did not attribute my seeing lights with a medicine, but instead said it was seizures.

My Shrinking Brain: Dancing as Fast as I Can ...A Book About Alzheimer's Disease, is the tentative title for the book I am writing.

I hope Larry is okay. I hope you are okay.

Let me rephrase that: You're Okay, Larry's Okay and I'm Okay too!!!

Email

From: Ann Hamilton

Sent: Monday June 17, 2013 9:09 PM

To: Barb Sharik

Subject: Re: Meds etc.

You are on a lot of meds but hopefully they will help slow the progression of this thing. Everything you're on seems to make sense, except for your BP meds, if your BP is already low you can probably get rid of that one.

I think you will write that book.

The more I think of the drug companies the madder it makes me. There probably are cures for all kinds of bad things but the drug companies don't want them. They would go broke keeping people well.

Thanks for the info. I think you are lucky with the doctor you have. He seems very caring.

Sent from my iPad

I AIN'T GOIN' NOWHERE

"I shot through my twenties like a luminous thread through a dark needle, blazing toward my destination: Nowhere."

(Carrie Fisher, Postcards from the Edge)

SUBJECT: WORK IN PROGRESS

Email
From: Barb Sharik
To: Mona L Hayden
Date: June 21, 2013 2:05 PM
Subject: work in progress
Mona,

If by chance you ever speak with the LSU Press folks again... let them know I am currently at work on a book titled *MY SHRINKING BRAIN: DANCING AS FAST AS I CAN ...A Book About Alzheimer's Disease.*

It is a layman's take on having been diagnosed with a shrinking brain... which happens to anyone who lives long enough, but there is shrinkage, and there is shrinkage. This is about being advised the parts that are shrinking in my head, are indicative of Alzheimer's Disease.

A death sentence?

Of course, but so is old age.

The difference is being diagnosed years before it actually shrivels beyond redemption, so that the few approved meds that help delay memory loss (nothing stops/cures Alzheimer's at this point), can be prescribed. Slowing the inevitable, will then, perhaps, with lots of luck and good doctor's care, allow a person to die of something besides Alzheimer's. Dying with dignity, as it were.

I do not know if this would be of interest, however, I am "dancing as fast as I can" in a determination to turn out this small book, in the hopes that it will give hope to others. After all, we've all been told Hope Springs Eternal. Trust you are doing alright.

My daughter, Theresa, her partner Carla and Carla's 8 month old grandson are coming to visit for the weekend. They will arrive late tonight, after they get off work and drive up from the gulf coast, and then will leave Sunday. So we have Saturday. I just finished making my always requested Lasagna... Theresa loves it... and the saddest thought flitted through my head... *My Last Lasagna.*

Goodness, I hope not. That is what reminded me that I wanted to let you know about my latest project.

Yes, I am in the midst of the sequel to *NORMAL*, and yes, I am taking notes and planning to do a fun book about Hadley... I'm probably going to title it *THE CORNER OF HADLEY AND GARRETT: A DOG STORY.* Since that's where he was rescued... His rescue is a beautiful story all by itself.

But, my mind has shifted gears and I am making a stab at this Shrinking Brain book...

See, that's what I mean by dancing as fast as I can... I also have an almost completed BooCat book penned together with former classmate Ann Hamilton... *BOOCAT: LETTERS FROM JACKSON & FRIENDS.* It is all but ready, just a couple things to finalize it.

I'm rambling... sorry.

Have a good weekend.

Barb

From: Mona L Hayden
Sent: Friday, June 21, 2013 4:21 PM
To: Barb Sharik
Subject: Re: work in progress

Hey sugar,

I'll definitely pass this info along to Margaret at LSU. They, like most publishers, are sooooooooooo slow with everything they do. You know that. So what type of book is this... first person with personal experience, just facts, or?

So tell me more about the shrinking brain. What are possible causes, what can stop it, can it be reversed.... I hate to hear this. You are one of the most special, intelligent, insightful, entertaining, charming people I know and after the year you've had, I only wish you fame and peace - definitely not another hurdle such as this.

Can't wait to read more from you. I have all your books in a pile for me to breeze through again during JULY, my 30-days of bliss.

I know you're going to have a great time with the company this weekend. Just don't wear yourself out.

DEFINITELY not your last lasagna. Can't be, I haven't had any yet!

Love you much,
Mona

***

Email
From: Barb Sharik
Date: Friday, Jun 21, 2013 11:19 PM
To: Mona L Hayden
Subject: Re: Re: work in progress

I will write with details later. I've known the diagnosis for awhile... and suspected before he confirmed, just by what he was prescribing.

But, it's all good.

The book, I see as a way to reach out and share something that might help others... first person, more layman than technical. Factual but covering the emotions involved.

Theresa and Carla texted about 25 minutes ago they were in Bastrop. Should be here soon. The corn is so high, they will have to come in by radar, can't see the house from anywhere except from above.

Thanks for kind words.

You know how I feel about you as well...

Goodnight. Barb

"Dreams may die, but they never grow old."*

(*Barbara Sharik)

SUBJECT: BIRTHDAY WISHES DO COME TRUE

Email

From: Barb Sharik

Date: Sunday, Jun 30, 2013 7:05 AM

To: Mona L Hayden & Carolyn Files

Subject: Birthday wishes do come true

Mona and Carolyn,

I've had a lot of birthdays... 69 now, in fact. I only celebrated one other (my 56th) that compares to this, my 69th. And it compares in a slightly different way. Thus, when you take two different things, it is difficult to determine how one might be better than the other when both are quite good individually.

Thus, comparably, except for the year my mom made me a homemade strawberry shortcake instead of the standard birthday cake (and I must've been somewhere between 6-9), at my request, yesterday was over the top!

Thank you.

Yesterday's celebration compared in a wholly different way from my 56th which was a complete surprise, held at the Oak Grove Moose Lodge and my mom was still alive... Jon, Mom and I drove over there... he needed to talk to somebody about something Jon said, then we were going to go out to supper for my b'day.

My now co-worker in Bonita, Tammi joined Mom and I as Jon disappeared with a promise to be right back. Not too long afterward, Tammi told Mom and I to come see what they'd done to the office... But on the way to the office, you pass the large hall that is rented out and where Saturday night dances are often held.

We veered off there. She opened the door, and Jon was onstage. He started singing the song he sang to me a million times... every Karaoke night at the Moose Lodge... at home with all our own Karaoke stuff... singing me to sleep... (He loved to sing & he wrote songs also), *"You Are Always on My Mind."*

He sang it and he ended it as he always did every time: *"I love you, Barbara."*

As an aside, he added *"I love you, Barbara"* so many times, that at a New Year's Eve party at my house one year, he sang it... and at the end Tammi popped up with: *"I love you Barbara"* and quickly added, *"Well, he was going to say it anyway!"* and everybody died laughing.

Then he said, *"Happy Birthday."* Everybody clapped and started singing *"Happy Birthday to You."* I was stunned. It really was a complete surprise.

And so, another happy memory is added to my life. Mona & Carolyn, you have no idea how much your friendships have come to mean to me. I've lived long enough that I have a lot of acquaintances... but, there is something so special about the bond we have built that puts ours in the *"Best Friends"* department. Best friends are special, they are unique. They don't grow on trees or out in cotton fields.

For the whole day, the delicious meal (albeit probably the most costly), the girl talk, the sightseeing, the laughter, the closeness... the gifts... over and over, Thank You!

It was wonderful!

And, I am eating leftover *Doe's Eat Place* shrimp for breakfast with my coffee. Yummy in my tummy! Happy in my heart.

I do love you both. Thank you,

Barbara

⌁

Email

From: Mona L Hayden

Date: Sunday, Jun 30, 2013 9:35 AM

To: Barb Sharik

Subject: Re: Birthday wishes do come true

And I love and cherish you even more!!!!

It was a splendid day

Mona

Sent from my iPhone

⌁

THE BEGINNING OF LIFE

"Maybe it's true that life begins at fifty.
But everything else starts to wear out,
fall out, or spread out."
(Phyllis Diller)

⌁

"A WHOLE LOTTA SHAKIN' GOING ON"*
(*Jerry Lee Lewis)

I had a preconceived idea about seizures. Of course, like many things, it turns out they are surprisingly different from person to person. Apparently, the difference between various seizures depends upon which part of the brain they stem from.

I want to comment on the use of *brain* and *stem* in the same sentence; a bit of humor. There is a term for it. But, because of my ISB (Incredible Shrinking Brain), I have forgotten the term. It is not an oxymoron. No doubt, tonight, when on the edge of sleep, it will make its way from between the deep, dark, shrunken recesses of my brain and pop on like the proverbial cartoon light bulb.

After being told I suffered at least one seizure, I read that one thing all seizures have in common is that the person remains alert and can remember what happens.

Can that be true? I always had a different take on that. I thought there were some seizures that put a person out of touch with reality. I thought they became so seized up, they were incapable of knowing what was going on.

By the way, as I sit here typing, it feels like my shingles are coming back. Can they come back?

It is always something. Why? Why must we always be tested? Pushed to the limit?

My seizures apparently are sensory. I have visual hallucinations… lights. Most always bright lights. Purple. Yellow. White, even. My brain knows I am a lover of colors, so why not let me enjoy the bright lights of various colors? I mean, if I have to have weird stuff going on in my head, let it be pleasant. Scary, yes, but pleasantly colorful.

I have heard a loud bang a time or two.

But, I do not see or hear things that are not here... other than the lights.

Recently, though, I had a problem talking. It was a weekend, a Saturday, so it did not affect my work. I knew what I wanted to say, but could not spit it out. A stroke? Seizures? Sometimes I have a difficult time finding the right word when writing, and occasionally when speaking. This is frustrating.

Is this because of a seizure, or is it the shrinking brain?

I want to say it does not matter, but it does. Of course it matters.

Anybody can get seizures. However, stroke, brain infection or tumors are the most common causes. No matter what, they are indeed symptoms of a brain problem.

Seizures manifest themselves with sudden, abnormal electrical activity in the brain. One of the first tests Dr Shelat did involved determining if there is abnormal electrical activity in my brain. There is.

Focal seizures, or partial seizures, happen in just one part of the brain. This is me. But, are seizures indicative of a shrinking brain? Of Alzheimer's developing? I do not know.

I will have to ask the doc. He told me not to go searching the Internet; that things posted there can be misleading. I am conflicted. I have the thirst to know. Yet, everyone knows a little knowledge can be dangerous.

So, I take it one day at a time. Today.

Yesterday is dead and gone. Yesterday is the train that has already left the station.

Tomorrow is out of sight. Tomorrow is unobtainable. Tomorrow never comes. It is always one day away.

So, one day at a time, sweet Jesus, just let me meander through life, one day at a time. That is all I ask. Let me travel with grace. Let me travel with lucidity. Let me continue to travel with a heart full of love, and not be tumbled over with fear.

⌐⌐

AN OLD MAN'S BRAIN

"And still the brain continues to yearn, continues to burn, foolishly, with desire. My old man's brain is mocked by a body that still longs to stretch in the sun and form a beautiful shape in someone else's gaze, to lie under a blue sky and dream of helpless, selfless love, to behold itself, illuminated, in the golden light of another's eyes."
(Meg Rosoff, <u>What I Was</u>)

⌐⌐

YOU NEVER MISS 'EM TIL THEY'RE GONE: JULY 3RD DOCTOR VISIT FOR ARTHRITIC THUMB

I had a doctor visit for my arthritic thumb July 3rd. They always ask, so I prepared a list of meds, surgeries and various ailments. It took forever to fill out all the paperwork.

Every time you go to a new physician, or one you have not seen for in a while, a new history is required, along with a current list of medications being taken.

They ask about allergies and a list of all surgeries (what we used to call operations).

This is boring reading, and has no pertinence and I recommend the reader skim over it. I only add it because it is what we must go through every time we go to a physician for the first time, and sometimes, if sufficient time has passed since the last visit.

Plus, there just may be a connection somewhere heretofore, or somewhere down the line, where something contributed to the development of my ISB.

There is not a single soul who has been to a physicians office that has not had to dig deep into their memories and begin recording personal medical information.

THE MEDICAL LISTS

Dr. Timothy Spires, Orthopedic Clinic

<u>MEDS</u>

<u>PREPARED JULY 3, 2013</u>

<u>Dr Shelat, Neurologist</u>

    Folic Acid 1mg 1x a day

    Namenda 10mg 2x a day

    Trazo-Done 50mg 1 at bedtime

    Donepezil HCL 5mg 1 at bedtime

    Primidone 50mg ½ 3x a day (ask if can do 2 a day, so small, cut in half, crumbles)

    Levetiraceta 250mg (Keppra) 4x a day

    1 whole aspirin 1x day

    Simvastatin 20mg 1x a day

    Calcium 1x

    Vitamin C 1x

    Cyanocobalam 1000mcginj- inject 1 cc im every 2 wks (vit B12)

Dr Khalil

Lisinopril 20mg 1x a day

LATEST DIAGNOSIS:

Shrinking brain/early onset Alzheimer's

ALLERGIES

Darvon

Demoral

Morphene

Mobic ??

SURGERIES

- 2 back surgeries. 1985(?) (Glenwood) & Nov 2000 (Shreveport)
- Removed blood clot first thought to be a tumor, inner right arm - 1971(St Francis)
- Remove right nipple: benign papiloma - 1975? (Morehouse General)
- Uveitis - extreme treatment/ injections into eyeball itself, etc. (left eye) Eye Clinic, West Monroe
- Cataract surgery left eye - 2008
- Cataract surgery right eye - 2010
- Laser eye surgery left eye - 2010
- "Retail Surgery" January 2010 (Glenwood)
  - » Rectal reconstruction
  - » bladder sling (A&P repair)
- A&P repair also somewhere in the 1970's
- Hysterectomy age 27, 1971 (left ovaries) (Glenwood)
- 1982: Endometriosis
- 3 wks later: Removal of both ovaries

- Meniere's Disease, left ear April 2001- surgery plus remove tumor behind left ear also

(Shay Ear Clinic, Memphis TN) - Associated with lifelong bouts of Tinnitus

PREVIOUS AILMENTS

- Stroke May 31, 2010 (maybe reaction to Mobic) (Morehouse General Hospital)
- Seizures Dec 2010 (Morehouse General Hospital)
- Rectal bleeding - colon - May 30, 2011: Ischemic Colitis (Glenwood)
- Several bouts with Diverticulitis / diverticulosis
- Smashed knees - surgery recommended (auto accident) but not done, 1999 or 2000

CURRENT AILMENTS

1. Left Thumb

   » Hurts at thumb joint, (nodule) stiff.

   » Never realize how much you use your thumb until it hurts to use it.

2. Neck crunches

   » Hurts.

   » Used a neck pillow for years; purchased an Orthopedic neck pillow 2 months ago; is helping.

   » Assuming, as with my back, may be bone spurs, narrowing, pinching nerves, etc....

3. Left thigh/hip

   » I cannot sleep lying on my left side; my hip hurts. If I turn sleep on my right side it does not hurt, but the pressure of the left hip in this position, makes the left hip hurt. I must sleep flat on my back.

   » My left thigh periodically erupts in the most horrible pain... a wrong move; to lift my leg, bending at the knee and upward, like to straighten a sock... and the thigh is grabbed with unbearable pain (i.e.).

4. Feet, calves, legs

   » Numbness in bottom of feet and toes mostly upon rising.

   » Cramps in my feet, legs, calves. Mostly in the early morning.

5. Shoulder.

   » Not 100% but better after PT end of 2012, first of 2013, twice a week. Bursitis?

   » I do almost everything left-handed except write and paint.

   » Used: Voltaren Gel together with PT.

6. <u>Shingles</u>

   » Back. 2nd round in less than a year. 6/13 (current)

7. <u>Esophageal Dilation</u>

   » This procedure came undone x 2 within a month, first of year, 2013.

8. <u>Tinnitus</u>. It never goes away.

<u>Seizures</u>

First diagnosed Dec 2010.

<u>Dr Vipul Shelat</u>

Occasionally, not long after I turn off the light, but not yet asleep... suddenly the whole room seems to light up. Every time, automatic reaction is to call out, "Is anyone there?"

The dogs and BooCat never stir. Of course, no one is there. Very fleeting, yet real. I am wide awake. The first couple of times, it was as though someone had shined a flashlight into the bedroom window except it appeared to light the whole room. Not a car passing; too far off the road, car lights don't shine in. No one prowling around the house: 5 outside dogs, 3 inside and BooCat...

Continues off and on... mostly colored lights behind my eyes when closed.

Also, see yellow splotches on plain surfaces; pages of books, but can read through them.

━━

JUST CURIOUS

"Why do men's shirts button on one side, and women's button on the other?"

━━

DIAGNOSIS AND TREATMENT

Dr Spires advised to hydrate and to squeeze a soft ball in a basin of warm water; simple physical therapy. He was prescribing a steroid, since I had a reaction to Mobic the last time I visited his office for tendonitis.

My appointment was late in the afternoon and it was after 4 when I left Monroe, heading to Bastrop to the pharmacy and then home. His office was to call the prescription into the pharmacy, however, even though it took me over an hour to go from his office to the pharmacy, no prescription.

When I called his office I reached the answering service. They knew nothing, of course. Therefore, I drove home without the prescription.

The next day was July 4th so I knew I would not be going back to Bastrop for my prescription. What happened to handing you a prescription so you can take it yourself? How much simpler for everyone involved. More and more physicians are contacting pharmacies directly; does it have to do with drug abuse or just attempting to simplify the overall kit and caboodle?

Kit and caboodle? Not sure if a kit and caboodle can be simplified since I have forgotten what a kit and caboodle is. I know I covered the expression in one of my columns over this past decade, but there you go… the shrinking brain hiding away another simple memory.

I am supposed to return to the doctor's office in two weeks for an evaluation. Without being able to start the prescription for several days, that puts a spanner in the works.

Why do I even mention this or any of the other broken-wings from over the years?

Because, *we do not know.*

We do not know what causes Alzheimer's and thus, we do not know how the conditions and experiences and happenstances we undergo might effect our brains. Surely any illness, even the slightest, takes its toll on the body, the immune system, the overall condition that my condition is in. Including, my brain. The center of my physical and mental universe.

Does a broken bone allow enzymes, or what kids used to call cooties, get into the system and work their way to the brain? I surely do not know. I expect there are studies into all phases of what does and does not affect our brains.

After all, scientists study what seem to some the most mundane, so why not? The air we breathe, the soil we inject, the fifteen spiders we swallow in a lifetime while sleeping… the germs coughed in our faces, spread from a handshake… all these things have an immediate, and oft times a long term, effect on each and everyone of us.

If these things were not in some way important, why then would the physicians ask each time you visit… *What's up, baby?*

Later at home, around 6:30, I received a text from the pharmacy that the meds were available. Being a 40 mile trip one way, I decided to wait until the weekend. I was very tired. It had been a very long and trying day. I had already traveled 120 miles, I could not see doing another 60-plus at 7 p.m.

Am I feeling my age? Would it be so strange if I were? Still, I seldom wind down completely. I liken myself to my Seiko Kinetic watch. Not a

Timex, mind you, requiring batteries. Because my Kinetic and me, neither of us require batteries. However, both of us, my watch and I, we may slow down, but once up and about, with a little motion, we pick up speed and continue for another day and another and another.

Until something goes haywire.

Haywire. Apparently, haywire has a tendency to have a mind of its own and while eventually containing the hay, it takes a bit of tenaciousness on behalf of the baler to get those bales baled in the first place.

TOOLS OF THE TRADE

Two elderly women were eating breakfast in a restaurant one morning. Tammi notices something peculiar about Barb's ear and says, "Barb, why on earth do you have a suppository in your left ear?" Barb, surprised, replies, "I have a suppository in my ear?"

She pulls it out and stares at it for a moment. Blushing, she replies, "Tammi, sweetie, thanks for letting me know. Now, I'm pretty sure I know where to find my missing hearing aid."

BUMBLEBEE BUGGY SIDE-TRACK

Sharp chest pain. Like electricity shooting throughout as I was writing my weekly newspaper column. Both arms went numb.

Confusion.

I went next door to Chuck's and told him about the episode. He told me to sit and rest. I decided to go to my bedroom, lie down and rest. Figure out what happened.

The furbies followed me to the bedroom. However, BooCat would not allow Hadley up on the bed. She snuggled next to me and he stood beside the bed looking pitiful. I told him to get on the bed. He tried, but Boo would not let him. She was hanging onto me. It was weird. Almost uncanny. It was like animal intuition that something was wrong with me.

Calmness.

I picked up my cell phone, opened my facebook app and posted about my experience. Then it struck me, *this is insane.*

Fear.

I got up to go tell Chuck I needed to go to the emergency room. He was already talking to Theresa.

Action.

We gave the little BumbleBee Buggy a run for its money.

BumbleBee Buggy? There is a story there. Let me veer away from my rush to the emergency room with a happy tale. Just hang on tight… shrinking brains have a way of jumping track. It is like having commercials injected in the middle of the serious stuff you are watching on TV.

I will be talking about one thing, think of something else… go there… come back… continue where I left off.

The following is an unpaid commercial.

I always mute commercials if I am watching TV. Hmmm.

Runnin' the Roads Just Got More Fun

Louisiana Road Trips
June 2013
I bought a car. Deciding to downsize, I traded an Impala with all the bells and whistles, albeit 7-years old, for the cheapest car on the lot at Ryan Chevrolet in Monroe.

Actually, considering the cost of cars these days, finding cheap isn't so simple. Downsizing meant not only car size but also payments. Thus, I'm happy to say, I got practically everything I wanted and can afford to buy gas too.

Brenda at the gas station is used to me stopping by once a week, filling up and writing large checks each time. Now, some weeks I just wave as I breeze by, and when I do fill up, it's but a fraction of the cost. Admittedly, it isn't just because it gets stellar gas mileage: the gas tank holds a mere 9 gallons. It makes making road trips not only fun but affordable.

Okay, it lacks one convenient bell I miss: keyless entry. It took about two weeks to break the habit of reaching for the car-clicker when approaching my car because there isn't one. I've been clicking a button to unlock my cars for so many years, it's a practice not easily eradicated. Oh well, I gave up smoking, drinking and running around... wait, no. That wasn't me. That's somebody in a country/western song. The habit I actually broke was daily dusting. You'd be surprised how long it takes before you have to dust the TV screen and still see the picture. I do it when Seinfeld starts looking like Bill Cosby. Also, when dust bunnies turn into dust dingoes and growl when I walk by.

Reality is, I began having expensive repairs on my Impala, so while in for a re-repair of the previous week, I left Chuck reading a magazine and meandered from the waiting room to the showcase of cars out front.

A ray of sunshine caught my eye: a little yellow Chevy Spark. I'd use the Southernism, 'Cute as a Bug in a Rug,' but I don't see many cute bugs, so I'll sum it up by simply saying it was absolutely adorable. Suffice to say, that's likely another euphemism but not as unpleasant as bugs in rugs.

While giving it a look-over, sales rep, Phil Hammett offered his assistance. We chatted. Likely, he saw a sucker begging to bite his bait. Correct assumption. He didn't need to yank the line too hard to hook me. I reeled myself in. He simply accommodated me in my moment of desire, making the deal palatable.

Halfway through the transaction, Chuck showed up, shaking his head and smiling. He said he knew when I didn't come back I was buying a car. He remembered times I'd returned with new cars when originally setting out to buy new tires, have a back window repaired or to get an oil change. Chuck, my best friend, says he doesn't always understand me, but he knows me.

All kidding aside, I don't know what Chevy was thinking when they doled out color names for the Spark. Wonderful array, yes, but to name the yellow one Lemonade could throw up red flags. In carspeak, the word "lemon" is a no-no. To negate any bad luck the hapless name might imply, I call it Sunshine yellow. I like sunshine on my shoulder, which makes me happy.

Second week on the road, Sunshine passed the Barbara-Test. I loaded one 50-pound sack and two 10-pound bags of dog food, a 10-pound bag of cat food, 25-pounds of litter, two 20-pound bags of wild birdseed, a 10-pound box of dog biscuits, a 3-pound box of cockatiel birdseed, one shaker of tropical fish food, along with salad makings, bananas and apples for me. Also, some decadent cookies to offset the healthy salad, bananas and apples. Already stashed was a box of my books: *NORMAL, a Novel; BooCat Unleashed; BooCat: Dancing Naked in the Rain; BooCat: Living in my Lap; BooCat Throws a Frisbee* and *Unquenched Thirst, the Crush that Lasted fifty Years*, leaving room to spare. Runnin' the roads, I picked up Carolyn Files and drove to Monroe for dinner with Mona L Hayden.

Actually, the Spark boasts more maximum cargo room than Fiat 500, smart for two, and Scion iQ while seating four comfortably. Just so long as there's room for BooCat, Hadley-Badly, and the batch of furbies to visit the vet or just joyride, it's all good. I even let Chuck drive it once after he got on his knees and begged.

I call it my BumbleBee Buggy and this isn't a commercial. It's just me being me. Now, if I can find a zealous antique broker and figure out how to downsize my living quarters and accumulation of stuff, I'll be good to go.

OBITS

I call the local newspaper and ask to speak to the person in charge of the obituary column. I am passed to the advertiser so I ask, "How much does it cost to run an obit in the paper?" "$4.00 per word," he says. I tell him, "Ok. Write this down: "Barbara Sharik is dead." "Anything else?" he asks. "Nope. That's it." "I'm sorry, there's a ten word minimum," he tells me. I'm thinking, why didn't you tell me that in the first place, but anyway, I tell him, write this down: "Barbara Sharik is dead. Sunshine yellow Chevy Spark for sale."

HAPPY 4TH OF JULY
EMAIL SUBJECT: HOME AT LAST

Back to reality.

Email
From: Barb Sharik
Date: Saturday July 6 2013 6:06PM
To: Ann Hamilton
Subject: Home at last
My goodness, what next?! However, according to the blood test, heart enzymes did not indicate a heart attack.

The test for blockage in arteries to heart and neck... neck was basically okay, but some blockage going into the heart itself. So, I am to call Monday and set up an appointment for a treadmill test.

They did breathing treatments while in the hospital because of shortness of breath, etc. And they kept me on oxygen. I did experience shortness of breath when I got up to bathe... hence the breathing treatments.

The BP fluctuated... but the pulse stayed around 50, too low.

What happened was, I was sitting at the computer composing my next week newspaper column (oh my, I need to get back to that & send to the newspaper)... and all of a sudden I had a painful, almost electrical surge fill my whole chest, and then both arms, which were sitting over the keyboard, went numb.

I first got up and went next door to Chuck's. He was cooking 4th of July dinner for us. I sat on his couch & told him what I experienced. He said rest a bit. I decided I'd go lie down.

Once in there, I picked up my cell phone and made my way to FB & did what was completely insane... I posted about this strange thing happening.

Well, a friend of Theresa's saw it & called her & told her to call me.

About this same time, I realized lying there was nuts. Something happened. I needed to go to the ER. So, I got up and was headed over to Chuck's and met him, as he was talking to Theresa, who was telling him to take me to the ER. Call the ambulance to meet us on the way. So, that is what we did.

About 20 miles from the house, we met the ambulance and made the exchange. They hooked me up to IV... and onto the ER. After lying in the ER and being tested, it was decided something was going on, something happened, hence the admission to the ICU. (I hope I haven't repeated myself in attempting to tell what happened.).

The rest is history. Sort of.

I feel like mystery meat when it comes to ailments.

BTW: The wonderful rainbow over Moab photo arrived. It is so outstanding. The content, the starkness, the colors. It is worthy of reproduction and framing... with Bobby being in this business ask him what he thinks, etc. I am in love with the picture and even though I have a million things hanging on my walls, this will find a special place once properly framed. I never can thank you enough for you kindness, generosity and friendship.

Ann, you are so special. Tell Larry I love him also... as my cousin Mike in NYC always closes his letters, Love to everybody who loves you... Barbara

<hr>

Email
From: Ann Hamilton
Date: Saturday July 6 2013 8:34PM
To: Barb Sharik
Subject: Re: Home at last

My God, so glad you're home. Are you still short winded. When I had my rib thing and thought I was having a heart attack, the medics at the fire station started running tests on me ASAP had me hooked up to leads, basically told me they didn't think I had a heart attack, but my chest hurt so bad, it hurt to breathe they thought it best to take me to ER.

Glad they kept you there for a few days. The ER doc told me they are good at figuring out what it's not, but not that good at finding out what it is.

That's when they did the CT scan of my lung and found the nodule. Still waiting for results from the second scan. Can't stand this waiting. Ones mind goes nuts.

Glad you like the picture, but it's from Colorado not Utah.

Yep, u had a lot of fb fans going for ya.

Love you and glad u r home. Yes we both have these weird things happen.

Sent from my iPad

⸺

THERE'S ALWAYS ROOM FOR CHOCOLATE

"I'm pretty sure that eating chocolate keeps wrinkles away because
I have never seen a 10 year old with a Hershey bar and crows feet."
(Amy Neftzger)

⸺

SUBJECT: HOPE YOU ARE HOME AND BETTER

From: Rosemary Ross
Sent: Friday, July 05, 2013 5:42 PM
To: Barb Sharik
Subject: Hope you are home and better
Hi, Barb, I am keeping up with all the updates on you on Facebook but wanted to send a note to say I am thinking of you.

Man, you have more people who love you than anyone I know except maybe my son.

Hopefully all the tests will clear you and you can be getting home soon. Your animals and all your friends and loved ones need you home!

Don't worry about writing til you are back on your feet, I will keep looking to Facebook for info.

Love you so much, sending healing energy. Rose

⸺

Email

From: Barb Sharik

Sent: Saturday, July 06 2013 8:10 PM

To: Rose Ross

Subject: Re: Hope you are home and better

Yeah, my sister Jan called and said I'd gone global on fb. Get well wishes from so many people & different countries, even Bangledesh (probably misspelled).

I've not been on fb since home. Too tired to fool with it.

Have to give Rosie benadryl. She's acting like she does when it storms. I don't hear anything yet but Tammi texted & said it is storming about 40 miles away. Rosie is pyschic. Children's benadryl helps her relax.

I must do the column. Got sheets changed. One blanket still in dryer. Not that we need blankets. Wkend task. You sleep with dogs and a cat, you change sheets no matter what. lol. Especially with all these black pets.

Sounds unsanitary but we are happy together. I didn't feel like changing sheets but… I took my time.

Chuck did good but didn't think about feeding my cockatiel & dove. George was very vocal when I came home. SnowBird let me know she missed me as well. George says "Goodnight" every night before I turn out the light.

What will happen to my furbies... no, I must never go there...

When I came home and laid down, Hadley laid his head up on my pillow beside my head, BooCat settled in about midsection, leaning on me, Taco curled up at my feet, Rosie came and rolled over on her back and looked at me upside down so I could rub her belly, and then went to the bottom of the bed to chew on a doggie chewtoy.

More later I promise. love to you and your son and everybody who loves you...

Your healing energy is surrounding me... I feel it. However, I also feel like mystery meat when it comes to ailments. Barb

SUBJECT: GLAD YOU ARE HOME

Email

From: Rose Ross

Sent: Sunday, July 07 2013 8:10 AM

To: Barb Sharik

Subject: Glad you are home

Wow, Barb, yeah, what next? Do you have any body parts left that haven't been in crisis? I am so glad that it didn't indicate a heart attack.

I have my own opinion. (Seen it in sci-fi movies). Maybe you have been thru so much, done so much good for people, are so beloved in this world, the other worldly beings (Orb people maybe) decided to give you a Jolt of totally healing forever energy and it came across as a lightning bolt across your chest. Healing everything!

Well, I can dream, can't I? I remember a psychic I knew… a real true one… who went thru 6 months of serious illness… seems like in bed… and came out of it newly psychic.

Really. Well, I choose to believe you will become much better now!

I was so glad to hear from you, my computer wouldn't let me online last night so I couldn't get your happily received e-mail. I'm having a rare morning at home, the hot weather gets to combined with still 4th of July-ing firework neighbors keeping me awake til midnight, so Geno said stay home til this evening.

I have a list a mile long of to-do's but writing you was No. 1. I can only imagine how thrilled the animals were to have you home. I am so glad you are able to catch up on your bed changing etc., the alternative is worse, but sure wish you didn't have too do that stuff. Wish I didn't have to either. There should be automatic paid maids for us older ladies who have done for everyone else all our lives. (Can you imagine what the Republicans would think of THAT idea??)

I again am so thankful you have a Chuck. Chuck's can be so wonderful! We would have all imagined you lying on your bed after your lightning flash unconscious with no one to check on you nearby. Was so glad to get the news that Chuck was taking you to the ambulance.

Though what happened to the 4th of July meal?? Knowing you guys it was a really good one, too. I'm sure hospital food didn't measure up.

Too much food in too few days but a lot of laughs and good company. After breakfast I came home, Geno and the kids were going back to his house, then he would rest. I was really tired as the neighbors had been Fireworking til midnight again, the cats were restless and me too.

I thought of sleeping at Geno's in the quiet country but as you know we can't leave the pets to the stress on their own.

Anyway it is now 10 a.m. here, need some breakfast, my schedule is messed up Being home. Have to eat and then get busy. Had a wonderful rain at 6 to 8 this a.m., needed it, the plants are happy. We have had a good rain season, like once a week, the crops are beautiful. Such a gorgeous time here in Michigan, lots of roadside flowers due to the rain. The orange roadside daylilies are blooming, do you get them there? Geno has them all around his house 3 ft. deep, so pretty with his redwood siding, they back my gardens so nice with the flowers.

We had them on Long Island when I was a kid.

I finally got down to Geno's Dad's Memorial tree garden and neatened it up. Geno had gone down with the tractor and mowed around it, he can mow as he's not on his feet, not good with hand stuff due to numbness but fine with tractors etc.

The mosquitoes are horrible. I got a bright idea and bought netting from Wal Mart, a buck a yard, and wore long sleeves and shirt and gloves, netting over the head. It worked pretty good to weed and mulch.

Still have flowers to plant down there but another day. I also went on line and found you can buy hoods of netting that would be great fairly cheap, will get one. Over a cap with a hat it would work great, also they said black netting is almost invisible to see thru, I had white and it was ok but I think black would be better.

One hint they gave me (amazon reviews) is to take off the hood before going in the house so you don't ferry a head full of mosquitoes in!

Enough of my rambling, I have to ramble to the other rooms and get busy cleaning. (I have been called Rambling Rose in my lifetime.)

So glad to hear you are home, hopefully feeling ok today enough to enjoy some of the weekend. Hopefully this will turn out to be just a fluke.

(OR the jolt from the Universe to change you to healthy? Well. I can dream!) I guess you need to just give a thank you to everyone not to on Facebook, how in the world could you answer them all?

We were so grateful that we got updates there. Such great people who love you so much. Maybe the fact that you DID write on Facebook when the shock happened caused all these people to send you love and healing thoughts and that kept it from being serious! Love you a lot, Rose.

NOTE

Rose and I graduated from Irvin High School, El Paso, Texas, together. She was an art student, as was I. Many, many years later, we reconnected through the wonders of facebook.

SUBJECT: IT'S GOOD TO BE HOME

Email
From: Barb Sharik
Sent: Sunday, July 07 2013 7:05 PM
To: Rose Ross
Subject: It's good to be home

What a wonderfully long Rambling Rose email. I really enjoyed reading about your happy 4th of July. It was a vicarious experience. lol. Since mine was celebrated at Spa MGH (aka: Morehouse General Hospital)...

Chuck was just finishing up a very special meal... pork loin roast, mashed potatoes, yellow squash from his garden, green beans, sliced tomatoes from his garden... and I missed it. So did he. I mean, he was able to eventually come home and eat... he had just finished it when I had my jolt of healing via Orb people (I like that also). And he did put a plate in my fridge... However, I didn't nibble on it for several days. Then, I shared with my furbies, but we won't tell Chuck. It was too much to eat.

I have to admit, the food I was served at *Spa MGH* was really quite tasty. Always hear bad stuff about hospital food, but this was all good. I will not say it is because I am used to eating cookies and one bit of this or one bit of that... because it is impossible to properly prepare for one person... not to mention I am lazy. The best food I eat is when Chuck cooks and shares.

Anyway, it was tasty. But, I was willing to give it up to get to come home to my cookies. I actually need to go to the grocery store someday soon and replenish something besides cookies.

This was not my idea of a way to spend an extended holiday. You see, our office is closed on Thursdays anyway, and we had Friday off as well... By the time I get the bills, no doubt it will feel like I am paying for a trip to a Spa. If you didn't count the testing, the sticks and blood drawing, having someone cook and serve and cleanup afterward, was kind of nice. However, next time I think I'll reserve a room at a real hotel up in the cool mountains instead. One that's pet friendly.

Oh how happy my babies were when I got home. Me too. I think it scared Hadley enough he is more clinging, and not so difficult to get his attention when I call him inside after a potty run. He comes bounding, smiling, tail wagging.

I do not know what I would do without Chuck. He likes working in the yard and he is always doing little projects and he has the place looking so nice. It is so reassuring knowing he is right next door too. I will forever owe him.

The day before I had been to the orthopedic dr about my inflamed thumb. You never know how much you use your thumb until it hurts every time you do anything, from pulling up your pants or whatever... everything. Anyway, I had an afternoon appointment & they said they'd call in the prescription and it was over an hour before I reached my Walmart pharmacy... and no prescription. I called the office and got the answer service. Well, I gave up. It was 5:30 by then. Once at home I got a text message from Walmart around 6:30 that my prescription was ready... frustration.

Anyway, I am supposed to go back to him in 2 wks but the hospital doc said not to start taking the prescription, even after I picked it up yesterday, because they are a steroid and he wants to figure out what's going on with-out adding something else in my system.

So, when it rains it pours. My thumb has hurt for close to a year... just never got better, so finally decided to check it out. So, I was tired when the prescription was filled, and I didn't feel like doing a 60-plus mile round trip for the prescription, and as it turns out, just as well.

I couldn't have a maid here either, Rose. My house has gotten so cluttered ... and filled with furbies. I made a conscious decision... clean house every day and have nothing left for me. I'd been doing that for so many years. I want to write. I want to paint. I want to read. I want to visit with friends on fb and email. I have to work. I have nothing left. There is not enough of me to clean house as it needs cleaning either. And how quickly things get cluttered.

I can declutter and before I know it, it is cluttered again. So I commiserate with you 100%.

I thought we had the most mosquitoes of anyplace else in the whole wide world... they are our state bird. I liked your idea of the netted up garden lady... made me think of a beekeeper. We need netting to work around here so much of the time. I just never thought of it. All our pets are subject to heart worms from the mosquitoes. We have outbreaks of bird flu every year... the one transmitted by mosquitoes. Swampy in some places, but don't need swamps. They hatch constantly. A drop of water, and there is a family of mosquitoes come morning. Never leave standing water, they advise.

However, it is impossible not to have some... drinking water for dogs, etc. They love dark places, like behind lawn furniture on the patio, if it's against a wall. They do ruin summertime. They get beneath every dark place.

Anyway, obviously you understand fully.

I had a ton of daylilies up and down the drive when I first put in my yard but over the years they were mowed down by uncaring ex husbands, there are only a few that remain. I do love daylilies. When we moved here and built a house, this was a former cotton field. We have cannas of every color. Lots of trees and shrubs...every one planted by me (and by Chuck too).

I have seen the photos you've shared with me of yours & Geno's... you are really a flower lady. I am more random, perfect wildlife and bird reserve. Or is that preserve?

I am not a pruner or someone who does flower beds. Too haphazard. I am awed by all the plants you put out every year between yours and Geno's yards. You get them out before it gets too hot, before the mosquitoes arrive, and then can sit back and soak up the glory of your labor.

There is no way I can thank everyone individually. I was wowed! So many people wishing me well. I finally got on fb earlier today and I went through and LIKED everyone and did comment on some.

If there is power in numbers, all these people pulling for my recovery must have moved something out there... wow.

Now I have to go back to work tomorrow. How I wish I had a few extra days to recuperate. But there is much to do. Must get the bills all paid and in the mail. etc.

I love you... Barb

WINDOW WITH A VIEW

I visited my doctor and asked him, "How do you determine whether or not an older person should be put in a nursing home?" He said, "Well, there is a formula. We fill up a bathtub and offer a teaspoon, a teacup and a bucket to the person to empty the bathtub."

Smart me, I said, "Ok. That makes sense. So a normal person would use the bucket because it is bigger than the teacup or spoon." "No," he says. "A normal person would pull the plug. Do you want a bed near the window?"

AS MUCH AS THIS IS GOING TO COST, IT'S LIKE A 4th OF JULY MINI-VACAY AT SPA MGH*
(*Morehouse General Hospital)

Chest pain. Like electricity shooting throughout as I was typing my weekly newspaper column. Arms numb. Fast and furious. Amazing to think, this is how quick a heart attack can kill a person. Had this episode been fatal, there would be no ten-count. No three-strikes and you're out. It would have been instant evaporation.

*"But don't think twice, it's all right."**

(*Bob Dylan)

Text Message
From: Mindy Diffenderfer, RN
Sent: Thursday July 4 2013
I saw ur FB post. Please call 911 and go to the ER! Chest pain is very serious!

Dr Cox is in there today working. He is wonderful. And I know you know this - time is of the essence with heart attacks.

Text Message
From: Mindy Diffenderfer, RN
Sent: Thursday July 4 2013
Im glad you came. If they'll let me I may stick my head in.

MAMA'S WARNING OF THE DAY

"Always wear clean underwear. You never know when you might wind up in the hospital."

Text Message
From: Jan Sharik Baker (from Maryland)
Sent: Thursday July 4 2013
Hey you. You OK?

Text Message
To: Jan Sharik Baker
Sent: Thursday July 4 2013
Going to ER. Will let you know.

Text Message
From: Jan Sharik Baker
Sent: Thursday July 4 2013
Good. Keep in touch. Love ya.

ATTENTION... SALUTE!

*"Old people are patriotic: Red cheeks, pasty white skin and blue veins!"**
(*Barbara Sharik)

Text Message

From: Theresa Tubbs

Sent: Thursday July 4 2013

Reinhard is trying to get in touch with you. He fb messaged me. I gave him ur cell #. Don't know if he tried to fb message u or not.

⚯

Text Message

From: Reinhard Hollink (from Holland)

Sent: Thursday July 4 2013

I tried to call you but you couldn't answer it what I can understand. I hope you are feeling better now. You scared me yesterday. I want to say that I do love you and being friends or family has nothing to do with facebook. Blood is thicker than water.

⚯

THE TRUTH OF THE MATTER

The reason men are elected president instead of women is because men are smart enough not to wear panty hose (which were likely invented by a man who hated his mama)*

(*Barbara Sharik)

⚯

Text Message

To: Theresa Tubbs

Sent: Thursday July 4 2013

He asked about asthma. That's when I thought to tell him about cpap. No asthma. But got very short of breath today when up bathing. Sleep apnea is a serious thing. Christine & Gary visiting Bob Crymes. Visited me too.

Kirk Doles here too. Said spider bite.

Anyway, don't worry. In as good a hands as anywhere these days. Plus I have a brain. Even if its shrinking can keep up & know whats happening. LuvU.

~

AGING EQUALS GROWTH

"It's very simple. As you grow, you learn more. If you stayed at twenty-two, you'd always be as ignorant as you were at twenty-two. Aging is not just decay, you know. It's growth. It's more than the negative that you're going to die, it's also the positive that you understand you're going to die, and that you live a better life because of it."
(Mitch Albom, Tuesdays With Morrie)

~

DAY 2, SPA MGH
FRIDAY, JULY 5TH

Text Message
From: Theresa Tubbs
Sent: Friday July 5 2013
Yeah I just talked to Chuck. Which test are they concerned with? Are you feeling any better? Get some rest!

~

Text Message

To: Theresa Tubbs

Sent: Friday July 5 2013

What he ordered is a breathing treatment. Moist air through nasal apparatus. Damned being deaf… everyone talks too softly. Lol.

Text Message

From: Theresa Tubbs

Sent: Friday July 5 2013

Yeah. Everyone is worried. I have tried to keep them informed all along the way. FB is a good way to keep in touch with everyone.

Text Message

To: Theresa Tubbs

Sent: Friday July 5 2013

Nurse said breathing treatment should hlp shortness of breath. Another one around 10.

Text Message

From: Theresa Tubbs

Sent: Friday July 5 2013

Ok. Let me know if you learn anything else. Hope everything is alright with tests.

Text Message
To: Theresa Tubbs
Sent: Friday July 5 2013
Just did the checking of neck veins… Blood flow. Next be doing something similar w/heart. This to see if any blocked arteries/veins. Whichever.

Text Message
To: Theresa Tubbs
Sent: Friday July 5 2013
Just had a bad reaction to nitroglycerine patch. Still trembling but slowly getting steadier. Got it off. Said it dilates all blood vessels & must have caused a rush. Will report to doc. Nurse sure I will b ok. Made heart pound. BP little low. This is how hosp kills people. Sure scared me.

Text Message
From: Theresa Tubbs
Sent: Friday July 5 2013
That's not good. They need to figure out what u do need!
Sounds like u don't need it anyway. U don't have high blood pressure and not showing signs of heart problem according to the tests.

Keep your oxygen on. They r gonna kill u in the hospital. Glad u can get some rest. Hope the tests r going well.

Text Message

From: Theresa Tubbs

Sent: Friday July 5 2013

Definitely tell the doctor as soon as you can. I don't know what else they need to do for you. Must be some kind of different meds to help with your episodes.

Well hopefully new tests tomorrow will give some answers. No more experimenting with new drugs. Get some rest.

Text Message

To: Theresa Tubbs

Sent: Friday July 5 2013

Nurse said nitro done by length… that was a qtr inch. A patch. Affects all blood vessels & heart. Mustve been too much at once. Said I have rite to refuse any meds. Shell let him know. First experience. Said usually used when bp real hi or something strenuous. My bp has steadily gotten lower. She educated my about nitroglycerin. Scared me. Ok now.

Text Message

To: Theresa Tubbs

Sent: Friday July 5 2013

I know. The blood enzymes did not show heart attack. The tests today for blockages to heart & not known when he ordered nitro this am. My bp was hi when came in. Steadily dropped ever since. See what thse results show.

Told me nitro will give headache. I better hurry & go home. Next time ill ride it out... Goodnight.

$\rightleftharpoons$

Text Message
To: Theresa Tubbs
Sent: Friday July 5 2013
Since stayed xtra day didn't plan on didn't bring cpap. Will use one of hosp tonight. Told them last nite. Sleep apnea can kill ya too. Sorry to text so late. Headache went away. Shortlived. I need a cookie. Night again. Im ok.

$\rightleftharpoons$

Text Message
From: Theresa Tubbs
Sent: Friday July 5 2013
Maybe nurses can find u a cookie.

$\rightleftharpoons$

"DAYLIGHT COME, AN' I WANNA GO HOME"

"Everyday is one less day."
(Tom Ford)

$\rightleftharpoons$

DAY 3, SPA MGH
SATURDAY, JULY 6

Text Message
From: Theresa Tubbs
Sent: Saturday July 6 2013
Hope u got a good night's rest. Has doctor made his rounds yet?

Text Message
To: Theresa Tubbs
Sent: Saturday July 6 2013
On way home. Nonspecific chest pains. Some blockage near carotid artery. Make appt for stress test… treadmill. VP fluctuated. Pulse stayed around 50. Very low. Hence stress test.

Mentioned halter monitor once but not again. Found a tiny tick burrowed under my skin. He wrote prescription for antibiotic for lymes disease. I said we don't have lymes disease here. He said I know but cnt tell u not to take it. I left the tick at icu stuck to pc of tape. I didn't get prescription filled yet. Chuck drove rite by walmart. Then asked if wanted to go back. Said no. Maybe get it Monday. Wearing him out enuff. So. That's it.

Text Message
From: Theresa Tubbs
Sent: Saturday July 6 2013
Well that sucks that they didn't find an answer yet. Maybe stress test will tell u more. Glad u get to go home though. Catch everyone on FB up!

Text Message
To: Theresa Tubbs
Sent: Saturday July 6 2013
Agree. Nonspecifics. Ifs. Maybes. Probably wont do fb til later.
Nonspecifically depleted. The spa wore me out.

HOW OLD IS OLD?

"Old is always fifteen years from now."
(Bill Cosby)

Text Message
From: Tammi Carroll Garner
Sent: Saturday July 6 2013
What did test say
R u hme

Text Message
To: Tammi Carroll Garner
Sent: Saturday July 6 2013
Some blockage in arteries into heart… Not in neck. Have to schedule appt
w/dr Monday for stress test/treadmill. He said the bloodtest enzymes did

NOT indicate a heart attack. I had shortness of breath, tightness & an electrical sensation filled my chest & both arms went numb. Was writing a column. It puzzled me then scared me. I did not message u bcuz u were supposed to b enjoying ur wkend. Figured soon enuf to tell u. Feel like the mystery meat of the medical world. BP fluctuates but on low side & pulse too low. Never over 50. Happy 4ᵗʰ late.

Are u home yet?

Text Message
From: Tammi Carroll Garner
Sent: Saturday July 6 2013
B hme 2mor it is stormy 2nite

THREE ABSENT-MINDED SISTERS

Three sisters, Barbara age 81, Jan age 83 and Michele age 85, live together. One night Barbara draws a bath for herself. As she sticks her foot in, she pauses. She yells to her sisters downstairs, "Was I getting in or out of the bath?" Jan shouts back loudly, "I don't know. Let me come up there and see." She begins walking up the stairs, but then pauses. She yells to her sisters, "Was I going up the stairs or down?" Michele is sitting in the living room, enjoying some tea. She listens to her sisters, shakes her head and mutters to herself, "I sure hope I never get that forgetful. Knock on wood." Then, Michele turns and shouts, "I'll come up there and help both of you as soon as I see who's knocking at the door."

SUBJECT: HI

Email
From: Ann Hamilton
Sent: Wednesday, July 10, 2013 8:29PM
To: Barb Sharik
Subject: Hi

Thinking about u, tomorrow, what time is your treadmill test. How did they know in the hospital that you had blockage without running tests on u? Several years ago Larry and I underwent a test for blockage, they injected something into our veins that made our heart race, took pics and it made us feel like we were having a heart attack.

Both of us were fine, no blockages, but that was 10 yrs ago. Hope they have improved on testing since then.

Been so hot don't feel like doing much of anything. I've done a number on my stomach these past five months worrying about that damn nodule in my lung, now that it's disappeared trying to relax my gut.

We found two more petrified rocks, one is bigger than the ones I sent you. I will send these to u also. They are interesting.

Let me know how u do tomorrow. Please.

Luv to all

Sent from my iPad

Email
From: Barb Sharik
Sent: Wednesday, July 10, 2013 7 10:29 PM
To: Ann Hamilton
Subject: Re: Hi

I am a little fuzzy with names of tests done to check veins/arteries in neck and around chest into heart area... they brought big machines into the room... some kind of sonar that could be read... it was behind my head, but I gathered it was like when they look at babies in tummies.

It didn't require any injections.... I had one of those years ago, into the vein at the groin... I think that must have been when I had that stroke; afterward.

They stuck and probed so much while there, but it was because of what this test showed, the blockage going into the heart, that prompted him to order the treadmill test. He said.

I hope the treadmill doesn't make me have a heart attack. I am used to a little bit of exercise but not extreme.

He was concerned because my pulse stayed at 50 and below the whole time I was in there, even though my bp was relatively normal after awhile.

I don't know. I will let you know. I have a cardiologist but he is out of the country with his family for this month.

And then, he wound up sending me up to ICU after I was in ER for about 4 hours and things were still not right... and the ICU doc took over from there. I will let you know what I learn, if anything.

Nothing after midnight, said to get registered at hospital at 8 a.m. Means I have to leave no later than 7... They will do it after that.

Chuck offered to go with me. I wasn't going to ask him. I hate asking him to take me so many places... the day before when I went to the orthopedic doc I went by myself. I was sooo tired afterward. It's like 65 miles to his office. Had so much paperwork to fill out. Then xrays. Finally saw him, and he told me to exercise my hand in warm water, squeezing a ball, and he said he'd give me a prescription for a steroid, since I couldn't take Mobic.

BTW, the stained glass people FINALLY came and installed the broken window panes (left from the tornadoes and hailstorms the first of the year). They had a problem ordering the blue they said. Anyway, I had written half the amount for what it would cost on March 23. This is how long it has taken to obtain stained glass.

Now I can call the insurance man so he can come see what's been done & maybe can get the depreciation back that they withheld from original insurance payment. I hope so. I have $2,000 deductible, had to have a new roof, replaced siding, replaced a metal screened-in front porch roof and a fiberglass patio roof. I replaced some of the trees and shrubs beaten and broken. Theresa gifted me with a couple garden globes, a bird bath and feeder, to help me piece my Argosy Garden back together.

The glass people were concerned about the blue glass not being same shade... but it is perfect... however, the amber is not the same. It looks more tan. I am just so grateful to finally have glass in the windows... Plastic covering the windows during hot and cold for so long... Close to six months, is not so good. It is out in the large room where Chuck lives. It used to be a big game room. I sold the pool table and we converted it into an apt for him. Has a bathroom & a kitchen with has a sink etc. So worked well. And it wasn't being used. Kids grown and gone. Nobody played pool. It just gathered junk after awhile. He pulled up the old indoor/outdoor carpet & put down tile & it looks nice.

I'm wondering since they said not to eat or drink after midnight if this stress test involves injections? Hell, who knows. I am just really tired.

Oh well, I have managed to pass enough time the furbies are begging me to come to bed. It's only a little after 10 I think, but it is time. I will miss my morning cuppa coffee. But I expect I'll live over it, as they say around here.

How exciting... petrified rocks. That is definitely what the ones you sent me look like. They are so neat! Unique might be more accurate.

I am so glad your nodule is okay.. so okay it is now gone. How are your shingles? I hope my shingles don't come back from all this stress... they were barely cleared up when the hand-basket took me to hell.

Harvey Rodman, fb friend, sent me a message that he wants an advanced copy this new Shrinking Brain book. How 'bout that?

I hope I'm not peeing up a rope and this turns out to be a good and worthwhile book... We'll know soon enough. It has over 60,000 words so it is not a very long book, but it will be enough, considering the subject.

Until I reread what I have written during the stress and strain and working etc., I really do not know if it is okay or not. I really did plan to proof what I'd written and finish it up over the 4th...

Oh, I believe I said that already. See, that's what shrinking brains do... they make you repeat yourself.

A little humor there.

Goodnight to both of you and you know I love you. You will not hurt my feelings if you and/or Bobby don't want me to use your photos... BUT, on the other hand, I sure hope I can.

Always, Barb

⌐

Email
From: Ann Hamilton
Sent: Wednesday July 10, 2013 10:56PM
To: Barb Sharik
Subject: Re: Re: Hi
Wow, don't know how you get all this done. U r amazing. Of course u can use whatever photo of mine, and I don't think Bobby would mind one bit, he would be flattered I think.

Bobby is watching the bears catch salmon in Katmai Alaska, he posted a couple of pics tonight.

They are without cell phone service, they have wifi.

Since they said not to eat anything sounds like they may inject.

I would be honored to read your latest book whenever you are ready.

My shingles are some better. Just working on my stomach now, trying to get it to relax.

You take care and keep me posted. Luv u.

Sent from my iPad

PUSHING UP DAISIES

"Here's to another year and let's hope it's above ground."
(Carol Shields, The Stone Diaries)

SUBJECT: THE SAGA CONTINUES

Email
From: Barb Sharik
Sent: Thursday 11, 2013 3:05 PM
To: Ann Hamilton
Subject: The Saga Continues
Well, that was a bust...

What happened was, I am all ready for the test, when the doc who is to administer the test comes in and looks over records & asks questions... and btw, there was a group of students going to watch the event as part of their training.

He asked if I had knee, hip or back surgery. 2 backs.

I told him the doc said he scheduled the treadmill because I have a blockage.

This doc says he does not do treadmill tests if a person has blockage and he does not do it if they have had knee, hip or back surgeries. He said these people cannot withstand the test properly and test results with the blockage, may be distorted.

He told the students that he watched how I stepped up on the machine, how I took hold of the railings... he was telling them that you observe everything about a patient.

Anyway, he called the doc & discussed what he felt, that he wanted me to have the stress test with the dye... like what you talked about... where it will speed up your heart etc.

So, that test was scratched & I went elsewhere & was signed up for next Tuesday at 7 a.m... and the lady there explained that the dye would be injected, then some pictures taken, then more dye, more photos, & more dye... anyway... seemed like 3 injections of dye. Whatever. Sigh. Said it would take about 3 hours.

I have not contacted my cardiologist; as I said the ER doc said he was out of country. So, I am still in semi-limbo and mostly I am just very, very tired. BUT, I am okay.

Theresa texted & asked if I'd walked a couple miles on the treadmill & I sent back, no... but I did it at Walmart. Dogfood, wild bird food, meds, etc... I got the prescription renewed for shingles. Definitely came back... must be stress for sure. How are yours?

I need to put all this stuff in the *Shrinking Brain* book. lol. I mean, you can't make this stuff up.

How is your stomach?

I am tired. I will write more later.

Love, Barb

Email

From: Ann Hamilton

Sent: Thursday, July 11, 2013 4:16 PM

To: Barbara Sharik

Subject: Re: The Saga Continues

I think that's why I was so confused about the treadmill test, I knew they didn't do those if they already knew there was blockage, and that they usually did the dye testing.

I hated it and Larry did too, but I've known several people who have had it with no problems and yes it will take about 3 hrs. They take lots of pics of your insides.

I did send Bobby an email telling him what u would like to do, don't know if he got it yet, they will be home from their bear watching excursion on Saturday, expect to see fantastic pics of bears.

At least this latest adventure of yours gave u more to put in the book.

So sorry your shingles came back, mine are a little better, I was so afraid they were going to land on my pelvic floor, they got very close, but not quite there. I'm trying to relax my insides.

More waiting for you, geesh. I'm laying down listening to meditation music and itching, now that's not supposed to happen is it. lol

Rest my friend I'll check with u later

Sent from my iPad

Email

From: Barb Sharik

Sent: Thursday, July 11, 2013 7:05 PM

To: Ann Hamilton

Subject: Re: Re: The Saga Continues

Well, you knew more than me... I suppose my ICU doc knew treadmills are called for, but not being an expert in the field, he requested one. Then, the doc who does these tests, because he *does* do these tests, he *did* know. And so, now, I'm not back to square one by any means, just had a roadblock to maneuver.

Detour ahead.

So what else is new? There appears to be one detour after another. I knew what you wrote about it, and that makes me cringe a tad. I mean, no tests are fun, and some are a little worse than others. And, as you said, not everyone reacts the same way to each test. This is why meds and everything come with a list of Possible-Side-Effects a mile long, starting with everything from indigestion to death at the end.

So, with my usual optimism, I will hope for the best. Perhaps there will be no uncomfy side-effects.

And yes, more for the book... I hope it will wind down and I can close it out and get it published. You see, though, the reason, I figure this should be covered is because not knowing what causes Alzheimer's we have to assume every onslaught will have an effect on our brains to some degree or another. And so, I question... how much does this contribute? Will it make a difference, or will it speed up the process?

But, Ann, look at us... I am 69 and you will be next month, and look at us. We are still upright for the most part, still have our mental faculties despite everything we have both gone through and come down with and gotten over and contracted at one time or another... because by comparing notes we do know that if it is an oddity, we are susceptible. No plain-Jane stuff for us. We are more like sisters-under-the-skin than any other non-related people I have ever known.

I have taken 2 out of 3 pills today for shingles. So I hope they will go away again... and stay gone. And likewise, I hope yours stays gone for awhile also.. although laying down and itching is not a good sign, you know?

I also hope your innards settle down... and that soon, we can both get back to thinking about things other than our ailments. Mind over matter. Go take a magnificent sunset over Mt Franklin. I'll reread my book... and try to bring it to a close. I still have a couple roosters to paint for a friend, and another children's book to illustrate... and... and... and... LuvU.

EASY COME, EASY GO

"You start out happy that you have no hips or boobs. All of a sudden you get them, and it feels sloppy. Then just when you start liking them, they start drooping."
(Cindy Crawford)

"I used to have rosebuds. Now I have hanging baskets."
(Barbara Sharik)

SUBJECT: FRIDAY EARLY A.M. COFFEE WITH BARB

Email
From: Rose Ross
Sent: Friday July 12, 2013 4:47AM
To: Barb Sharik
Subject: Friday early a.m. coffee with Barb
Here I am up early and well rested, for once, must be the fire-work fanatics in my neighborhood have run out of torture

equipment. I fell asleep early so am feeling good. Wondering how you made out yesterday with the tests and hoping for good news.

Before I forget, I was remembering all the things you had going on before the 4th and remembered you'd dealt with shingles again and it made me wonder if the lightning strike feeling you had could maybe have been associated with the shingles. I looked it up and did see some people describing that, plus this after the shingles thing that can cause stuff like feelings of electric shock afterwards. Did the Drs. check out that type of thing? You are surely making me consider the shingles vaccine, have heard there can be side effects though so will check it out.

Got to go. Love you! Me

THE TIME MACHINE

The huge round lunar clock was a gristmill. Shake down all the
grains of Time—the big grains of centuries, and the small grains
of years, and the tiny grains of hours and minutes—and the clock pulver-
ized them, slid Time silently out in all directions in a fine pollen, carried by
cold winds to blanket the town like dust, everywhere. Spores from that clock
lodged in your flesh to wrinkle it, to grow bones to monstrous size, to burst
feet from shoes like turnips. Oh, how that great machine…dispensed Time
in blowing weathers."
(Ray Bradbury, Farewell Summer)

SATURDAY, A DAY OF REST

I am doing what I thought I would be doing July 4th weekend. I am proofing what I have written to the best of my besotted brain's ability. No, "besotted" is not the right word.

See, it is already starting. I am typing and "besotted" automatically pops into my head and from there, onto the page. Then I pause. No. That's not the right word.

Besotted: *Smitten, obsessed, fanatical, head over heels in love, infatuated, love-struck.*

Nope. Wrong word. I wanted to say "my sodden brain…" Perhaps. Sodden: *Saturated, sopping, soaked.*

It is full to overflowing. It is saturated.

But, still, there is another word… I grope. It is saturated but it is heavy laden also. In other words, it is overloaded. In danger of short-circuiting. Zap! Fried.

I started this book a little over a month ago. I made folders and put away all my notes planned for the Hadley book. I simply have not been back into the document saving the sequel to *NORMAL… ALMOST NORMAL*.

I have had to work full time. I have had to keep up with my pets and everyday duties. My floor needs mopping right now. It is on my To-Do List.

I got interrupted with the visit to Spa MGH, or else I would have been closing this book out, getting it ready to upload to the publisher. But, with the events of the Independence Day weekend, I have added chapters. Until I have the next test on next Tuesday (oh my goodness, I forgot to reschedule for the thumb checkup… I started those meds after I got out of the hospital, so there will not be a true reckoning and I am scheduled for a followup visit next Wednesday).

I have an appointment with Dr. Shelat Thursday. I told him last month I was going to write this book. Now, I have to relate to him what happened over the holidays; the chest pains, the testing.

The publishing process itself overall takes several months. Will the music end before I finish? Will the "Swan Song" begin before I finish? I feel as though my clock is ticking louder and louder.

In fact the Tinnitus in my ears is practically roaring. It must be a reaction to one of the meds. It is always here, it is never quiet in my head. But this is so loud. So very loud.

Then, my brain jumps back to the statement about the clock ticking louder and louder, and my mind thinks: It has to click louder and louder; you're deaf as a dormouse.

Are dormice deaf?

Is that even the correct expression, or was it like using the word "besotted" when I meant to use "saturated?" Do I have to google "dormouse" to find out? I cannot continue unless I know. I would look it up in my old dictionary, but dear Hadley chewed its edges and I put it up. I have shoes and chewable things stowed on every upper level. He is getting better. I do not think he has chewed anything in about two weeks. This is progress. He is a little over a year old.

My school principal, all those years ago, said, *Learn a new word everyday.*

While I probably still do learn new words on occasion, right now, I am trying to ascertain an old word.

This is what happens when the brain shrinks. This is what happens with the onset of Alzheimer's disease. This is what I am fighting with every inch of my being.

Another insane thought. Mind over matter. How can I use mind over matter, when the matter in my mind is fading away?

Ah, it makes me sigh. I am not yet fearful but I am on the edge of a certain sadness. I am not depressed but I am realistic enough to know that all the laughter in the world will not completely stop the inevitable.

Maybe when I sit in the sunshine, overlooking my magical Argosy Garden, I will be surrounded not by dust motes, but instead, fairy dust. That likely means I still have a couple wishes left. I am certain my garden is filled with fairies, and fairies do grant wishes, don't they?

SUBJECT: FAIRIES & ORBS & SNAPPING BANANAS

Email

From: Barb Sharik
Sent: Sat, 20 Jul 2013 20:10:59 -0500
To: Rose Ross
Subject: Fairies & Orbs & Snapping Bananas

I am not okay yet. However, the test taken with dye going into the heart valves or whatever it did, was "within the norm"... that is what was reported to me. When I went to neurologist & told him what happened, he said I must think positive that it was not a heart attack.

The results from the radiological dye in vein test showed to be within the norm... so I am back at square one. Or not. Something happened. But if the results do not indicate a heart attack, this is a good thing.

I went to Dr Shelat & told him everything that happened. He said actually, something similar to carpel tunnel syndrome can cause what I experienced... and he told me to feel positive, because the tests ruled out a heart attack. He wants me to come back next month again.

It's easy enough to think positive, but I really wish I knew what did go wrong. I know it was not a panic attack, it was real, my bp bottomed out per usual... and is still low. Every time I've had weird attacks... this is the 3rd since 2010, that is one of the main symptoms, low bp. But this is the first time I felt such severe pain in my chest. Still an occasional flutter. Whatever that means.

I am thinking positive but I am so tired, my ankles are swollen, my legs are heavy... I am not right. Whatever happened, it happened and physically affected me. However, I am attempting to be positive... And I love you for your care and friendship.

BTW, Ann has introduced me to a new Geriatric Exercise that is both healthy and fun. A new sport for the Over 60 Gang... Banana Snapping.

She said to grip a banana, curved side up, in both hands and just snap! Viola! It snaps in half every time... in the skin. (Then you eat the banana of course... that's where the healthy part comes in).

When I told her I tried it and it worked she said she was glad I found it as amazing as she did. She laughingly called it "Our new hobby."

Back to this book, I really, really think it is going to be a winner. I hope so. Between Ann's photographs, Bobby's cover, the human interest personal stories shared, the facts included and my confused commentary, I believe it will prove to be beneficial reading for everyone concerned.

I contacted CreateSpace, so it is beginning... Additionally, in the book I do talk about my Argosy garden being full of orbs and fairies... and why not. I report it lightly, but, you, me, Ann... we believe in something special floating around out and about. Makes life much more fun. Orbs show up in our photographs, why not have fairies prancing around in our gardens. Somebody to watch over us as we smile our way through life... In any case, one thing the three of us have learned, we always take time to smell the flowers and to laugh at adversity.

Now, I have to go buy more bananas.

Stairway to Healing

Photo by: Ann Hamilton,

Las Cruses New Mexico

Look up. This is the stairway to healing. Right up there... You see? At the very top... it will be. It will be.

A LETTER TO MY BRAIN

Dear Shrinking Brain,

Alzheimer's disease will not go away on its own. It will not get tired. It will not give up. We cannot wish it away.

Not you, my amazing shrinking brain, nor me, the residue of your amazingness. We are at present stuck with the process.

Wash in cold water only. Oh, if it were only so simple.

Twinkle, twinkle, little star... Oh, I think I did that one already. It did not work either.

My fingers are crossed, but I am taking my meds too. I've been foolish, but I'm no fool. *Good golly, how many times have I been foolish? Too many to count. Too many to lament over. Learning everyday from yesterday's mistakes.*

You sit on the tracks, a train will eventually run over you. This is what I said about people with addictions. Stop abusing yourself. But, what do you do when lightning strikes out of a clear blue sky and Alzheimer's is the result? Did I sit on the tracks too long and not even be aware? Where did I think I was sitting? At the Taj Mahal?

My lifestyle abuses have been eating too much; becoming fluffy. I call it fluffy but I saw the term *obese* written on my chart at Dr Shelat's office. There is not an uglier word than obese, I thought at that time. So, I lost 70 pounds. Now I have regained 20. I am a yoyo. A frustrated fluffy yoyo.

Also, now, I have learned there is an uglier word than obese. It is Alzheimer's. It is simple enough to pronounce and it is not hard to spell. But it is damned difficult to look at and think: this is me. Me.

I repeat: *Alzheimer's disease will not go away on its own. It will not get tired. It will not give up. We cannot wish it away.*

I read these facts in association with cancer somewhere and they stuck in my head. Same difference with Alzheimer's disease. Ultimately terrible. Dead-end terrible.

(Except some cancers do go away… Alzheimer's never does).

What is needed to eradicate cancer is the same thing needed for Alzheimer's disease. *We need leading-edge research and innovative clinical trials in the relentless pursuit of a cure.*

Just as with cancer, and many other dread diseases, Alzheimer's researchers must discover why and how it comes about, how it works. Only with this knowledge substantiated can it be stopped in its tracks… cured.

Do I have an after thought? Something more to add? No. Not really. It is more a fresh thought I never had reason to give much consideration to previously. Everything needs to be cured. Everything needs to be stopped in its tracks. All the dread diseases of the world.

However, I cannot stand upon the bandwagon for all the dread diseases of the world. So, I stand here waving my flag… *Attention! Attention! Calling all scientists. Keep up the good work, but let's speed up the process, okay? Time is of the essence. That music you hear? That's not "You gotta get up, You gotta get up in the morning." Revelle. Nope. That's the "Dying Swan Song."*

Somebody, somewhere, please… time really is of the essence.

There used to be a commercial warning about drug use. The main line was: *A mind is a terrible thing to waste.*

Yes. Yes, it is.

Sincerely, Yours truly.

⌒

WAVE BYE-BYE

One's doing well if age improves even slightly one's capacity to hold on to that vital truism: "This too shall pass."

(Alain de Botton)

⌒

FYI: A LITTLE LEGALESE

Living Wills:

No. I have never thought about a living will. I mean, I am a notary public for the state of Louisiana, and have been since 1970, so I can write and execute wills. Louisiana notaries have a good deal of power, compared to some states. Of course, with this power comes responsibility. (I also served as a Justice of the Peace for eight years). But a regular will is different from the document known as The Living Will.

A Living Will gives individuals the right to participate in developing and implementing their own plan of care. It allows them to make informed decisions regarding their care and treatment in the event they are hospitalized.

What does this mean? Well, it gives an individual the right to be notified about the status of his/her health and the right to not only receive treatment, but also to refuse treatment… and the right to implement an advance directive.

Advance Directives:

What is an advance directive? This in essence is the essence of the Living Will, because it is a document that tells an individual's healthcare providers and family what medical care he/she does or does not want in the event they are unable to make their own medical decisions.

Do you leave the decision to your family, or do you determine for your own self? Suppose you contract a terminal illness or are involved in a serious accident, and are unable to communicate?

I will not go into the problems that are erased before they are ever allowed to eventuate, by preparing a Living Will. Not to mention, there have been times when a judge has to step in and appoint someone to do your bidding, on your behalf, if you have not prepared to handle such a tragic situation. And, these situations come to be everywhere, all the time.

Bear in mind, an advance directive only comes into play if you are incapacitated to the point where you are incapable of making your own medical decisions.

Declarations:

I have learned that in Louisiana, since this is where I reside, advance directives are also called Declarations. An individual must be 18 years of age to implement one. And, again, they only go into effect when a person is hospitalized with a terminal or irreversible condition such as a coma that renders the individual incapable of making or communication his/her own medical decisions.

A Living Will is generally composed so that the individual can describe the types of life-sustaining procedures that he/she wants or does not want, however, in order to appoint a particular individual to make medical decisions for that individual, a Durable Power of Attorney is required.

Hospitals are receptive to adding your Living Will to your medical records.

LaPOST:

Approved by the Louisiana Legislature in 2010, the LaPOST *(Louisiana Physician Order for Scope of Treatment)* is an advance directive that is written in the format of a physician's order and allows a person to document his/her wishes concerning specific types of life-sustaining care.

It is recommended for individuals diagnosed with terminal or irreversible conditions and do not expect to live for more than one year.

When placed in an individual's medical records, it is used as a physician's order.

Durable Power of Attorney:

The Durable Power of Attorney allows an individual to appoint someone he/she trusts to make medical and end-of-life decisions on his/her behalf in the event he/she has a terminal or irreversible condition and cannot communicate his/her own medical wishes/decisions.

Bear in mind, that a durable power of attorney not only gives consent for this person to make medical decisions, but also end-of-life decisions on the individual's behalf.

Individuals appointed—close friend, relative or clergy member—should be someone the patient trusts to make serious decisions… because when this person is called upon, it will mean serious decisions must be made.

Do Not Resuscitate:

Another important issue to consider concerns if a person's physician determines that he/she has a terminal or irreversible condition, whether or not to be resuscitated.

This is the "Do not resuscitate" order that lets healthcare providers be aware that in the event a person's heart stops beating or they stop breathing, do not perform cardiopulmonary resuscitation (CPA)… in an attempt to revive.

The State of Louisiana Declaration:

This is a form that can be filled in and used as a living will and durable power of attorney.

Steps to take:

1. Fill it out in front of at least two witnesses who can attest you were in a sound state of mind when you made the Declaration.

2. Witnesses must be at least 18 years of age, cannot be related to you by blood or marriage, and cannot be entitled to any portion of your estate if you die.

3. Declarations can be notarized, but it is not mandatory. I can inject, as a long-time Notary Public, I would recommend it be notarized, just for your own peace of mind, and then placed in your medical records.

4. It is also not necessary to involve an attorney to prepare your Declaration. However, bear in mind, that an attorney will be able to assist you in making your intentions completely clear. Again, just as having it notarized, it will give you peace of mind.

LaPOST:

The state of Louisiana has a form that can be filled out if someone feels the LaPOST is more appropriate for their needs.

Steps to take:

1. The form should be filled out by you or your legal representative in conjunction with your physician.

2. This form must also be signed by you or your legal representative AND your physician.

Obtaining the forms:

1. Your healthcare provider can assist with obtaining the appropriate forms.

2. Call your local AARP

Websites:

1. U.S. Living Wills Registry

www.uslivingwillegistry.com/individuals.shtm

Choose: Advanced Directive Forms on top toolbar.

Choose: The Forms.

Choose: Appropriate state

2. Office of the Secretary of State

www.sos.louisiana.gov/tabid/215/Default.aspx

Choose Living Will on he left sidebar.

3. LaPOST

www.La-POST.org

More information and the document are available for download. It is recommended the form be printed on gold paper so that it is easily identifiable in the medical record.

Registering your form in Louisiana:

You can register your Declaration or LaPOST with the Secretary of State for a small fee. However, it is <u>not</u> mandatory and if you determine not to register it, it is still effective and valid.

To register, send a <u>certified copy</u> or the <u>original</u> to:

Office of the Secretary of State

PO Box 49125

Baton Rouge, LA 708014-9125

Attention: Publications

For more information, including current fee, contact the Office of the Secretary of State at 225-922-0309.

What next?

Talk to your physician, your family, your friends, and clergy, about your advanced directives in order to make sure everyone is aware of your intentions… and that they are completely understood.

Make several copies of your Declaration or LaPOST so you can easily provide them to your healthcare provider at the hospital.

P.S.

<u>You can change your mind.</u>

You can revoke your Declaration or LaPOST.

…Simply express your intention in writing, destroying the document or verbally voicing your desire to revoke the <u>Declaration</u>.

You can change your document.

…However, if you change your document, you should rewrite the entire Declaration or LaPOST and as before, have it signed and witnessed.

If you registered your Declaration or LaPOST with the Office of Secretary of State for Louisiana, it can still be revoked if you so choose. However, it will be necessary to send in a <u>revocation request in writing.</u>

~

TAKING RESPONSIBILITY.

"I reckon responsible behavior is something to get when you grow older. Like varicose veins."
(Terry Pratchett, <u>Wyrd Sisters)</u>

~

"THE END OF THE LINE"*
(*Traveling Wilburys)

Did I mention I ordered a third Bluetooth?

I got a notice from amazon.com, it has been mailed. I will have to keep a lanyard around my neck so I will not lose it, so that Hadley will not eat it.

Of course, I already mentioned it. That is what happens when your brain shrinks. You forget. But, only for a moment. Right now, I only forget for a moment.

What is down the road?

Speaking of roads, I bought a new car a last month. I already mentioned that also.

You see how my mind works? This is why lists are a must... something to keep me organized and on track. This is why I sometimes mislay things. I am on the way to bed, with cell phone in hand so I can plug it up for charging overnight, and I see something that needs doing. I set the cell phone down *unconsciously* and then, when whatever it was I felt I simply had to do at that very moment in time, I go into the bedroom, and am immediately reminded: *charge cell phone.*

So, where is my cell phone? I had it in my hand moments ago.

That is when the backtracking begins.

I calm my panicking brain, and commune with myself that it is here. It is somewhere between the bedroom and wherever I was when I stopped to feed the fish... the aquarium full of fish I suddenly remembered I had not fed this morning.

Sidetracked. It is called getting sidetracked.

Two things forgotten. Feeding the fish before leaving for work and where I set down my cell phone.

Naturally it does not take long to retrieve it. The path is short enough, and it must be somewhere along the way. It is not in a logical place, however. It is just where my hand opened at the same time my brain was telling me to feed the fish, and left it sitting. That could be on the arm of the couch, on a desk, on the kitchen table.

The hunt, the search, is not difficult. I know it is here. I know I had it in my hand. I know everything except the exact location.

It is all about backtracking. I also know it is not like my Bluetooth, lost somewhere out in the galaxy. No. It is within a forty-foot section of the house. Between my home office where I picked it up after shutting down the computer, and the bedroom, where I know it is not. The bedroom is where I realized my hand was empty.

Will this sort of thing escalate? Is that what shrinking brains and Alzheimer's comes to?

I left an orange in the fruit bin too long. Somehow, it got overlooked and eventually shriveled up.

My brain. A forgotten orange. Shriveled beyond re-hydration. Beyond redemption.

Above and beyond the call of duty? Yes, and no. That term, *above and beyond the call of duty* indicates pushing the limit, going to the edge, accomplishing something amazing. But, if you think about it, when a brain has gone above and beyond the call of duty, it means it is no longer a viable organ. Duty may call, but it can no longer respond. It is above and beyond. It is no longer in working condition.

When my brain dies, so will my body.

Like love and marriage, horses and carriages, you really cannot have one without the other.

Tomorrow I will begin eating healthy.

Tomorrow.

Tonight I am plugging my cell phone into the charger. I am going to bed. I am shutting down negative and scary thoughts. I have lived my life blocking negatives.

Detour. Road Work Ahead.

OLD FRIENDS

Two elderly ladies, Tammi and Barb, had been the best of friends for over 50 years. Over the decades they had spent together, they had worked together, lived next door to each other, and even vacationed together with their husbands. In their golden years, they would meet every afternoon to play cards. One day, as they were wrapping up a game of pinochle, Barb looks at Tammi sheepishly and says, "Now please don't get angry with me. I know we've been friends for a long time, but I just can't seem to remember your name! I've been wracking my brain for the past hour but it still escapes me. Please remind a forgetful old lady!" Tammi glares angrily at Barb. For five minutes, she doesn't speak, only giving her friend stares of disappointment. Finally, Tammi asks, "How soon do you need to know?"

"911. WHAT IS THE NATURE OF YOUR PROBLEM?"

The term, Alzheimer's disease, dates back to 1906 when a German physician, Dr Alois Alzheimer, presented the case history of a 51-year-old woman who suffered from a rare brain disorder, before a meeting.

The autopsy of her brain identified the plaques and tangles that still, to this day, characterize Alzheimer's disease.

There is no cure. There is no proven way to prevent Alzheimer's either. It is a progressive, degenerative disorder that attacks brain cells (neurons) which results in loss of memory, thinking and language skills, and behavioral change.

The brain short-circuits. Short-term memory fails when the disease destroys nerve cells in the hippocampus. Language skills and judgment decline when neurons die in the cerebral cortex.

The most positive report released suggests the only way to lower your risk of Alzheimer's disease is to reduce your risk of heart disease.

According to Mayo Clinic, *Many of the same factors that increase your risk of heart disease can also increase your risk of Alzheimer's disease and vascular dementia. Important factors that may be involved include high blood pressure, high blood cholesterol, excess weight and diabetes.*

Probably the most important thing I have learned while doing superficial research is that, while Alzheimer's disease is the most common cause of Dementia (loss of intellectual function) among people aged 65 or older, Alzheimer's disease is *not* a normal part of aging.

However, the second most important thing I learned is that there is *no* cure.

So, what does this mean in the grand scheme of things?

I will let you know as soon as I know. Stay tuned. I am not out of here yet. At this moment, every day is a brand new day (no pun intended), and I know everything will be okay. One way or another, it will be okay.

So, don't rock the juke box, I'm saving the Last Waltz for you.

And you.

You too.

EPILOG

Then… what do I hear? A call in the night, a voice in the dark.

What do I see? A light suddenly shining. A bright, guiding light.

Yes!

I reach out my hand, touch his hand. He closes his fingers over mine. I am no longer alone. I am rescued.

However, this is not a spirit from the unknown; this is someone very familiar. I know him. I do.

My rapid fearful breath slows. My pulse rate drops. My heart stops pounding in my chest. I was lost, but now I am found.

He hands me a prescription.

I look, read. It is for memory loss. Medicine to improve memory. Magic? No. Not unless you call modern medicine magic.

Well, then, maybe it is. Maybe it is magic after all.

I swallow the pill. It is all coming back to me now. I do not have to live in a dark cocoon. I emerge. I unfold and spread my wings.

Looking down at myself, I first see greenness. Green? A Luna Moth? Surely, not a Luna Moth. Lovely Luna Moths live only a dozen days; they have no mouths. They cannot eat. They emerge from their cocoons, look beautiful, and then they die.

My magic pill has bought me time, but to what end?

I take another pill, look down again. Not a Luna Moth. No. I see orange. Beautiful orange and black. A Monarch Butterfly. Monarchs are the most magnificent of all butterflies, and the most fascinating. Their quest for life is amazing. Remarkably, Monarchs of the fourth generation will live for eight or nine months and travel over two-thousand miles to Mexico; a place they have never seen before. Before migrating, they gather in huge numbers at departure points such as Presqu'ile Provincial Park, on a peninsula sticking out into Lake Ontario.

There is no other creature in the kingdom that does what the Monarch does. When these butterflies migrate in reverse, head back to Mexico and California, they will live for six to eight months in hibernation. When they come out of hibernation, the whole process begins all over again.

I like that I will be among the most beautiful and the most fascinating, but most of all, I like that I will continue life's journey. I received a second chance.

On the verge of losing it metaphorically and physically. I was lost but now I am found. I am making my way back home. My house key again fits my front door. I am given a second chance.

How long will the key continue fitting this same lock, before a new lock must be installed, a new key cut? That is a shoulder-shrugging question. I cannot worry about that. Nobody is promised tomorrow. All I ask is to let me have today one day at a time and I am good to go.

Most of all, I like that I will continue life's journey.

I am given a second chance.

My house key again fits my front door.

I am home. For now, I am home.

THE END

AND

THE BEGINNING

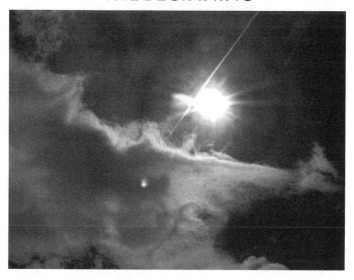

Hope

Photo by: Ann Hamilton,

Even in the darkest sky, eventually the sun shines. There, there is the answer just waiting to be discovered. And, it will be. Maybe not in my time. Maybe not even in yours. But, rest assured... please, rest assured... it will be discovered.

ADDENDUM

OLD GUYS ARE GETTING HARDER TO FIND THESE DAYS

Column for week of July 23, 2013

It started with a pain in my chest that proceeded to shoot like lightning bolts down both arms, numbing them as I was sitting at the computer typing a newspaper column. It took my breath away and hurt like the dickens.

I went next door to Chuck's. He advised I sit and relax. He was in the midst of cooking 4th of July dinner to share with me. It's difficult to cook nutritious meals for one, therefore, if either of us gets the urge to do more than heating up a can of soup or mixing up a can of tuna, we share.

Restless, I advised I'd go home and lie down. Once down, BooCat immediately snuggled, holding the three dogs at bay. Written all over Hadley's handsome face was "Why can't I snuggle too?" He was so pitiful. Boo was so bad.

I like Facebook very much but scorn folks who post their every thought. "Get a life," I mumble. Yeah, I'm old and cranky sometimes.

However, although my cell phone's ancient, I can get into FB and I did. I posted what I experienced for all the world to read.

Catching my breath, realizing this is nuts, I got up and headed back to Chuck's to ask him to take me to the ER. I met him midway. He was on the phone with daughter Theresa.

A friend of hers saw my post, called her and told her to call me. Just that fast. Theresa was telling Chuck to take me to the hospital. So much for that delicious 4th of July meal.

Chuck cranked up my little BumbleBee Buggy and we headed toward Morehouse General Hospital. I called the ambulance; they met us outside Mer Rouge where we made a transfer. I became less frightened as we headed for the ER.

Long story shorter, I wound up being admitted to ICU where I spent the holiday at Spa MGH. The meals were delicious, the service good (if you don't count the needles, prodding and poking), and likely when I get my bill, it will cost like going on vacation to a Spa.

Blood enzymes didn't show a heart attack. Later outpatient tests showed blood flow into heart within the norm. I'm not alright, very shaky still, and weak as a kitten. I don't know what happened; something did. My blood pressure remains very low; and the couple times I've had serious incidents (stroke and seizures) the low BP was so troubling one doctor spoke of the possibility of a pacemaker.

However, I'm still alive, sitting here typing a column and thanking everybody who posted to my fb page… Over 400 posts, of course I had to heal. There was even a phone call from a friend in Pakistan. (Please don't tell NSA). There was too much praying and well wishes crossing the airwaves not to heal. But, I feel so old.

I commented as much to friend Mike Lytle which prompted him to say, "You know, the older I get the harder it is to find an old guy anymore." Naturally I caught his joke. Used to be, he said, when he needed something from someone with experience, he went to the old guy; now we ARE the old guys. He also pointed out that there are fewer and fewer of us old guys. Point taken, but not jumping with joy at having it pointed out.

Not to mention jumping with joy is another thing of the past. Old people don't jump for joy. We stand up a little straighter, teeter on our toes, and smile because we're still upright. Upright's good.

(Bastrop Daily Enterprise, Bastrop, Louisiana)

⌒

BREAKING NEWS

(The following are news releases offering promising hope for Alzheimer's disease)

Late Retirement May Prevent Dementia
Monday, 15 Jul 2013 10:03 AM

New research boosts the "use it or lose it" theory about brainpower and staying mentally sharp. People who delay retirement have less risk of developing Alzheimer's disease or other types of dementia, a study of nearly half a million people in France found.

It's by far the largest study to look at this, and researchers say the conclusion makes sense. Working tends to keep people physically active, socially connected and mentally challenged — all things known to help prevent mental decline.

"For each additional year of work, the risk of getting dementia is reduced by 3.2 percent," said Carole Dufouil, a scientist at INSERM, the French government's health research agency. NEWSMAX

Retiring Later May Help Prevent Dementia, Study Finds

By MARILYNN MARCHIONE 07/15/13 08:28 PM ET EDT

BOSTON — New research boosts the "use it or lose it" theory about brainpower and staying mentally sharp. People who delay retirement have less risk of developing Alzheimer's disease or other types of dementia, a study of nearly half a million people in France found.

It's by far the largest study to look at this, and researchers say the conclusion makes sense. Working tends to keep people physically active, socially connected and mentally challenged – all things known to help prevent mental decline.

"For each additional year of work, the risk of getting dementia is reduced by 3.2 percent," said Carole Dufouil, a scientist at INSERM, the French government's health research agency.

She led the study and gave results Monday at the Alzheimer's Association International Conference in Boston.

About 35 million people worldwide have dementia, and Alzheimer's is the most common type. In the U.S., about 5 million have Alzheimer's – 1 in 9 people aged 65 and over. What causes the mind-robbing disease isn't known and there is no cure or any treatments that slow its progression.

France has had some of the best Alzheimer's research in the world, partly because its former president, Nicolas Sarkozy, made it a priority. The country also has detailed health records on self-employed people who pay into a Medicare-like health system.

Researchers used these records on more than 429,000 workers, most of whom were shopkeepers or craftsmen such as bakers and woodworkers. They were 74 on average and had been retired for an average of 12 years.

Nearly 3 percent had developed dementia but the risk of this was lower for each year of age at retirement. Someone who retired at 65 had about a 15 percent lower risk of developing dementia compared to someone retiring at 60, after other factors that affect those odds were taken into account, Dufouil said.

To rule out the possibility that mental decline may have led people to retire earlier, researchers did analyses that eliminated people who developed dementia within 5 years of retirement, and within 10 years of it.

"The trend is exactly the same," suggesting that work was having an effect on cognition, not the other way around, Dufouil said.

France mandates retirement in various jobs – civil servants must retire by 65, she said. The new study suggests "people should work as long as they want" because it may have health benefits, she said.

June Springer, who just turned 90, thinks it does. She was hired as a full-time receptionist at Caffi Plumbing & Heating in Alexandria, Va., eight years ago.

"I'd like to give credit to the company for hiring me at that age," she said. "It's a joy to work, being with people and keeping up with current events. I love doing what I do. As long as God grants me the brain to use I'll take it every day."

Heather Snyder, director of medical and scientific operations for the Alzheimer's Association, said the study results don't mean everyone needs to delay retirement.

"It's more staying cognitively active, staying socially active, continue to be engaged in whatever it is that's enjoyable to you" that's important, she said.

"My parents are retired but they're busier than ever. They're taking classes at their local university, they're continuing to attend lectures and they're continuing to stay cognitively engaged and socially engaged in their lives."

—

AP Medical Writer Lindsey Tanner in Chicago contributed to this report.

⌒⌒

Why DELAYING retirement can make you less likely to develop dementia

Those retiring at 65 are 15 per cent less likely to suffer from the condition than those retiring at 60, finds authoritative French study

- By <u>Daily Mail Reporter</u>
- **PUBLISHED:** 15:50 EST, 15 July 2013 | **UPDATED:** 15:50 EST, 15 July 2013
- Get to work Grandma: New research carried out in France suggests that delaying retirement can make people less likely to develop dementia
- It is the dream of many to be successful enough in their professional life to retire early and enjoy their golden years in a splendid state of carefree relaxation.

But new research suggests that delaying retirement can make people less likely to develop dementia.

A French study believed to be the largest ever of its kind found someone retiring at 65 was about 15 per cent less likely to develop the condition that someone retiring at 60.

The findings back up previous studies suggesting that continued intellectual stimulation and mental engagement may ward off the tragic cognitive decline caused by Alzheimer's and similar illnesses.

They suggest professional activity may be an important determinant of intellectual stimulation and mental engagement, which are thought to be potentially protective against dementia.

Study author Carole Dufoil and her team at the Institut National de la Santé et de la Recherché Médicale (INSERM) analysed the health and insurance records of more than 429,000 self-employed workers.

Analyses showed that the risk of being diagnosed with dementia was lower for each year of working longer.

Even after excluding workers who had dementia diagnosed within the 5 years following retirement, the results remained unchanged and highly significant, the researchers said in a release.

'Our data show strong evidence of a significant decrease in the risk of developing dementia associated with older age at retirement, in line with the "use it or lose it" hypothesis,' said Dr Dufouil.

'The patterns were even stronger when we focused on more recent birth cohorts.'

Around 35million people worldwide suffer from dementia, with Alzheimer's the most common type, CBS News reported.

The illness is expected to become a particularly acute problem in Western nations in coming decades as members of the baby boom generation reach their dotage.

But with retirement ages being delayed in many countries worried about the impact of so many new pensioners on social security safety nets, it appears it could have the unintended consequence of actually keeping them healthy for longer.

Dr Dufouil, director of research in neuroepidemiology at INSERM, said: 'Professional activity may be an important determinant of intellectual stimulation and mental engagement, which are thought to be potentially protective against dementia.

'As countries around the world respond to the aging of their populations, our results highlight the importance of maintaining high levels of cognitive and social stimulation throughout work and retired life, and they emphasize the need for policies to help older individuals achieve cognitive and social engagement.'

The researchers presented their findings today at the Alzheimer's Association International Conference in Boston, Massachusetts.

Don't Trust Online Tests For Alzheimer's Disease

Gary Drevitch, Contributor

Thinkstock

Do you sometimes not know why you walked into a room?

Do you often forget your ATM PIN number?

Have you ever forgotten the weather report you heard yesterday?

If you answered yes to any of these questions, you may have Alzheimer's disease … but probably not.

A number of online tests for Alzheimer's disease have cropped up on the Internet in recent years, claiming to be able to diagnose the much-feared condition through a Web surfer's answers to 10 or 20 questions, usually focused on memory. But a new report released today at the Alzheimer's Association's International Conference in Boston finds such claims to be scientifically invalid and characterizes their hosts as unethical and often predatory in their pursuit of profits through sales of sketchy prevention tools to a beleaguered, vulnerable older population.

The study's lead author, Julie Robillard, a postdoctoral fellow at the National Core for Neuroethics at the University of British Columbia in Vancouver, asked an expert panel — including geriatricians, neuropsychologists and neuroethicists — to rate 16 representative, freely accessible online tests for Alzheimer's disease. The experts scored the sites on scientific validity and reliability; human-computer interaction; and a range of ethical factors. Three-quarters of the tests were rated as "poor" or "very poor" for scientific validity and reliability and all 16 got "poor" or "very poor" grades for their ethical standards, including overly dense or absent confidentiality and privacy policies, failure to disclose commercial conflicts of interests and failure to word test outcomes in an appropriate or ethical manner. (The majority of the sites were rated as "fair" for appropriateness of human-computer interface for an older adult population.)

The sites hosting the online tests that were reviewed for the study had unique monthly visitors ranging from 800 to as many as 8.8 million.

More than 5 million Americans live with Alzheimer's disease, according to the Alzheimer's Association, a number the group estimates could reach 13.8 million by 2050. It is the sixth-leading cause of death in the United States.

The Impact of Fake Diagnoses

Clinical colleagues of Robillard's had noticed an uptick in the number of older adults coming to their waiting rooms claiming to have read something online that convinced them that they had Alzheimer's or were at high risk. Their stories inspired her to take a closer look at the type of material about the condition available on the Web. "I took a peek at these diagnostic tests and it struck me as an important issue to address," she says. "What we found online was distressing and potentially harmful."

It's important to know, first of all, that there is no valid online test for Alzheimer's disease, which is notoriously difficult to diagnose with accuracy. Doctors rely on a complex set of mental and physical tests, sometimes including brain scans, to determine if a patient has the condition. "There is no test that you can do sitting at a computer by yourself," Robillard says.

That hasn't stopped companies from launching "diagnostic" sites, some with quizzes featuring 10 or 20 questions, often quite general, with vague answers that are seemingly designed to yield maximum fear and concern in the online audience.

It's not surprising that Alzheimer's disease has been the focus of such sites, Robillard says. "It has a couple of interesting features that makes it especially vulnerable to this kind of site." First, it's not like diabetes, which has to be diagnosed with a blood test. "And people think it's easy to test memory," she says, adding that there's a widespread misconception that "if you have bad memory, there's Alzheimer's disease."

For all these reasons, Robillard says, "These tools have very low scientific validity or scientific reliability. If people have concerns, it's an understandable behavior to try to find information online. But when it comes to seeking a diagnosis, the tests are not an appropriate solution."

Predatory Practices

Beyond the obvious ethical problems with purporting to diagnose Alzheimer's online, Robillard says, there are further, serious concerns. Many of the test sites are hosted by companies or groups that market products or tools claiming to help prevent the disease. Robillard's study does not identify any of the evaluated sites by name. "They were fairly homogenous," she says, "and the point is to say that, as a whole, there are serious issues with these tools." But she says that they are "a mix of organizations and individuals. It's not solely scam vitamin sellers."

The tests, Robillard found, are often worded in ways that almost assure doubts are raised in the minds of the user. "Some tests make it really hard for you to score well so that at the end you'll buy the tools and products they might be selling," she says. "It's a predatory marketing strategy in a population that's vulnerable to start with." She cited a recent widely publicized UCLA study that found older people may be more susceptible to fraud and scams because of changes in the aging brain that weaken the ability to discern untrustworthy sources.

Even computer-savvy adults may be fooled by some of the Alzheimer's testing sites. "It's not always obvious that these are commercial sites," Robillard says. "It's very difficult to tell — and if I had a hard time, I imagine others would have a hard time as well."

All other issues aside, these sites are scary. Doctors take care when they share a diagnosis of dementia with a patient or family. "Should people be alone in their home when they find out they have Alzheimer's disease?" Robillard asks. Even if the diagnosis is not real, the fear is. "That's part of the whole predatory marketing strategy. It's one of many possible harms."

Robillard hopes her study shines new light on unethical practices. "It's absolutely a small part of a larger problem," she says.

The preponderance of invalid diagnostic Web sites has wider implications. "When you're told online that you have Alzheimer's disease," Robillard says, it's only logical that you'd race to your doctor with the news. "That creates a burden on an already burdened health care system as people respond to a result with a demand for health care services that may or may not be appropriate."

Sharing her results with physicians who treat Alzheimer's, Robillard believes, could help enlighten them about the scope of the issue. "People are going to come into their clinics who may have taken these tests and they could have a printout and say, 'I have a 46! I have Alzheimer's!'" she says.

Even if someone takes an online test and gets a good result, it could negatively impact their care, Robillard adds. Some sites advise people who get a perfect score on the test that they don't need to consult with their doctor about cognitive issues for a year or more, but those positive scores don't prove there are no underlying issues that need addressing. A quiz site's results could lead you to delay getting care you actually need.

Finding Reliable Information

Of course, families should not avoid the Internet altogether when seeking information about Alzheimer's and dementia. The Alzheimer's Association and government sites like <u>alzheimers.gov</u> provide useful facts and explanations, along with links to other resources that have been screened for accuracy and legitimacy. "Just don't expect to find a diagnostic tool," Robillard says.

The new study also does not call into question legitimate sites offering lists of criteria which caregivers and adult children can use to help determine if they should be concerned that a loved one may be suffering from dementia or Alzheimer's. Brochures like, even from the Alzheimer's Associarion do not pretend to diagnose any condition, but encourage people to talk to a doctor if they have concerns about someone's mental state.

Gary Drevitch is senior Web editor for Next Avenue's Caregiving and Health & Well-Being channels. Follow Gary on Twitter @Gary Drevitch.

VITAMIN B-12

July 19, 2011
By Charis Grey
Lawrence Berkeley National Library/Photodisc/Getty Images

Vitamin B-12 is the most chemically complex of all the vitamins, and it is essential to the production of red blood cells, the synthesis of genetic materials and the function of your nervous system. Your nervous system is your body's communications system; it includes your brain, spinal cord and peripheral nerves. Deficiencies in vitamin B-12 can result in symptoms related to nerve damage and have also been linked to brain function and dementia, according to the Office of Dietary Supplements.

Vitamin B-12

Cobalamin is another word for vitamin B-12. This is a reference to the presence of a cobalt ion within the chemical structure of the B-12 molecule. B-12 is found in animal-based food sources. Steamed clams and steamed mussels are especially high in B-12, containing 84 mcg and 20.4 mcg, respectively, per 3-oz. serving. Eggs, milk, cheese, meat, fish and poultry also provide B-12. For those over the age of 14, the recommended dietary allowance of B-12 is 2.4 mcg per day. Pregnant women should consume 2.6 mcg daily, and breastfeeding woman should consume 2.8 mcg.

Effects of Deficiency

B-12 deficiency causes megaloblastic anemia, a condition wherein your red blood cell count decreases and abnormally large, immature red blood cells are produced. B-12 also affects your neurological system, which is where brain lesions become a concern. Though the connection between B-12 deficiency and nerve damage has not been completely elucidated, lack of B-12 may affect the outer insulating layer of nerve cells, called the myelin sheath.

Research

According to a study in the February 2009 issue of the "Journal of Neurology, Neurosurgery and Psychology," low B-12 levels are associated with increased severity of white matter lesions in the brain, an effect that may be related to decreased integrity of the myelin sheath. A case study published in the April 2009 issue of the journal "Rinsho Shinkeigaku," or "Clinical Neurology," describes a 39-year-old man whose seizures and multiple brain lesions were improved through B-12 supplementation therapy.

Causes of Deficiency

Because B-12 is found in animal-based foods, deficiencies based on dietary consumption alone are not common. The exception to this is in those who abstain from animal-based foods, such as those who follow a completely vegan diet. More commonly, B-12 deficiencies are due to disorders and conditions that make it difficult for your body to absorb B-12. These include the autoimmune disorder known as pernicious anemia. Older people whose gastrointestinal systems no longer produce enough hydrochloric acid to properly digest foods may also have difficulty obtaining enough B-12 deficiency.

APPRECIATION AND RECOGNITION

Angels in people's clothing (which is so much better than wolves in sheep's clothing), I say thank you.

Unless recognized otherwise specifically, thank you in no particular order: Ann (RuthAnn Wilson) and Larry Hamilton… who have been a shoulder of strength even though many miles away, Robert G "Bobby" Arrington, Rosemary "Rose" Ross, Tammi Carroll Garner, Mona L Hayden, Carolyn Files, Ron Crown, sister Jan Sharik Baker and husband Kevin, Pat Claiborne Latham, Carol Holston, Wes Helbling, forever sister-in-law Linda Babb Crymes, James "Jim" Perry, (The Honorable) Michael "Mike" Lytle, daughter-in-law Carla McGee, daughter-in-law Cindy Tubbs, granddaughter Alisha Danielle Tubbs, cousin Mike Sarik, sister Michele Sharik and husband Brian Pituley, Mindy Diffenderfer, RN, (Director Clinical Resource Management, Morehouse General Hospital), Dr Wyatt Webb, Dr Shelat, Dr Kahlil, Dr Walters, Dr Cox, Dr Coats, Dr Spires, Dr Bhandari, Dr Marx, and all the angels in nurses' clothing (which is actually people's clothing but comes with a helpful hand and a happy heart beating with every step).

Each of you fill my heart to overflowing… in fact, it is so overflowed, I likely left off a name or two. Blame it on my ISB. (You remember what that means, don't you? My Incredible Shrinking Brain). Everybody needs a heart that overflows because, after all, it definitely beats a shrinking brain, incredible or otherwise.

Bet you thought I was going to use the original expression: *It beats a blank…* Well, actually, it *is* the same difference… Another favorite idiom of mine… *same difference.*

I'm bad about using double negatives… Or should that be *good* about using double negatives?

I love our language! I will miss it when I lose it.

FACEBOOK FRIENDS

July 6, 2013, upon being released from intensive care, I was overwhelmed by the many facebook friends who wished me well. Two-hundred, three-hundred, four… However many of you commented with heartfelt wishes, This is to each of you… and also a special thank you to my fb friend from Pakistan who called to inquire about my health after I got home from the hospital.

Dear Facebook friends:

Ok. I am home. I have some blockage going into the heart, so they will schedule a treadmill test.

The blood enzymes did NOT show a heart attack!!! This is good, however, it doesn't answer the heaviness on my chest and shortness of breath that is the residue from the original attack.

Something happened. Just not sure exactly what yet.

I look back at my initial response... lying down AND POSTING to FB about the incident... what was I thinking?

I suppose I wasn't.

However, even as I was making my way to friend Chuck to ask him to drive me to the ER, a friend had called daughter Theresa & told her to call me... she called Chuck, and he was on his way to get me to go to the ER.

We called the ambulance & they met us about 20 miles from the house, and we transferred me from the car to them, north of Mer Rouge... and then headed to the ER.

At first the BP was high. Then it kept fluctuating. But, soon my pulse dropped to 50 and below and would not go higher.

I am of the age when things can go south and never return north... so I am pleased I am still kicking.

I mean, still upright. Not exactly kicking. lol.

Dr Cox, ER physician, admitted me, and turned me over to Dr Coats. I am not sure Dr Coats knew how to take me and my humor. Believe me, when I die, I will die telling a joke.

In fact, I was in the midst of writing my weekly humor newspaper column when this incident happened.

THANK YOU ONE AND ALL... I am awed. I am overwhelmed. I cannot tell each of you how very much I appreciate your responses, your thoughts, your prayers, your love and caring.

I wish I could list each name individually, because after all, each of you individually posted and took me into your hearts of love. How could I not begin healing? The odds! My goodness, the odds! My healing was a given.

On a lighter note, this gives me another chapter in this.

Having been diagnosed with early onset Alzheimer's disease, I decided to write a book from a layman's point of view... real information, impressions, humor, are within these pages. I write because I must. It keeps my shrinking brain operating. I am no expert, I am a participant. I cannot offer medical facts, but I can offer firsthand experience instead.

And on that note, I received a check from my first publisher, Clark Kenyon, Camp Pope Publishing, for the sale of five more *BOOCAT UNLEASHED* books, my first published book.

At this moment, my chest feels heavy and slightly painful on the left side. I am tired, naturally. Even though I was calling my stay at Morehouse General Hospital *SPA MGH*, it is very trying to undergo lots of tests. However, I am still kicking. And I love and thank each of you.

Barbara

ABOUT THE AUTHOR

Author photo by: Mona L Hayden
Bayou DeSiard, Monroe, Louisiana

BARBARA SHARIK is a freelance writer, a newspaper and magazine columnist, an author and painter.

As a fun aside, one year she was among eight finalists in a *Jay Leno Comedy Challenge,* (ULM, Monroe, La.) and is still called upon to speak before organizations and groups where she delivers her own brand of humor.

Several months ago she spoke to the Bastrop Optimist's Club and in August she will speak to the Mer Rouge Lion's Club. Her constant goal: *I hope I make you laugh.*

July 3, 2013 Summary:

- I experience tremors in my left hand occasionally ever since the original stroke, May 2010.
- I see multicolored lights behind my eyelids at night.
- Yellow blotches fill the pages of my books, and any plain surface.
- My feet and toes get numb, even when I am barefooted. The feet and ankles swell.
- I recently started getting muscle cramps in my feet, calves, stomach even.
- My memory for the most part is good.
- My senses seem sensible.
- I have written and published six books/novels since 2010.
- I've published 4 BooCat books *(BooCat Unleashed; BooCat: Dancing Naked in the Rain; BooCat: Living in my Lap ; BooCat Throws a Frisbee),* 1 erotic romance, *Unquenched Thirst, The Crush that Lasted Fifty Years* & 1 psychological thriller, *Normal, a Novel.* (see www.amazon.com)
- When I finish this book, *My Shrinking Brain: Dancing as Fast as I Can …A Book About Alzheimer's Disease,* a firsthand experience being diagnosed with early Alzheimer's disease, I will resume the sequel to *Normal,* titled *Almost Normal,* and *BooCat: Letters from Jackson & Friends* (written with Ann Hamilton), and *The Corner of Hadley & Garrett: A Dog Story.*
- I illustrated a child's book (for ages 4-8) written by Lila Shelton, and available on amazon.com, *Eddie Bugbear and his Fearsome Growl.*
- Visit my facebook page, also *BooCat Unleashed* fb page and BooCat's webpage.
- I work fulltime as the clerk for the Village of Bonita.
- I serve as Commissioner-in-Charge at the election polls.
- I am active in several civic organizations (Morehouse Tourism Commission: president; Morehouse Sales Tax Commission; Jones-McGinty Water System, secretary; Village Museum, curator et al).
- I write successful and popular weekly humor columns for the *Bastrop Daily Enterprise. (Life in the Last Lane)*

- I write monthly humor columns for *Louisiana Road Trips* magazine. (*Runnin' the Roads*)
- I keep a notebook by my bed so I do not lose a thought that might be important, might be paramount in a column or book. I get my column fodder from everywhere and everything.
- I have name recognition; big fish in a little pond.
- I have an active facebook account with beaucoup friends.
- I never cry.
- I *try* to make a point of thinking before I set down my car keys, try to make a conscious effort not to do anything "absent-mindedly."
- I read constantly.
- I paint intermittently.
- I am a whiz at crossword puzzles, acrostics, Boggle and Scrabble.
- I do dog rescue and adoption and am owned by eight dogs: 15-year old TacoBelle, 11-year old Rosie, Collie, Cotton, Cheeto, Betty Lou, JezeBelle (Jezzy), and 1-year old Hadley.
- Also, completely owned by the famous BooCat, a 20-year old cockatiel named George and 10-year old white dove named SnowBird, a tank of guppies and a recently rescued Musk Turtle named StinkiePooPoo.
- I work in the yard and have created a beautifully peaceful place I call my Argosy Garden (which is full of magical fairies).
- I feed the wild birds and squirrels.
- I do not keep the house as clean as I used to. It is about priorities.
- I function... but I hurt very badly physically much of the time; that could drain me if I did not keep the plug in place. But, I do. Firmly in place.
- I sing in the sunshine and I dance in the rain... as fast as I can...

ABOUT THE PHOTOGRAPHER

ANN HAMILTON, is an amateur photographer who makes her home in El Paso, Texas with husband, Larry. She is the mother of three children, Bobby, Kristi and Kenny, and two stepsons, and also mom to three loving dogs and 25 turtles.

Daughter Kristi Albers is a famed woman golfer, son Bobby, R.G. Arrington, a renown Alaskan photographer, Ken, is a bank manager in Phoenix, Arizona and one stepson serves on the police force in El Paso and the other is on the Ft Stockton police force.

Ann says, *actually, my photography hobby started in El Paso where beauty is hard to find. I started looking to the skies for my beauty, and found the clouds, beautiful clouds everywhere. Clouds are probably my favorite subject.*

I am married to a fantastic guy, Larry, and since retiring, we like to travel. Although photography is just a hobby, I never leave home without my little point-and-shoot camera. I just enjoy beautiful images. Once I started looking at the world through a camera lens, I discovered a combination of beauty and uniqueness everywhere I looked.

INTERIOR PHOTOGRAPHS by Ann Hamilton:

1. Pushing up Daisies
Photo by: Ann Hamilton,
Anchorage, Alaska

2. The Old Man
Photo by: Ann Hamilton,
Arches, Utah, May 2013

3. Entering the Unknown
Photo by: Ann Hamilton,
Monument Valley, Utah, May 2013

4. Life's Highway
Photo by: Ann Hamilton,
Monument Valley, Utah., May 2013

5. A Far and Distant Shore
Photo by: Ann Hamilton,
Sunset in Maui, Hawaii, December 2011

6. The Biggest Bolder
Photo by: Ann Hamilton,
Monument Valley, Utah, May 2013

7. Too Many Mountains to Climb
Photo by: Ann Hamilton,
Mt. McKinley aka Mt. Denali, August 2013

8. Rocky Horizon
Photo by: Ann Hamilton,
Monument Valley, Utah, May 2013

9. In the Mist
Photo by: Ann Hamilton,
Sunset at Monument Valley, Utah, May 2013

10. Staying Balanced
Photo by: Ann Hamilton,
Balanced Rock, Canyonlands, Utah, May 2013

11. Wilson Arch
Photo by: Ann Hamilton,
Arches National Park, Utah, May 2013

12. Let there be Light
Photo by: Ann Hamilton,
Summer in the Valley, El Paso, Texas, 2012

13. Stairway to Healing
Photo by: Ann Hamilton,
Las Cruses New Mexico

14. Hope
Photo by: Ann Hamilton

RESOURCES & ASSISTANCE:

Living Wills: Louisiana Hospital Association Trust Funds

∽

Alzheimer's disease - Wikipedia, the free encyclopedia

*en.wikipedia.org/wiki/**Alzheimer's_disease**?Alzheimer's disease* (AD), also known in medical literature as *Alzheimer disease*, is the most common form of dementia. There is no cure for the disease, which **...**

Alzheimer's disease - MayoClinic.com

*www.mayoclinic.com/health/**alzheimers-disease**/DS00161?Alzheimer's disease* — Comprehensive overview covers symptoms, causes, treatment of this debilitating disorder.

Alzheimer's Disease & Dementia | Alzheimer's Association

*www.alz.org/**alzheimers_disease**_what_is_**alzheimers**.asp?*Learn about *Alzheimer's disease*, dementia and memory loss symptoms, causes and risk factors and understand their relation to normal aging and brain **...**?The basics - ?Symptoms - ?Changes in the brain - ?Plaques & tangles

Alzheimer's Disease Fact Sheet | National Institute on Aging

*ww.nia.nih.gov/**alzheimers**/publication/**alzheimers-disease**-factsheet?Alzheimer's disease* is an irreversible, progressive brain disease that

289

slowly destroys memory and thinking skills, and eventually even the ability to carry out the ...?Alzheimer's Disease Genetics - ?Diagnosis - ?Symptoms - ?Caregiving

NIHSeniorHealth: Alzheimer's Disease - What Is Alzheimer's Disease?
hseniorhealth.gov/alzheimersdisease/?.Alzheimer's disease is a brain disease that slowly destroys memory and thinking skills and, eventually, the ability to carry out the simplest tasks. It begins slowly ...

Signs of Alzheimer's Disease: 10 Things You Should Know | PBS ...
*www.pbs.org/.../signs-of-alzheimers-disease-10-things-you-should-know...?*May 29, 2013 - Rebecca Wyant (left) is the primary caregiver for her mother Mary, who suffers from *Alzheimer's*. Photo by Mike Fritz / PBS NewsHour.

Alzheimer's Disease Causes, Symptoms, Stages, Signs, Treatment ...
www.medicinenet.com/alzheimers_disease_causes.../article.htm? by Dr. William Shiel - in 50 Google+ circles Learn about *Alzheimer's disease* causes, stages, symptoms, signs, dementia, treatment, and medications.

Mild-Moderate Alzheimer's
www.myalzheimerssupport.com/

Alzheimer's Symptoms?
*www.alzheimerstreatmentoption.com/*Learn About **Alzheimer's** Symptoms and Know What to Look for.?

Alzheimer's Foundation - alzfdn.org?
*www.alzfdn.org/***Alzheimer's** Foundation of America Reach out to us for help.?About AFA - Reach Out to Us for Help - Make a Donation

Alzheimer Disease Stages?
*www.izito.com/**Alzheimer**+**Disease**+Stages*Find **Alzheimer Disease** Stages In 6 Search Engines at Once.

alz.org®| alzheimer's ℺ association

24/7 Helpline: 1.800.272.3900

Our vision is a world without Alzheimer's
Formed in 1980, the Alzheimer's Association advances research to end Alzheimer's and dementia while enhancing care for those living with the disease.

National Headquarters
Alzheimer's Association National Office, 225 N. Michigan Ave., Fl. 17, Chicago, IL 60601
Alzheimer's Association is a not-for-profit 501(c)(3) organization.

Made in the USA
Middletown, DE
05 March 2016